PENGUIN BOOKS

REIMAGINING SINGAPORE'S HISTORY

Matthew Oey is an associate editor at Tuttle Publishing, part of Periplus Publishing Group. Previously, he was a research assistant at Columbia's Graduate School of International and Public Affairs, where he worked with Professor Stuart Gottlieb and former US National Security Advisor Robert O'Brien. Matthew was the lead organizer of the Reimagining Southeast Asian History conference at the Asian Civilisations Museum, on which this book is based, held on August 23, 2023. He holds a Bachelor of Arts in History summa cum laude from Columbia University and is a Juris Doctor candidate at Harvard Law School.

REIMAGINING SINGAPORE'S HISTORY

Essays on Pre-Colonial Roots and Modern Identity

Edited by
Matthew Oey

PENGUIN BOOKS
An imprint of Penguin Random House

PENGUIN BOOKS

Penguin Books is an imprint of the Penguin Random House group of companies whose addresses can be found at global.penguinrandomhouse.com

Published by Penguin Random House SEA Pte Ltd
40 Penjuru Lane, #03-12, Block 2
Singapore 609216

First published in Penguin Books by Penguin Random House SEA 2025

Copyright © Matthew Oey 2025

All rights reserved

10 9 8 7 6 5 4 3 2 1

The views and opinions expressed in this book are the authors' own and the facts are as reported by them which have been verified to the extent possible, and the publishers are not in any way liable for the same.

Please note that no part of this book may be used or reproduced in any manner for the purpose of training artificial intelligence technologies or systems.

ISBN 9789815323757

Typeset in Garamond by MAP Systems, Bengaluru, India

This book is sold subject to the condition that it shall not, by way of trade or otherwise, be lent, resold, hired out, or otherwise circulated without the publisher's prior consent in any form of binding or cover other than that in which it is published and without a similar condition including this condition being imposed on the subsequent purchaser.

www.penguin.sg

Supported by

The views expressed here are solely those of the author(s) in his/her private capacity and do not in any way represent the views of the National Heritage Board and/or any government agencies.

Dedicated to my grandmother, Chia Meow Huay (1934–2025), who grew up in the colony of Singapore, and, together with her generation, built the country that we know today. The strongest woman I know—your love, kindness, and curiosity have been my greatest inspiration. Rest well, ahma.

Contents

Acknowledgements and Reader's Guide — ix
Prologue: From Nusantara Local to Maritime Global: Singapore and the Reimagining of Southeast Asia — xi
Introduction: The Dialogue between Past and Present in the Reimagining of Pre-Colonial Singapore — xxv

Part I: The Material: Twin Breakthroughs in Archaeology and European Archives

Preface to Part I — 3
Chapter 1: Sources for the Study of Singapore before 1800 — 7
Chapter 2: Archaeology in the Writing of Singapore's History — 43

Part II: The Reassessments: New Perspectives on the 1819 Paradigm

Preface to Part II — 63
Chapter 3: Confronting 'The Singapore Story': Colonial Rule and the Power of History-making — 67
Chapter 4: Marginal Notes to a Treaty: The Quibble of the Malay Princes — 107

Part III: The Theoretical: Orientalism, Eurocentrism, and Raffles

Preface to Part III	127
Chapter 5: Raffles and the Coloniality of History	131
Chapter 6: The Myth and the Man: Bringing Singapore's History Out of Stamford Raffles' Shadow	147

Part IV: The Possibilities: Revisiting Malay Perspectives in Modern Singaporean History

Preface to Part IV	171
Chapter 7: Sultan Ali's Reign and the Impact of the 1855 Treaty: A Reassessment	175
Chapter 8: Colonialism, the Historical Construction of 'Tanah Melayu', and its Significance to Malaysia's and Singapore's National Narratives	199
Bibliography	235
Author Biographies	265

Acknowledgements and Reader's Guide

The idea for this book began with a conference titled Reimagining Southeast Asian History, which was hosted at the Asian Civilisations Museum in August 2023. Together with many of the authors in this volume, we wanted to communicate to the public how narratives on Singapore's history, particularly its treatment of colonialism, have changed over the last few decades. The positive reception of the conference blew us away—people of all ages were shocked to learn how much the curricula had transformed since they left school. By popular request, we uploaded the conference proceedings to YouTube so that audience members could share with their friends, and so people could continue to engage with the ideas online. We thus came up with the idea of curating an essay collection around the conference themes to continue the ongoing dialogue around perspectives on Singapore's history.

In this spirit, the volume is about bringing together the diverse voices and viewpoints that have contributed to enriching Singapore's history over the past few decades. Our project is supported by a grant from Singapore's National Heritage Board (NHB) based on its merits in contributing to the broader discourse on Singapore's history and historiography. However, we would like to emphasize that while the NHB has provided funding support for this publication, the views and interpretations presented here are those of the individual contributors and do not reflect or represent the official position of the Board. We would also like to thank them for their help.

I—the editor—would like to give a special thank you to Professors Kwa Chong Guan, Peter Borschberg, and Wang Gungwu for their support and mentorship ever since taking a chance on me at the Reimagining Southeast Asian History conference. In introducing me to the wonderful world of pre-colonial Southeast Asia, you have given me the equivalent of a college education in the subject despite my having no prior background in it. Thank you also to my Columbia classmates, Luc Hillion and Stephanie Chan, who were instrumental in running the original conference. Finally, to my parents and grandmother, who have supported me in everything.

In terms of how to approach this book as a reader, we want to emphasize that it is not so much about history as a series of facts and figures. Rather, it is about dialogue, discourses, and narratives—and, in particular, how they affect our understanding of history. Therefore, we implore readers to treat this book more as a tool for conversation than as a definitive answer to Singapore's history and its many questions. We urge readers to critically engage with the diverse perspectives presented and to use these viewpoints as starting points for further queries, reflection, and discussions about historical narratives and how they change. Above all, we hope that readers leave with a newfound appreciation for how much Singapore's history has been reimagined over the last few decades, and the painstaking work that has supported those changes behind the scenes.

Prologue

From Nusantara Local to Maritime Global: Singapore and the Reimagining of Southeast Asia

Wang Gungwu

Imagining and Reimagining, Past and Present

I am fascinated by the themes raised in this volume, which cover many of the problems that have been on my mind for quite a while.[1] They reinforce an important and recurring matter in the study of Singapore's past: how different times lead us to approach history differently. In other words, we recognize a distinction between *history* and history written by historians. They are sometimes completely different. We can never fully know *history* as it happened. On the other hand, our task as historians is to

---

[1] This prologue is a transcribed and edited version of the paper that I presented at the Reimagining Southeast Asian History conference held in August 2023, titled 'From Nusantara Local to Maritime Global'. See: Wang Gungwu, "Wang Gungwu: From Nusantara Local to Maritime Global (RSAH Conference 2023)," August 26, 2023, Asian Civilisations Museum, Singapore, 1:04:52, https://www.youtube.com/watch?v=tJnBU4o77Uo.

capture some of the realities behind what we *imagine* might have happened from the sources and information available.[2] This begs the question, who are the historians and where are they writing from? What is their perspective? How have the politics of the present shaped their views? As you will read in the other essays, the complexity and variability of historical sources obscures a 'correct' and 'objective' interpretation of them. This is to say that we are 'reimagining' the past all the time—whether we are conscious of it or not.

Therefore, the present influences how we write about and understand the past, and that has always been true. In the history books and textbooks that we read, we are constantly reminded that whoever writes history determines the way the narrative is told. Recall that overused aphorism: 'History is written by the victors.' We are influenced by the viewpoint of the historian whether we like it or not. That perspective, more often than not, is a reflection of the values and ideas of the present, the times in which the historian lived and wrote. This begs several fundamental questions about the process through which 'history' is made. Who is reimagining history? Who is guiding you in that reimagining? Are you reimagining it for yourself? Are you reimagining for your community, for your nation, or for your particular group? Are you reimagining it for your particular interests, be those ethnic, political, or religious? The purpose of this prologue is not to leave you with satisfying answers to these big questions. Rather, it is to show that history itself is an open, ongoing inquiry that is constantly subject to reimagination.

I want to use this prologue to explore and introduce these themes within a context that has long interested me: The establishment of Southeast Asia as a discrete region with borders. This is pertinent to the study of Singapore because, as this volume will highlight, many of the facts and terms we rely on

---

[2] The seminal text on the relationship between historical imagination and the writing of history is Hayden White, *Metahistory: The Historical Imagination in Nineteenth-Century Europe* (Baltimore, Maryland: JHU Press, 2014).

to explain Singapore's past are relatively recent inventions. Prior to 1819, Singapore was always part of a complex geographical, ethnocultural, and political space that we refer to as 'Southeast Asia'. However, it was not the Southeast Asia that we recognize today. States did not exist. Borders did not exist. Sovereignty, as it is often understood now, was still being worked out through wars, revolutions, and treaties in Western Europe. Part of the difficulty in studying Singapore before Raffles is, precisely, that it was always part of some larger entity or network that cannot be easily distilled into familiar concepts.

We now call this general space 'Southeast Asia'. But that requires us to ask, then, what was 'Southeast Asia' in the first place? Because if we start with the premise that there was a 'Southeast Asia', then I ask, was there really one to begin with? The term itself is a recent invention and has always been challenged and reshaped, as this prologue will articulate. Singaporean history as an element of that space thus had to be constantly 'imagined' and 'reimagined' in ways that were intelligible to people living within its borders at each particular point in time. Its most recent reimagining, the topic of this volume, is very much a product of developments in the twenty-first century. While this will be explored throughout the volume, I want to zoom out to Southeast Asia—and Singapore's place within it—to provide an overarching view of the thematic project that this book is undertaking. Moreover, I reflect on my own experience reimagining Southeast Asia throughout my career as a historian, and how that has changed over the years.

A Region with Borders

My starting point is the fact that Southeast Asia as a region did not have a name until very recently. There were a few loosely applicable terms—'Nusantara', an Old Javanese term for the Malay Archipelago, for example. But none of them truly capture what Southeast Asia is today. The primary difference is that Southeast Asia today has a *border*, and borders are new to our part of the world. For most of its history, the region has not seen formal borders, much less of the particular kind that we now recognize. Borders were invented in the modern period. Exactly when is debatable, but Southeast Asia as a region with discrete borders is a modern concept.

I contend that those borders were introduced during the Second World War.[3] Towards the end of Second World War, the term 'South East Asia Command' was created by British strategists in London and headquartered in Sri Lanka. The Americans later adopted it. But it was the British who first thought in these regional terms as they were strategizing about the future. They were not talking about the past. It was a name that they created for a command to perform a particular military task: drive the Japanese out and restore British imperial interests in the region. In any case, the South East Asia Command was born out of a military strategic vision. Southeast Asia suddenly had regional borders—India to the west and China to the north.

Southeast Asia was thus peculiar because it was a region developed for the purpose of forward thinking—the idea that the Second World War had fundamentally reshaped the world. Empires were coming to an end. Decolonization, a word not yet used but one that would gradually circulate in the coming years, was inevitable. This was determined not only by the people of the region but also by leaders of the West. After all, the biggest proponent of decolonization was the United States, the rising Western hegemon. They decided that the future must be a world without empires. The lessons of the First and Second World Wars were that national empires would fight each other to the bitter end and cause tremendous damage to the world's economic system. America's idealistic leaders recognized this and, building on the

---

[3] To explore this argument in further detail, see Wang Gungwu, "Before Southeast Asia: Passages and Terrains," in *ISEAS at 50: Understanding Southeast Asia Past and Present*, ed. Lee Hsien Loong, Leonard Y. Andaya, and Wang Gungwu (Singapore: ISEAS-Yusof Ishak Institute, 2018). Many of the empirical details for this prologue can also be found here.

enlightenment project of the eighteenth century, envisioned an empire-less world as necessary for the future of humankind. Otherwise, wars and continual destruction would ultimately lead to the destruction of humanity itself.

Recognizing the necessity of decolonization, empires began to withdraw from Southeast Asia. But what were they withdrawing from? They were not withdrawing from a discrete region, but an area where every geographical space was a colony of one kind or another. There were different ones under the Dutch, under the French, under the British. There were even the Americans in the Philippines, who had taken it from Spain in 1898 and kept the name. Thailand was independent but was, in effect, under the dominion of the French and British for most of the period. All of Southeast Asia was a patchwork of imperial colonies of one kind or another—in some cases protectorates. It was within this context that Southeast Asia was invented as a recognizable region that was distinct from India and China.

Why India and China? Because British strategists recognized that a united and independent India and China would be hostile towards the West. If they wanted to keep British interests protected in the region, they had to do something about Southeast Asia. Therefore, the strategy was to keep Southeast Asia—divided or otherwise—separate from nationalistic India and communist China. Then and only then could they preserve some of their economic and other interests in the region. On this point, Australia and New Zealand were relevant. Southeast Asia was the bridge that maintained Britain's imperial linkages to these appendages of their empire. Southeast Asia was thus strategic for a whole range of reasons, but most of all for economic interests. Without direct colonial control over the empire, their business interests would still be vital to the British economy as a whole. There are many other complex issues, but the key point is that 'Southeast Asia' was first imagined as a conglomeration of the residual interests that former empires identified as they vacated the region. The primary ones were economic and the need to separate it from India and China. If they could do that then they could at least retain their freedom of operation to protect their interests in the region. From their point of view, this was rational. The literature of the period explicitly states this.[4]

Overall, the important point, as I have stressed, is that the region had borders. Once you recognize China on one side and India on the other, all the territories in between can now be easily categorized as part of a region called 'Southeast Asia'. That is how the concept was born. Singapore is a prime example—as pre-colonial records can attest, the Temasek of the fourteenth century knew no borders. If it was part of any kind of region, that did not have a common name. I suggest that we use the Malay word 'Nusantara' to refer to the maritime territories of Southeast Asia. But for the mainland, there was no single name given by anybody that I know of. When the French and British tried to sort out what to do with the main peninsula of the region, they called it 'Indo-China' and the 'Indo-China Peninsula'. The French used the name for their colony because there was no alternative, even though there were already numerous distinct political entities, from the large area that now covers Thailand, Myanmar, Cambodia, and Laos to the three parts of Vietnam that came under French control. In other words, nobody could decide what to call the region. So, they left it as Indo-China, an engineered, nineteenth-century term that refers to a much older and culturally diverse geographical space.

Nobody saw Indo-China as a discrete region. However, as borders manifested after 1945 and started being recognized, people within the region started using them more widely. They suddenly became conscious of their freedom and embarked on building new nations independent of Western empires. They became aware of the fact that they were now part of Southeast Asia.

---

[4] From war histories and documents to various histories by Western, Indian, Chinese, and Japanese scholars. See the bibliography in Paul H. Kratoska, Remco Raben, and Henk Schulte Nordholt, *Locating Southeast Asia: Geographies of Knowledge and Politics of Space* (Singapore: NUS Press, 2005).

But what does that mean? If you look at the histories of the period published between 1945 and 1960, you will find very few, if any, books about Southeast Asia by local scholars of the region. They were written by foreigners—by British and Americans, joined later by Dutch, French, and Germans, then followed by a few Chinese, Indian, and Japanese scholars. The common denominator is that they all came from outside the region. However, they saw a utility in recognizing this region as such because, again, it demarcated a clean border between India and China. And I want to underline this because it is significant that Southeast Asia was defined in the negative as *not* India and China. Therefore, what we might conclude is that the 'discovery' of Southeast Asia—or what you could call its 'first imagining'—was actually done from perspectives external to the region.

Imagining from Outside

Local scholars began to write the histories of their respective nascent nations at the same time. Some saw advantages in separating their histories from those of China and India, others saw their primary task as sifting out the roots of a national identity. In doing so, questions arose as to which colonial borders should remain and which should be redrawn. The politics of national histories added another difficult dimension to 'imagining' the region. Nevertheless, the efforts to define and enrich local histories greatly supplemented our store of knowledge about distinct subsections of the region and thus contributed to the macro-regional constructions being made by scholars from outside.

The main imaginings of Southeast Asian history were done exogenously. This began to change when the Association of Southeast Asian Nations (ASEAN) was formed in 1967. That event is emblematic of the Cold War's impact on the region. It began when the largest non-ruling Communist party in the world—the Communist Party of Indonesia or PKI—was totally obliterated and Sukarno was replaced by Suharto's anti-communist government, which would rule for about three decades.[5] Elsewhere, the Americans were already committed to preventing the spread of communism by intervening directly in the Vietnam War. The Cold War was no longer 'cold' here; it was a hot war fought on the battlegrounds of Southeast Asia.

What could the countries do in this hot war that spawned from a European cold war? On their own, very little. But as that hot war went on for another decade, a sense of 'Southeast Asian' identity began to emerge within the region. I don't think many people there consciously thought about what that implied or what it would ultimately mean at the time. Even though ASEAN first converged as an anti-communist organization, it was not apparent. Interestingly, the members of ASEAN did not want to be seen simply as an anti-communist organization. They preferred being more or less neutral. Each rejected the notion of becoming a vassal state of some external power. Each wanted some modicum of independence. So, when the Cold War ended, take note of how quickly ASEAN invited the former pro-Soviet countries of Indo-China—Vietnam, Laos, Cambodia, and Myanmar—to join it. Here was ASEAN, at least its leaders if not its people, seeking to determine what the future of the region would be like. In other words, a group of political leaders in Southeast Asia was already charting a region that they recognized as consisting of ten, rather than five, independent countries by joining Indo-China to what had previously been just the area of Nusantara.

Before the end of the Cold War, I don't think this configuration would have been conceivable. You can see how reimagining depends on changes in contemporary politics. So, we have to take into account whether we were reimagining an anti-communist Southeast Asia or a non-communist one, which would be quite different. Singapore's leaders were very diplomatic and invented a third term: 'not anti-communist'. You can thus see how historians can operate within a system that is constantly

---

[5] Alex De Jong, "The Indonesian Counter-Revolution," February 1, 2019, Jacobin. Archived from the original on 24 April 2024.

changing, with perspectives changing around who is who, what is what, and which countries are which. It was almost a matter of guessing which countries would produce what kind of leaders, and in what direction they would lean. Who would have thought that Vietnam today would be more and more associated with the US in order to defend itself against China? Again, this takes me back to the original premise of Southeast Asia as a discrete regional body separate from China.

Vietnam knew exactly what it was doing when it accepted the invitation to join ASEAN. It sought to distinguish itself from China, a country whose history had been long intertwined with theirs. I remember noticing that, for quite a while, Harvard University's East Asian programme included Vietnam but not Southeast Asia because they saw Vietnam as part of the Chinese framework of nations, as it had been in the Sinic civilization orbit for centuries. So, Harvard had no Southeast Asian studies programme, but it did have Vietnam studies as an addendum to East Asian studies. In short, there were academics who did not always agree with all of the historical transmutations taking place. Vietnam, of course, recognized that much of its culture and civilization is closely tied to that of China, but they saw an opportunity in accepting the invitation to join ASEAN so as to become a separate national entity. And this, in turn, endowed Vietnam with a different perspective on the world and changed the way that its history would be written thereafter. It is now a history contextualized within Southeast Asia's geographical space and no longer in the East Asian civilizational zone that had orbited China for millennia. Such is the messy process of 'reimagining' history. In short, external forces have always shaped the way that Southeast Asian history is presented.

The View from Singapore

I was a student in 1949 at the University of Malaya in the Bukit Timah campus in Singapore when I was exposed to the Singaporean perspective on this novel concept of Southeast Asia.

In fact, it was there that the idea of 'Southeast Asia' was given prominence within the faculty of arts as a whole. The first book of geography on Southeast Asia as a region was written by a professor of geography, E.H.G. Dobby. The first history of Southeast Asia was done by Brian Harrison of our history department. These were the first two books that fleshed out the regional concept of Southeast Asia along geographical and historical lines. A fuller history by Professor D.G.E Hall from another British colonial university, University of Rangoon, was published shortly afterward. Indeed, it was the British colonial university system that focused on and sought to 'imagine' the region's history for the first time. Elsewhere, Southeast Asian historical research received close attention at the School of Oriental and African Studies in London and Cornell University, which built on the early work of D.G.E. Hall.

Looking back and asking who first imagined Southeast Asia, I would point to the British strategists. But among scholars, I would name Dobby, Harrison, and Hall. Interestingly, Dobby's book included the Philippines, even though the British South East Asia Command did not. The Philippines was part of the American sphere of Pacific interests, not the British. For Dobby, it could not be ignored. In terms of geographical space, he cognized that the Philippines had to be part of Southeast Asia. His colleague Harrison concurred. The first edition of D.G.E. Hall's history, however, did not include the Philippines because he followed the borders of the British South East Asia Command. It was only in his later, revised edition that he added the Philippines. This illustrates how imagining and reimagining is ingrained in the process of doing history. It also suggests that Singapore's location near the heart of the region gave it an advantageous perspective from which to look outwards onto it.

Singapore's early prominence in writing and teaching about the region reminds me of that first generation of scholars that was engaged in connecting the Nusantara archipelago to a 'maritime global'. This work began slowly in Europe's early modern history and reached its peak during the nineteenth century, when Singapore was joined to the chain of British imperial ports and woven into the history of European national empires. When the British retreated after the Second World War, it expected the city-state, as a nation-in-progress, to serve as an Anglo-American bastion in Southeast Asia. The island's leadership was smart enough to build on this foundation to eventually succeed as a global city that could also double as the region's financial centre.

For the first decades after 1945, the University of Malaya and its offshoot in Kuala Lumpur played a pivotal role in manifesting Southeast Asian history. Many of their teachers, mainly from the British Commonwealth and America, focused on work that shaped the region's past as a *region*. The first generation of students there responded, some more rooted within the region's poorly documented history and others turning to the imperial interests that gave the region its current identity. Expatriate historians continued to be attracted to use the campuses to support what had started as a strategic military vision. Local historians did learn from them but also recognized the urgent need for their national histories to be written. By the second and third generations, with more universities launching in every country, the early differences between expatriate and local historians gave way to areas of convergence. Here, again, Singapore's port city position, compared to the national priorities that their colleagues elsewhere in the region had to privilege, enabled its historians to remain more ready to use the past to empower a regional outlook. Their 'reimaginings' may not be shared by others but they carried with them the capacity to project a longer-term view of Southeast Asian history that others could accept.

A Singaporean History of the Future

This takes me back to what 'reimagining' could mean for us today. When I listened to my friends and colleagues at the Reimagining Southeast Asian History conference, on which this paper is based,

I was led again to think about how much our contemporary 'reimaginings' are influenced by events in the present.[6] History is a product of current affairs. We are reimagining Southeast Asia today in the context of major global change. We are no longer in the simple world of a United Nations framework dominated by the US and the West. There is much talk of new challenges to American dominance and hegemony, which were inconceivable a few decades ago. People are beginning to think more naturally of a multipolar world, a world that is unacceptable to many Europeans and Americans. After all, the idea of the UN coalesced in the aftermath of the Second World War around the belief in sovereign, independent—most of all, equal—nation-states. Definitional equality at least, though reality is never so simple. But the result was that, in 1945, an international system was invented by the most idealistic people at the time—and for good reason. They were trying to avoid a world in which people kept building empires to pillage, fight, and kill each other. They were trying to bring about peace in the world. Who would not support that? Everybody can agree it was a wonderful aspiration. Except that it didn't work. Almost immediately, we entered the Cold War, where two major powers didn't dare fight each other because they both had nuclear warheads. Instead, they fought each other through proxies, some of which took place in Southeast Asia. Other people carried the burden of fighting and killing. And they're still doing that. Nothing has changed, even though the Cold War has officially ended.

This unipolar world in which the UN served as an arbiter did not answer questions for all humanity. It did not really get off the ground. The Cold War ended, and the idea that America would be the sole superpower was quickly challenged as they got into wars that they could not win so easily; they found it too costly to fight and police everybody else's wars. In the middle of all those

---

[6] Wang Gungwu, "Wang Gungwu: From Nusantara Local to Maritime Global (RSAH Conference 2023)," August 26, 2023, Asian Civilisations Museum, Singapore, 1:04:52, https://www.youtube.com/watch?v=tJnBU4o77Uo.

challenges, new nation-states were established. Each of them had its own reasons for not wanting to be dominated by another power or group of powers. They wanted some semblance of equality in the world of nation-states. This was their road to reimagining. In that context, the reimagining of Southeast Asia as a separate, distinct region with its own identity that is not influenced by any major powers in a multipolar world further drove the project of establishing ASEAN. To that extent, we cannot avoid contemporary affairs when discussing history.

A case in point is the fact that Southeast Asia is in a different position today from where it was ten years ago, much less twenty or more. As the world changes, and as we try and look to history to learn from the past, we are also in some way reading that past into our future. Because our future will be different, that in turn will determine how new histories can be rewritten. Somebody in the future will write a history of the past in a different way from how we are conceiving it today. I will leave you with that uncomfortable thought. You have to accept the fact that history gets written by new victors, and every victor determines that only its history will count and tries to use that to dominate the narrative for future history writing. Except that it never remains stationary. Whether that's for better or worse, it is never going to be comfortable. Historians are always going to be on the soles and tips of their feet, trying to figure out where they stand and how they should look forward.

In this context, Singapore within ASEAN is the product of unique circumstances and will continue to play its distinctive role in that regional organization. I draw that conclusion from having lived in proximity and having been peripherally involved in its growth from colony to independence as a city-state. I had to observe its nation-building efforts mainly from afar but then lived and worked there for the past three decades. This gave me the chance to study how Singapore grew into an exceptional global city as Southeast Asia was being reimagined. I have had the privilege of seeing how its new generation of scholars, some of whom have contributed to this volume, examines the changing perspectives to unexpected changes that both the city and the region have experienced. It has given me an understanding of reimagining that has made me more sensitive to all the previous efforts that Southeast Asia went through even before it had a name. The set of essays here illuminates some of the ways in which Singapore has been described and imagined over the past seven centuries. How that was done as the Nusantara islands and the continental peninsula interacted without borders has added multiple dimensions to the reimaginings that are now taking place in an age of nation-states. That should remind us that the historian's task is an unending one—as Southeast Asia continues to adopt new roles on the world stage, so too will its history continue to be reimagined.

Introduction

The Dialogue between Past and Present in the Reimagining of Pre-Colonial Singapore

Matthew Oey

Nestled among the sleek skyscrapers that dot the Singapore River is a pristine statue of Sir Thomas Stamford Raffles. The site commemorates the spot where Raffles disembarked in 1819 and set up an entrepôt for the East India Company (EIC), ushering in over a century of British colonial rule in Singapore-Malaya. Raffles' 'genius and perception', we are told from the plaque under the statue, 'changed the destiny of Singapore from an obscure fishing village to a modern metropolis'. In 1961, when the Dutchman Albert Winsemius reported for service as Singapore's chief economic advisor, he laid out two stipulations for the country's development. First, rid the country of communist subversives. Second, keep the statue of Raffles.[7] Though seemingly unrelated, both were seen as central to the project of Singapore's modern state-building. A recently decolonized state sixteen miles wide, Singapore had no natural borders, no natural resources,

---

[7] Lee Kuan Yew, "A Tribute to Dr Albert Winsemius," December 6, 1996, National Archives of Singapore.

no industrial base, and no powerful allies. For Winsemius, emboldening Singapore's Western roots using the iconography of Raffles was part of a broader economic strategy to its geopolitical quandary: Signal a friendly disposition to Western businesses and Singapore could modernize by consolidating overseas (predominantly Western) financial investment. The plan worked. Today, Singapore has among the highest GDPs per capita, manages one of the largest sovereign wealth funds in the world, and is widely celebrated as the quintessence of rapid, state-driven modernization. When Winsemius first arrived in the 1960s, Raffles' statue was surrounded by one-to-two-storey shophouses with clay-tiled roofs. The tallest building was the sixteen-storey Bank of China building. Now, it is dwarfed by the mega skyscrapers of Singapore's bustling business district.

The story behind Raffles' statue provides an insightful lens into the construction of Singapore's history—how it has been shaped and moulded by decisions in the present. In other words, its 'historiography'. For many generations, Singapore's past was inextricable from the story of Raffles and the subsequent period of British colonialism. It had a clear starting point in 1819, the year that Raffles 'discovered' a fishing village in Singapore, and his prescience in recognizing its strategic location explained its contemporary success, neatly intertwining past and present. This '1819 paradigm' of Singaporean history, as this book will refer to it, served additional purposes: It tethered Singaporean national identity to the West and, by so doing, helped legitimize the political and legal institutions that the post-colonial state inherited from the British.[8] The 1819 paradigm rested on the foundational, self-serving claim that nothing of importance happened in Singapore before the British. Implicit in that claim was the assumption that the history of Singapore is contained within this 200-year arc from Raffles' landing to today's metropole. Until the 1980s, historians of Singapore took this narrative and its

---

[8] Alfian Sa'at, Faris Joraimi, and Siew Min Sai, eds., *Raffles Renounced: Towards a Merdeka History* (Singapore: Ethos Books, 2021), 1–2.

assumptions for granted. They even partook in perpetuating the 1819 paradigm, believing proudly that Singaporean history had been fully written.[9] There was simply nothing left to discover.[10] To most Singaporeans of working age today, this is the version of the past they find most recognizable.

However, the 1819 paradigm is but one epoch in Singapore's longer history. In the fourteenth century, Singapore experienced a golden age as a highly sophisticated and cosmopolitan Malay port city under the name Temasek. It benefited from the maritime trade that connected the empires of the Middle East and Central Asia regions with the Ming Dynasty in China. These were, at the time, the most prosperous civilizations in the world. Temasek did not abruptly disappear at the end of the fourteenth century, as previously believed. It experienced a revival in the sixteenth century as an appendage of the Johor Sultanate. Between the time of Temasek and Raffles, it was a place of great interest to other European powers—mostly Dutch and Portuguese—as well as regional empires. Knowledge about pre-colonial Singapore and Temasek has always been available. Why did it take so long for Singapore to learn about its pre-colonial history? How did we come to know about this history? Long after independence, why was it still overshadowed by the story of Raffles and the era of British colonialism? These interrelated questions form the crux of this book. It poses two fundamental tensions for studying the history of Singapore. One deals with historiography, the other with colonialism.

The Challenges of Singapore's Historiography

The historiographical problem can be summarized by what Kwa Chong Guan calls the 'paradox of Singapore history': If Singapore

---

[9] Cheah Boon Kheng, "*The Makers and Keepers of Singapore History* (review)," *Journal of the Malaysian Branch of the Royal Asiatic Society (JMBRAS)* 84, no. 1 (2011): 110.

[10] Derek Heng, "Casting Singapore's History in the Longue Durée," in *Singapore from Temasek to the 21st Century: Reinventing the Global City*, ed. Karine Delaye, Karl Hack, and Jean-Louis Margolin (National University of Singapore Press, 2010), 55.

was gifted by geography, why did it fail to develop into a major trading hub before the nineteenth century? And why did historians fail to account for this? The question was first posed in a 1981 publication by Wong Lin Ken, Raffles Professor of History at the then-University of Malaya (today's National University of Singapore [NUS]).[11] His predecessor, Kennedy Tregonning, famously asserted that nothing of contemporary relevance to Singaporean history happened before Raffles' arrival. That injunction has since framed the orthodox historiography centred around the 1819 paradigm.[12] Wong, Tregonning, and other contemporaries were aware of Singapore's fourteenth-century existence as a Malay port city. However, together with another influential historian of Singapore, Constance Mary Turnbull, they dismissed Temasek as irrelevant to Singapore's contemporary history of burgeoning modernity.[13]

Their contention was not that this history was non-existent, but that it was not *meaningful* to the current project of nation-state-building. Turnbull's nation-state-centred approach, *A History of Singapore, 1819-1975*, dominated the history curriculum in the late twentieth century. It reaffirmed a chronology that began with British colonialism in 1819. A foundational premise of this narrative was that Temasek met a violent demise at the end of the fourteenth century, ushering in what the literature calls the 'dark space' or 'fallow period'. And this assumption was peddled to dismiss Temasek's relevance to the nineteenth century.

---

[11] Wong Lin Ken, "A View of Our Past," in *Singapore in Pictures, 1819-1945*, ed. Yik Lee and C.C. Chang (Singapore: Sin Chew Jit Poh and Ministry of Culture, 1981), 15. This refers to the infamous quote by Tregonning that underpins the orthodox historiography: 'Modern Singapore began in 1819. Nothing had occurred on the island prior to this has particular relevance to an understanding of the contemporary scene; it is of antiquarian interest only.'

[12] Kennedy Gordon Tregonning, "The Historical Background," in *Modern Singapore*, ed. Chiang Hai Ding and Ooi Jin-Bee (Singapore: Singapore University Press, 1969), 14.

[13] Kwa Chong Guan and Peter Borschberg, eds., *Studying Singapore Before 1800* (Singapore: National University of Singapore Press, 2018), 3.

Until about 2014, students could go through the entire education system having learned very little about pre-colonial Singapore, a testament to how successfully the 1819 paradigm entrenched itself in the collective historical imagination.[14]

Newer generations of scholarship have challenged this framework, arguing for the importance of situating modern Singapore within a longer chronology that begins with Temasek in the thirteenth century. There are several key claims in this revisionist school. First, that Singapore's longer 700-year history should be seen as a series of cyclical ups and downs, of which British colonialism is just one recent uptick. Second, the perceived 'dark space' between the fall of Temasek and Raffles' landing is an oversimplification bordering on myth. Using a tapestry of archaeological records, non-English sources, and non-textual sources, the pioneering works of archaeologist John Miksic and Peter Borschberg have cogently argued that Singapore did not simply disappear for several centuries. Rather, it was swept up by regional and international currents—more on this later. These revisionists offer a powerful alternative to the 1819 paradigm and have even affected the way that public authorities engage with their country's past. In 2014, the Ministry of Education updated secondary school textbooks to encompass the 700-year arc, pushing back the start date of Singapore's history to 1299.[15]

The recent 2019 Bicentennial commemoration marked another watershed. Although the tradition was established in 1919 to venerate Raffles on the centennial of Singapore's colonial birth, the government decided in 2019 that the official theme of that year's commemoration would be to raise awareness about

---

[14] Kevin Blackburn and ZongLun Wu, *Decolonizing the History Curriculum in Malaysia and Singapore* (New York: Routledge, Taylor & Francis Group, 2019), 154.

[15] This features in the new standard secondary school textbook on Singapore history, published in 2014: *Singapore: The Making of a Nation-State, 1300-1975. Textbook. Secondary One* (Singapore: Curriculum Planning & Development Division, Ministry of Education, 2014).

Singapore's 700-year history and its Temasek roots. British colonialism and 1819 were now just one—albeit important—episode in a much longer story.[16] The Singapore Bicentennial Office, a subcommittee of the Prime Minister's Office mandated to manage the events, even released the publication of Peter Borschberg, Kwa Chong Guan, Derek Heng, and Tan Tai Yong's *Seven Hundred Years: A History of Singapore*. The book has since established itself as a key reference point in the newer historiography.[17] The 2019 Bicentennial can thus be seen as public and national histories aligning themselves with the newer revisionist vogue of scholarship on early Singapore.[18] While the dominant view today remains that of a 200-year history with colonialism as its driver, the 2019 Bicentennial was a commendable undertaking by the Singapore government to recognize newer approaches to its history.

The second issue posed by the 1819 paradigm deals with the impact of coloniality on the writing of history. By this, I mean how the institutions and intellectual frameworks of British colonialism continued to impact the writing of history long after decolonization. This discussion revolves around a basic question: Why did Singapore, one of the great post-colonial success stories, root its history in Raffles, a colonial founder, and British colonialism? Why did academics and officials willingly accept

---

[16] Kwa Chong Guan, "Editorial Foreword: The Singapore Bicentennial as Public History," *Journal of Southeast Asian Studies* 50, no. 4 (2019): 469; Alfian Sa'at, Faris Joraimi, and Siew Min Sai, eds., *Raffles Renounced*, 147; Singapore Bicentennial Office, "About the Singapore Bicentennial," The Singapore Bicentennial, 2020, https://www.sg/sgbicentennial/about/.

[17] This is an updated edition of Kwa, Heng, and Tan's 2009 book, *Singapore, a 700-year history*—with the addition of Peter Borschberg—based on advances that had been made since its original publication, for instance leveraging Borschberg's research to abridge the 'dark period' of Singapore history between the fall of Temasek and the arrival of the British.

[18] This is the thesis of Kwa, 'The Singapore Bicentennial as Public History'; see also Kwa Chong Guan, ed., *1819 & Before: Singapore's Pasts* (Singapore: ISEAS Publishing, 2021), 7.

this narrative to the preclusion of its rich, pre-colonial past? The short answer is political expediency—one might even argue it was necessary for survival. This brings us back to the story behind keeping Raffles' statue. As a nascent micronation looking out into a global, Western-dominated international economy in the 1960s, Singapore's adoption of the 1819 paradigm was part of a pragmatic approach to the multifaceted quagmire of nation-building in a post-colonial world.[19] When the People's Action Party (PAP) rose to power in the late 1950s, it championed decolonization and sought further integration within the larger political body of the Malaysian Federation. In fact, Raffles' statue was targeted for removal because of anti-colonial sentiments in the recently decolonized state; Winsemius was trying to assuage this sentiment when he strongly urged Lee Kuan Yew to keep the statue as a friendly signal to Western businesses.[20] In 1965, Singapore was separated from Malaysia. Facing the threat of interracial violence, Singapore now needed a 'neutral' national history that would distinguish it from that of Malaysia without inciting any 'communal cleavages'. The Singapore government was fully transparent about the political utility of this decision. Minister for Foreign Affairs S. Rajaratnam explained:

> Raffles was deemed to have a role to play in multiracial, multicultural Singapore: as an Englishman, he was 'a neutral' so there would be no dissension among the communities for him to be recognized as the country's founder, unlike putting up the first Malay, first Chinese, first Indian or first Indonesian.[21]

---

[19] Alfian Sa'at, Faris Joraimi, and Siew Min Sai, eds., *Raffles Renounced*, 151–52.

[20] Lee Kuan Yew, "A Tribute to Dr Albert Winsemius," December 6, 1996, National Archives of Singapore.

[21] The *Straits Times*, "Raffles: How He Nearly Came off His Empress Place Pedestal," August 7, 1969. For more on Rajaratnam's views on Singapore's history and its treatment of Raffles, see Sinnathamby Rajaratnam, "Speech by Mr S Rajaratnam, Second Deputy Prime Minister (Foreign Affairs), at a Seminar

Such is the social construction of historical inquiry—how the study of the past is constantly framed by the needs of the present.

The purpose of this book is not to pass value judgments about the 1819 paradigm of Singapore's history or to dismiss it altogether. Rather, it is to show that there is no singular objective framework that can account for the pluralism and complexity of Singapore's history. The 1819 paradigm was but one variant that was developed for a practical purpose at a particular point in time—nation-building and geopolitical insecurity in the 1960s. The Singapore of today is a world away from its precarious predicament over fifty years ago. To better study Singapore's history in the twenty-first century thus not only requires that we move beyond the 1819 paradigm but also take it seriously as an object of meta-historical inquiry. In other words, the 1819 paradigm should be seen as one lens among others that in tandem helps us paint a fuller picture of the past, one that no single lens can capture on its own.

There is not one but many different versions—many different ontologies—of Singapore's past, each with its distinct functions, each with its unique advantages and limitations. The revisionist shift to a 700-year view of Singaporean history, just like the 1819 paradigm, was itself subject to the currents of the present. For instance, one reading of the newer historiography is that its emphasis on transnational forces is more suited to capturing the complexity of Singapore's current position in a twenty-first-century, hyper-globalized economy—a position that the 1819 paradigm was not able to account for on its own. We should thus understand these divergent paradigms of Singaporean history as complementary rather than mutually exclusive. This newer model of Singapore's past should not be seen as simply 'better' but as an alternative that improves shortcomings and

---

on 'Adaptive Reuse: Integrating Traditional Areas Into The Modern Urban Fabric' Held at the Shangri-La Hotel on Saturday, 28 April 1984 at 10.30 A.M.," June 13, 1984, Archives & Oral History Department Singapore.

addresses paradoxes in the original literature. In the future, this may even be replaced by further developments and discoveries.

The purpose of this book, therefore, is to account for the transition to this newer, pluralistic historiography by tracing major developments in the study of pre- and post-colonial Singaporean history. Its overarching message is that history is not 'natural'. It is not discovered. It is not an objective collection of facts. Rather, we should understand history as a mode of inquiry defined by the questions we consciously *choose* to ask. Indeed, as a malleable dialogue shaped by the politics, institutions, and changes in the present. We hope to show, moreover, that Singapore's history is now deeper, more diverse, and more diffuse than ever. There are a multitude of avenues for further research. Forty years ago, it was believed that Singaporean history had reached its limit. This has been disproven, thanks to new evidence from archaeology, maritime history, and climate science, as well as breakthroughs in non-English archival research, literary analysis, and historical cartography. This introduction will plot the evolution of these major developments in Singapore's historiography. It will provide a brief overview of these new methods and sources and will explain how they have expanded the scope of knowledge about pre-colonial Singapore. It will summarize the main contentions of the newer historiographical school, known as the 'longue durée', and how they have reckoned with the issue of coloniality in Singapore's history.

This book is about historiography as much as history—the study of how history is made, its shapers and movers. The making of history does not happen in a vacuum. It is a fluid and messy process. Yet, it is the unpredictability of that process that makes its study deeply interesting. Singapore's history is no exception. Therefore, by engaging with Singapore's historiography, we can gain a better understanding of how the present shapes the past—as well as a better appreciation for our heritage.

The Recursions of Pre- and Post-Colonial Singapore

The primary contention of this introduction is that Singapore's history has always been shaped by developments in the present. To better understand it thus requires that we look at how knowledge about the past has evolved alongside contemporary preoccupations. Along these lines, the scholarship on pre- and post-colonial Singapore has broadly developed around addressing three interrelated problems.

First, what can we know about pre-colonial Singapore? And *how* do we know about it? I term this the epistemic and ontologic problems of historicizing 'Singapore' before modernity. By ontologic, I mean what *was* Singapore before the British came along, and how do we determine which aspects of it are important? For example, if you tell the story of Singapore as a geographical space you get a completely different picture than, say, the political history of its rulers or a trade history of its maritime commerce. By epistemic, I refer to a closer look at the sources used to historicize early Singapore, with attention to their capabilities and limitations. The issue of coloniality adds a layer of complexity because of the tendency of older canons to view 'Singapore' through the lens of Western concepts and using colonial archives.

Prior to 1819, the geographic space that we now call 'Singapore' went by many different names and passed through numerous empires. As Borschberg has argued, the name 'Singapura' has, in different instances, referred to a settlement, an island, one of two straits, a river, a bay, a polity or kingdom, a hinterland, a promontory or cape, or a mountain ridge.[22] Singapore as an independent nation-state with discrete borders is thus a recent construction—statehood as we know it today is, after all, a modern concept. Prior to this, Singapore's vague and disjointed existence partially accounts for the difficulty that historians faced in reconstructing the pre- and post-1819 period and conjoining them in a singular

---

[22] Peter Borschberg, "Singapore's Longer History," *Jahrbuch Für Europäische Überseegeschichte* 19 (December, 2019): 55.

narrative.[23] The revisionist study of pre-colonial Singapore has thus been framed by attempts to correct faulty assumptions in the colonial-era historiography, such as Tregonning and Turnbull's injunction that pre-1819 has no contemporary relevance or that there was a discontinuity between Temasek and British Singapore. Benjamin Khoo and Peter Borschberg's recent book, *Knowing Singapore*, which delves into the state of public information about early Singapore in pre-1800 Europe, has shown that almost every colonial power was interested in Singapore long before the nineteenth century—the idea that it was a place 'forgotten by time' is, therefore, a back-projection of contemporary assumptions onto the past.[24] This is one example of how studies on pre- and post-colonial Singapore engage in a recursive dialogue.

A second preoccupation of the revisionists has been to explain—if knowledge about pre-colonial Singapore always existed—why 1819 was taken as the starting point of its national history, especially after 1963 when Singapore officially joined a post-colonial state. In other words, why had pre-colonial Singapore been deliberately ignored in the historiography? While the political reasons for this have been discussed above, this section focuses on the professional study of history by trained historians. As Kwa and Borschberg show via the studies collected in *Studying Singapore Before 1800*, there were numerous colonial-era academics who knew about early modern Singapore.[25] One of the earliest sources on ancient Temasek is the *Malay Annals*, a literary epic dated to the fifteenth or sixteenth century that narrated the rise and fall of the Melaka Sultanate with the political goal of building legitimacy. However, the source was dismissed by colonial

---

[23] Derek Heng, "Casting Singapore's History in the Longue Durée," in *Singapore from Temasek to the 21st Century*, 73.

[24] Benjamin J. Q. Khoo and Peter Borschberg, *Knowing Singapore: The Evolution of Published Information in Europe, c.1500–1819* (Malaysian Branch of the Royal Asiatic Society, 2023), 13, 50.

[25] Kwa Chong Guan and Peter Borschberg, eds., *Studying Singapore Before 1800*, 15–22.

historians on the basis that it was apocryphal and full of literary embellishment; if it could be used as historical evidence, the question then was *how*—again, an epistemic problem. Moreover, it was assumed that the fall of Temasek in the late fourteenth century ushered in a 500-year-long decline, known in the historiography as the fallow period or dark space, until the arrival of Raffles in the nineteenth century. Because of the epistemic problems that plagued pre-colonial Singapore and its presumed dark space, it was easy to dismiss this early period as irrelevant to its modern history. In uncovering Singapore's pre-colonial past, today's historians have thus grappled with this tangential question of why the first generation of post-colonial historians, notwithstanding the availability of knowledge, ignored the pre-colonial era.

The third problem concerns structure and narrativity. Here, I am invoking the pioneering work of Hayden White's *Metahistory*, which suggested that history requires a coherent and intelligible story to be meaningful. Further, it is the onus of the historian to create that 'narrativity' from a set of facts. Because the pre-1819 period has been pieced together from a diffuse array of sources, it can seem, at a cursory glance, like a jumble of disparate, overlapping snippets with no organizing logic. This made it difficult for historians of the post-colonial period to fit these facts into the overall narrative of a modernizing nation-state. They were easy to dismiss as meaningless.

There is also the complementary concern of relevance: Why *should* we study Singapore's early history and what can it tell us about the present moment? As alluded to previously, the issue of narrativity is fundamentally intertwined with the above problems. It was precisely on the grounds of relevance and continuity that twentieth-century historians dismissed Temasek—it was framed as an esoteric and antiquated preoccupation, one far removed from the modern success story that made twenty-first-century Singapore. This argument both benefited from and helped reify the 'dark space' assumption that the fall of Temasek and Singapore were separated by 500 years of virtual non-existence, conveniently supporting the decision to then begin Singapore's 'history' in 1819. Overcoming this myth has been the major historiographical contribution of Borschberg's archival research and Miksic's archaeological findings. By proving that Temasek never disappeared but rather underwent a series of up and downs as it was assimilated into different entities and jurisdictions, Borschberg and Miksic paved the way for finally sequencing Temasek and Singapore within one continuous story, rather than as two disjointed episodes. This has facilitated the metanarrative of the longue durée approach, which suggests that early modern Singapore is important to understanding how Singapore's successes and declines have always been shaped by regional and international forces, the present being no exception. The revisionist study of pre-colonial Singapore has thus always revolved around this issue of 'narrativity', both in response to the previous historiography and the need to present new evidence in a digestible fashion.

Evolutions in the Study of Early Singapore

The orthodox view of Singapore's history as a nineteenth-century, Raffles-centred story was initially consolidated by British colonial writers such as John Crawfurd, the second resident of Singapore, Frank Swettenham, governor of the Straits Settlement, and Raffles' wife, Lady Sophia Raffles.[26] L.A. Mills, in 1924, was the first to use the British EIC's records to ground a study of Singapore's history, in which it was seen as nothing more than the 'establishment and development of a colonial state'.[27] Mills' research significantly influenced subsequent historians, namely

---

[26] Benjamin J. Q. Khoo and Peter Borschberg, *Knowing Singapore*, 48; Kwa Chong Guan, ed., *1819 & Before: Singapore's Pasts*, 2.

[27] Kwa Chong Guan and Peter Borschberg, eds., *Studying Singapore Before 1800*, 16–17.

Tregonning and Turnbull, who elaborated on his model and perpetuated this Anglocentric view of Singapore's history well into the late twentieth century.[28] They carried on with a nascent history department at the University of Malaya, established in 1949, which trained a generation of historians to focus exclusively on the archival records of the British EIC and Colonial Office.[29]

A product of this milieu, Turnbull's *A History of Singapore* was designated by the Ministry of Education as the primary reference for teaching Singaporean history; in 1984 it was adopted as the model for Singapore's national history curriculum.[30] She was the first to historicize Singapore as an autonomous subject in English, before which its history had been integrated with that of British Malaya. It thus served a distinct political function in the 1970s: the need to separate Singaporean from Malaysian history for the building of a national identity after its independence in 1965. For its time, Turnbull's work was revolutionary and important—though easy to critique with hindsight, it should not be denigrated. Despite decades of revisionism, Turnbull's work was extended twice, the most recent in 2006, with concession that the newer scholarship on pre-colonial Singapore will be difficult to ignore.[31] She even reworded the title to specify it deals with 'modern' history only. The endurance of Turnbull's work is a testament to the continued relevance of the 1819 paradigm.

---

[28] Ibid.

[29] Ibid.; Kwa Chong Guan, Derek Heng, Peter Borschberg, and Tan Tai Yong, *Seven Hundred Years: A History of Singapore* (Singapore: National Library Board and Marshall Cavendish Editions, 2019), 3; Benjamin J. Q. Khoo and Peter Borschberg, *Knowing Singapore*, 10; Kwa Chong Guan, ed., *1819 & Before*, 2.

[30] Tan Bonny, "Constance Mary Turnbull," in Singapore Infopedia (Singapore: National Library Board, 2016). See also: Kevin Blackburn and ZongLun Wu, *Decolonizing the History Curriculum in Malaysia and Singapore* (Abingdon: Routledge, 2019), 149–152; Kwa Chong Guan, *Singapore Chronicles: Pre-Colonial Singapore* (Singapore: Straits Times Press, 2017), 7–8.

[31] C.M. Turnbull, *Journal of the Malaysian Branch of the Royal Asiatic Society* 78, no. 1 (288) (2005): 122–124.

The first major challenge to this edifice came in 1984 when the old National Museum invited Miksic's to conduct a dig at Fort Canning. Over the next few decades, Miksic and his team unearthed tons of archaeological artifacts, which confirmed the legends of ancient Temasek.[32] Miksic's groundbreaking findings were summarized in a 1985 publication, 'Archaeological research on the "Forbidden Hill" of Singapore', and later extrapolated further to larger historical studies of Singapore, such as *Early Singapore, 1300s–1819* and *Singapore and the Silk Road of the Sea, 1300–1800*, which situated early Singapore within the maritime trade routes between Europe and Asia that converged on the Straits. Miksic's work paved the way for using material contributions to expand the state of knowledge on early Singapore. More recently, this has been taken up by maritime archaeological projects.[33] Miksic's research also helped legitimize ancient texts, which were previously taken less seriously as historical evidence.[34] In arguing that Singapore remained an active trading hub until the 1600s, his work further contributed a major historiographical revision to the fallow period, or the dead space in Singapore history prior to British arrival, which he effectively shortened to between the seventeenth and nineteenth centuries. This replaced the hitherto conventional view that traced it to the fall of Temasek at the end of the fifteenth century.

The next breakthrough is what I call the 'non-English and non-textual turn'. This began in the 1990s when Borschberg, whose study of the Dutch jurist Hugo Grotius brought him to Southeast Asia, was the first to locate Singapore within the archives of the Dutch East India Company (VOC). He later

---

[32] Kwa Chong Guan, ed., *1819 & Before*, 2–3; Kwa et al., *Seven Hundred Years*, 12–13.

[33] For a summary of recent maritime archaeological findings and their contributions to Singaporean history, see Kwa Chong Guan, *Shipwrecks and the Maritime History of Singapore* (Singapore: ISEAS Publishing, 2023).

[34] John N. Miksic, *Singapore & the Silk Road of the Sea, 1300–1800* (Singapore: NUS Press, 2013), 20.

expanded his search to a plethora of non-English European archives including Spanish, French, Portuguese, German, and Italian records. The colonial-era historians Ian MacGregor and C.A. Gibson-Hill had previously investigated Portuguese perspectives on Malaya in the 1950s, however, their work was not succeeded until Borschberg's research in the 1990s.[35] Borschberg's approach was thus groundbreaking in that it drew on a wider range of non-conventional and non-English historical sources and expanded the Anglocentric methodology of the field, which he used to fill in the remaining gaps of the fallow period. He situates seventeenth-century Singapore within the context of Luso-Dutch rivalry in the region; from the late seventeenth century to 1819, he argues, Singapore did not simply disappear but also entered a state of protracted decline due to several local and transregional shifts, such as the Jambi Wars of the 1670s and the tightening of the VOC's commercial monopoly respectively.[36] Borschberg's work has shown that almost every major colonial power, at one point, considered setting up a fort or trading post in Singapore. These non-English sources have expanded both the epistemic and ontological scope of Singapore history—what we previously understood as the fallow period or dark space, a core axiom of the orthodox historiography, was merely an absence of English-language sources on the period. Singapore did not mysteriously disappear from the world between the fourteenth and nineteenth centuries, we were just looking for the wrong things in the wrong places.

Borschberg's research, in exposing the reductionism of the 'dark-age-to-colonialism' arc, has been instrumental in facilitating a new historiographical school that frames Singapore's 700-year history as a series of up and down cycles according to macrotrends in the world. This new view applies the concept of 'longue durée' from the French Annales school of the early twentieth century,

---

[35] Kwa Chong Guan, ed., *1819 & Before*, 5–6.
[36] Peter Borschberg, "Singapore's Longer History," 52–53.

a structural approach to history that foregrounds long-term economic, political, and social changes in place of individual and group agency. The framework is, of course, in dialogue with the orthodox school of Singapore history, which accords primacy to the machinations of Raffles and British colonialism. In the longue durée model, Singapore's modern rise is but one upturn among several in its longer history—the British undoubtedly accelerated it but were by no means its sole movers.

Although there are different variations of the longue durée, it has provided the analytical backbone for the revisionist literature and is expounded on in works such as *Seven Hundred Years: A History of Singapore* and *Singapore from Temasek to the 21st Century*.[37] Let us recall that a crucial element of the orthodox view of Singapore's pre-colonial history is the alleged 500-year dark space, which made it impossible to establish a single, unified narrative. The longue durée is thus one answer to coalescing the pre- and post-colonial periods into one contiguous whole. It insists that pre-colonial Singapore is not a disjointed appendage to the present but central to understanding how Singapore's history has been, and continues to be, shaped by transnational forces larger than itself.

The longue durée, in its emphasis on macrostructural agents, can therefore be viewed as the expansion of Singapore's history from a colonial and nation-state-centred story to a regional and international one. With the possible exceptions of the 1300s and today, Singapore was always part of 'a much larger [political] entity: Srivijaya, Siam, Majapahit, Johor, Dutch dependency, British crown colony'.[38] It, therefore, makes no sense to study pre-colonial Singapore in isolation from its region, *European*—not

---

[37] For a summary of the different variations of the longue durée and how they differ from one another, see Kwa et al., *Seven Hundred Years*, 6–11; Derek Heng, "Casting Singapore's History in the Longue Durée"; Peter Borschberg, "Singapore in the Cycles of the Longue Durée," *Journal of the Malaysian Branch of the Royal Asiatic Society* 90, no. 1 (2017): 29–60; Peter Borschberg, "Singapore's Longer History."

[38] Peter Borschberg, "Singapore's Longer History," 55.

just British—involvement in Southeast Asia, and macrostructures such as the 'Silk Road of the Sea', the moniker that Miksic gave to the maritime trade that connected the Middle East and China via Southeast Asia. The logical consequence of this argument is that the oscillations of Singapore's history are merely a reflection of regional and international trends in trade, geopolitics, and nature.[39] In short, Singapore is just a mirror of the many overlapping spaces that it inhabits.

International history approaches to pre-colonial Singapore have located it within the rise and fall of Southeast Asian empires, European colonial rivalries, and the ebbs and flows of regional trade. Kwa Chong Guan's recent book, *Shipwrecks and the Maritime History of Singapore* argues that the 'development of Singapore was very much dependent upon the monsoons and currents swirling around [it], determining when and how ships could sail into and out of Singapore, the connectivity of shipping lanes ... and its port facilities'. He implores us to bridge Singapore's local-national history with a global history of its surrounding seas. International history approaches have also positioned Raffles' nineteenth century moment of 'discovery' within Anglo-Dutch rivalry in India, the rise of the British Raj, and the need to defend its transoceanic routes to China.[40] These perspectives prompt a reconsideration of the agency traditionally accorded to Raffles and force us to recognize that Singapore was an axel in a 'globalized' world system many centuries before the British arrived.

These competing visions of pre-colonial Singapore address fundamental philosophical problems in the study of history. Because the record on early Singapore is fragmented and diffuse, relying on the historian to weave together an intelligible story, the narrative framework that one adopts is bound to influence the content under investigation. Borschberg and Khoo's article,

---

[39] Karl Hack, Jean-Louis Margolin, and Karine Delaye, eds., *Singapore from Temasek to the 21st Century*, 15; Kwa Chong Guan, *Shipwrecks and the Maritime History of Singapore*, 6, 16.

[40] Kwa Chong Guan, *Shipwrecks and the Maritime History of Singapore*, 3.

'Singapore as a Port City, c. 1290–1819', provides a comprehensive overview of how the various approaches used to historicize pre-colonial Singapore have also had a performative impact on how it is understood and subsequently represented.[41] This alludes to a reoccurring theme in Borschberg's research—that 'Singapore' as a signifier refers to a different physical entity depending on where we locate it in history. Because nation-states are European products of internationalism and modernity, pre-colonial 'Singapore' is an anachronism. This forces us to approach Singapore through a lens that is open to the pluralities of its existence in a world before borders. The study of it, as such, is a question for the philosophy of history as much as it is a historical problem. Put differently, the study of pre-colonial Singapore is fundamentally caught up in basic questions about the nature of historical craft. What is history? How do we study it? How do we interpret it? And what is its purpose? Becoming conscious of *how* we approach Singapore's history is as important as the investigation itself.

Reckoning with the Post-Colonial Ledger

Although the original writers of Singaporean history were members of the British imperial administration, the model that they pioneered far outlasted the era of colonization. The political impetus behind maintaining a British-centric view of Singaporean history at the level of government has already been discussed. This section delves into complementary aspects of coloniality that facilitated its perpetuation in academic circles long after independence, and how historians have studied and addressed these problems. It first discusses how the 1819 paradigm developed under British patronage and then moves on to how it was shaped

---

[41] Peter Borschberg and Benjamin J. Q. Khoo, "Singapore as a Port City, c.1290–1819: Evidence, Frameworks and Challenges," *Journal of the Malaysian Branch of the Royal Asiatic Society* 91, no. 314 (2018): 19–20.

by the material vestiges of empire—institutional archives. Lastly, it briefly discusses how the hagiography of Raffles has created a self-perpetuating discourse that further reinforced the 1819 paradigm.

First, in studying early Singapore, it is crucial to remember that, with the Conquest of Melaka in 1511, it was the Portuguese and then later the Dutch who engaged with Southeast Asia long before the nineteenth century—the British in 1819 were thus entering the scene as a disruptive power looking to arrogate influence from their European rivals and exploit the dynamics between indigenous rulers. In answering the question of why the colonial historiography failed to engage with early Singapore despite the availability of information, Khoo and Borschberg argue that it simply 'did not serve the British political and imperial cause'.[42] The first commentators on Singapore history, who set the framework for historians well into the twentieth century, were members of the British colonial administration.[43] There was thus a utility in presenting a version of Singapore's history where its contemporary success was reduced to the sole drivers of 'British ingenuity, foresight, initiative, and policies'.[44] By setting the template for Singapore's history, they perpetuated the complementary view that information on pre-colonial Singapore was 'non-existent, fragmentary, vague, and contradictory'.[45] They discouraged the study of it as a frivolous and antiquated enterprise.[46] This orthodox view of Singapore's history as an Anglocentric story beginning in 1819 was maintained in the twentieth century by historians such as Tregonning and

---

[42] I am here referring to the previously-mentioned colonialists, such as John Crawfurd and Frank Swettenham, whom the historiography has identified as the progenitor of the colonial origin myth and orthodox version of Singapore's history.

[43] Benjamin J. Q. Khoo and Peter Borschberg, *Knowing Singapore: The Evolution of Published Information in Europe, c.1500–1819*, 50.

[44] Ibid. 49.

[45] Ibid.

[46] Ibid.

Turnbull who simply adapted the colonial historiography to the present and used it to explain Singapore's success after independence. Pre-colonial Singapore had no place within the story of forward-looking modernization and state-building, which had become the thematic substrate of both the colonial and post-independence-era historiographies.

A complementary approach to the problem of coloniality has been found in meta-analyses of how Singaporean history as a discipline was singularly defined by colonial archives and institutions. The EIC, and the overarching British Empire, were also data-gathering machines that created, disseminated, and instrumentalized knowledge for efficacious governance.[47] Newer scholarship has argued that archival knowledge must be situated within their social and political contexts, rather than be treated as 'depositories of [fact]'.[48] This subset of post-colonial historiography has focused on elucidating the impact of archive-centric epistemology on Singapore history.[49] They emphasize that the archives collected by the British government are not neutral recollections of the past, but administrative documents which served a specific, political purpose: managing the empire. Focusing on these archives exclusively thus constructed a myopic view of Singaporean history from the top-down eyes of administrative and policy concerns, which can be dangerous if dogmatically accepted as 'fact'. Indeed, the paradigm erected by early colonial writers fetishized British archives as the

---

[47] Farish A. Noor, *Data-Gathering in Colonial Southeast Asia 1800-1900: Framing the Other* (Amsterdam: AUP, 2020).

[48] Benjamin J. Q. Khoo and Peter Borschberg, *Knowing Singapore*, 10; Kwa Chong Guan and Peter Borschberg, eds., *Studying Singapore Before 1800*, 16–17.

[49] For more on this approach, see Kwa Chong Guan and Ho Chi Tim, "Archival Records in the Writing of Singapore History: A Perspective from the Archives," in *The Makers and Keepers of Singapore History*, ed. Loh Kah Seng and Liew Kai Khiun (Singapore: Ethos Books, 2010), 48–64; Kwa Chong Guan and Ho Chi Tim, "Archives in the Making of Post-Colonial Singapore," in *Colonial Legacy in South East Asia: The Dutch Archives*, ed. C. Jeurgens, T. Kappelhof, and M. Karabinos (The Hague: Stichting Archiefpublicaties, 2012), 125–150.

only objective arbiter of historical knowledge. This mindset was then institutionalized by the history department established at the University of Malaya in 1949, which inculcated a generation of historians to use the archives of the EIC and Colonial Office as the final yardstick for Singapore history.[50]

Such a myopic epistemology naturally amplified a view that Singapore existed as nothing more than an administrative microcosm of the British Empire, contributing to a lopsided focus on the rulers rather than their subjects. Pre-colonial Singapore could thus be easily dismissed because its sources came from outside the institution-backed methods of 'proper' historical craft—remember that most of the major breakthroughs in knowledge about pre-colonial Singapore were in disciplines adjacent to history, which forced historians interested in pre-colonial Singapore towards creative interdisciplinarity. Even Borschberg's archival research was originally met with scepticism for using non-British records.[51] The colonial historiography thus set a rigid for how 'history' was defined and how it was to be made. Pre-colonial Singapore, in its reliance on a tapestry of non-traditional sources, constituted a heterodox approach to history altogether—one that, as a result, took a long time to gain traction in the anglophone academy. The prior aversion towards investigations of pre-colonial Singapore can, therefore, be read as the obduracy of an approach to historical epistemology and methodology that exalted archival research above all else.

The final sub-aspect of this literature has examined Raffles' status as a great man of Singapore's history. Raffles is an interesting case study in historical consciousness because, at the time of his death in 1826, he had a polarized reputation in colonial circles; it was only decades after his death that his memory was aggrandized

---

[50] Kwa Chong Guan and Peter Borschberg, eds., *Studying Singapore Before 1800*, 16–17; Kwa et al., *Seven Hundred Years*, 3; Benjamin J. Q. Khoo and Peter Borschberg, *Knowing Singapore*, 10; Kwa Chong Guan, ed., *1819 & Before: Singapore's Pasts*, 2.

[51] Based on conversations with Professor Borschberg.

and began to take on a life of its own, in large part thanks to the posthumous memoirs published by his widow Sophia.[52] Ever since, Raffles has been apotheosized to such an extent that Raffles the man and Raffles the construct have become almost two separate entities. Most English-language biographies of Raffles portray him as 'heroic, honourable, visionary, [and] morally impeccable', with critical portrayals being few and far between, until recently.[53] The Dutch were always critical of Raffles, but their views did not have a major impact on the Anglophone world. As discussed earlier, Raffles was then honoured in the post-colonial period to facilitate Singapore's success as a financial outpost for Western business and to explain its rapid modernization.

Raffles' hagiography has been invariably linked to the orthodox colonial version of Singapore history, and his iconography continues to pervade the landscape of modern Singapore. The last few decades have, however, witnessed a gradual shift in the English scholarship towards more balanced and critical appraisals of Raffles' life and legacy.[54] A landmark in this literature is sociologist Syed Hussein Alatas' *Thomas Stamford Raffles: Schemer or Reformer*, which was the first to challenge Raffles' hagiography in the vogue of Fanonian post-colonial theory. Alatas examines Raffles' political philosophy and recounts some of the overlooked yet unscrupulous facets of his life, such as his hand in opium trafficking.[55] Originally published in 1971, the book's original reception was full of criticism and controversy.[56] However, that it would today be considered more in line with the contemporary, revisionist view of Raffles is a testament to how Alatas was ahead of his time.

---

[52] See Chapter 6 of this book titled 'The Myth and the Man: Bringing Singapore's History Out of Stamford Raffles' Shadow' by Tim Hannigan.

[53] Ibid.

[54] For an overview of evolutions in the historiography of Stamford Raffles, see Alfian Sa'at, Faris Joraimi, and Siew Min Sai, eds., *Raffles Renounced*, 103–105.

[55] Syed Farid Alatas, "Introduction," in *Thomas Stamford Raffles: Schemer or Reformer?*, by Syed Hussein Alatas (Singapore: NUS Press, 2020).

[56] Syed Hussein Alatas, "Preface," in *Thomas Stamford Raffles: Schemer or Reformer?*.

Conclusion

As this historiographical review has shown, evolutions in sourcing information about pre-colonial Singapore—from archaeological and archival findings to closer readings of existing texts—have, in turn, expanded the scope of knowledge about Singapore's past. What the historiography previously called the 'dark space' was simply a symptom of an Anglophone academy that searched for the wrong information in the wrong places. The study of Singapore's history in the 1960s and 1970s was framed by the practical need to rapidly build a post-colonial state, abetted by an academic system that inherited colonial databases for history-making. Temasek and pre-colonial Singapore simply did not fit the needs of the time. The shift over the last half-century towards a 700-year history can be understood in a similar vein. As Singapore continues to embed itself in an international and globalized economy in the twenty-first century, there is now more pressure to recognize its longer lineage and continuity—to show that it has always played a role in the history of trade, commerce, and globalization. Such is the recursive nature between the pre- and post-colonial historiography, a conversation between the past and the present. Moving beyond a colonial framework of history-making thus requires that we also study the *why* and *how* of that shift. It implores us to consider historiography alongside history.

The essays in this collection are divided into four sections, each of which tackles a particular problem or theme in Singapore's history revolution. As you will realize, the themes are by no means discrete. They overlap, complement, or complicate each other, and address many of the same subjects but through different lenses. The essays in this volume often float between the many overlapping ideas in that constellation. The different sections are thus not meant to be a rigid classification but to highlight the different historical and historiographical issues at play. The first section looks at the novel information that has been uncovered about pre-colonial Singapore through archival and archaeological work. The second revisits common tropes surrounding Singapore's founding in the 1819 paradigm and illustrates a much more complicated and interesting story behind the establishment of Singapore as a British colony. The third section moves beyond history to the world of post-colonial theory. Focusing on the commonly-held stories about Thomas Stamford Raffles, it gives a model for how theories about knowledge and perspective have contributed to new interpretations of Singapore's history. Finally, part four addresses the impact of the Malay world and its rulers on modern Singaporean history, a perspective that, until recently, was often omitted from mainstream narratives.

As Wang Gungwu eloquently put it, a crucial part of 'reimagining' is asking who imagined Singapore in the first place.[57] Indeed, it was the British colonial administration and its environs that set the original paradigm for the history of Singapore, defining both its scope and methods. For centuries, the assumptions embedded in this version of 'history' precluded investigations into Singapore's substantial pre-colonial heritage. Borrowing from Edward Said's *Orientalism*, the project of decolonization thus requires that we recognize how colonial structures have shaped the production of knowledge, even long after the age of empire. It is not about tearing down Raffles' statue or moving beyond European archives. The solution is not so reductive and radical. As this volume will show, non-English European archives have played and continue to play an important role in the discovery of pre-colonial Singapore and uncovering local perspectives.

Instead, this book is about subverting simple solutions. It is about being conscious of the process through which historians and institutions, gradually and painstakingly, challenged the colonial mould of history-making, the reasons for that shift, and what it teaches us about the relationship between coloniality and

---

[57] Wang Gungwu, "Wang Gungwu: From Nusantara Local to Maritime Global (RSAH Conference 2023)," August 26, 2023, Asian Civilisations Museum, Singapore, 1:04:52, https://www.youtube.com/watch?v=tJnBU4o77Uo.

historiography. Although the disjointedness of Singapore's pre-colonial past has been previously cited to justify its futility, one may argue that it is also what makes the study of early Singapore deeply fascinating. Where one sees a disjointed patchwork of events, an intrepid historian sees variability and plurality, and an opportunity for future scholarship. To borrow from Borschberg, there is not one but many Singaporean *histories*—and thinking about how the present shapes these different histories is the task of 'reimagining'.

Part I

The Material: Twin Breakthroughs in Archaeology and European Archives

Preface to Part I

The Material: Twin Breakthroughs in Archaeology and European Archives

At the heart of any history book is a story. There is a beginning, middle, and end. There are protagonists and antagonists. There is even a narrative structure infused with a larger theme or idea. However, it is the historian who puts this tapestry together from a cluster of disparate facts, sources, and data. This is what I call the 'raw material' of history writing. It is the starting point from which the historian begins to weave together their grand narrative and convey it to an audience in a digestible way.

But before we get to the narrative, there are a number of questions about what counts as 'raw material' and how we sift through it. In the particular case of Singaporean history, two major new-material breakthroughs were made over the past thirty years. The first was in archaeology, which found its big break with Professor John Miksic's Fort Canning excavations in 1984 and drew huge support for the field thereafter. The second was in non-English European archives, which Peter Borschberg pioneered over the last few decades. Both of these were truly revolutionary because they challenged previous beliefs that the available information on Singapore's history—particularly of the pre-colonial period—had been fully exhausted. The putative wisdom in the academy was that there was simply nothing new left to uncover. However, today, we now have more information on pre-colonial Singapore than ever thought possible.

Borschberg's essay will show how much of this new information came from non-English European archives. The irony is that the information was and has always been there; historians were simply looking for the wrong information in the wrong places. This was partially due to the Anglophone emphasis of the scholarship on Singapore—English speakers naturally privileged English archives. Another piece of the puzzle was the self-fulfilling and self-perpetuating assumption that Singaporean history was an exclusively British story. In other words, it was expedient to forget about Dutch and other European interventions in the region. In addition to both of these issues, Borschberg's essay touches on the state of scholarship in the field when he first arrived in the 1990s, the challenges he faced in conducting non-English archival research, and the difficulties of drawing conclusions from complex and incomplete sources.

Kwa's essay will look at the history of archaeological investigations in Singapore, and how its findings have expanded our knowledge base of its pre-colonial past. Again, there is a similar dynamic at play here, where misleading assumptions perpetuate themselves. As Kwa shows, there is a rich tradition of archaeology in Singapore pioneered by the Raffles Museum in the early twentieth century. However, efforts were focused on the Malay Peninsula, particularly in areas around the Johor Sultunates, rather than in Singapore itself.

Therefore, 1984 was a turning point because it was the first dig on Singaporean land, and a hugely successful one at that—within two weeks, Miksic and his team found overwhelming evidence that confirmed the existence of Temasek, a fourteenth-century port city on the island. Why was this so significant? Before the Fort Canning digs, the main source for Temasek was the *Malay Annals*, a text written between the sixteenth and seventeenth centuries—300 years after Temasek's demise—and was classified as a heavily embellished literary work. Historians could thus easily dismiss the source as apocryphal and historically irrelevant. By providing concrete evidence of Temasek, the Fort Canning excavations turned it into an indisputable historical fact and confirmed its location in Singapore in the fourteenth century. Thirty years ago, there was little interest in archaeology in Singapore and Temasek. Today, Temasek is the single most archaeologically well-documented port city in Southeast Asia. As Kwa concludes, the benefit of archaeology is that it complements existing documentary evidence and offers insights that written texts alone cannot.

Both of these breakthroughs speak to the creative and intrepid ways through which historians have discovered pre-colonial Singapore. They also speak to the multifaceted nature of history writing. Part of why the previous 1819 paradigm of Singaporean history proved so enduring was that it relied on easily accessible and available sources: English-written colonial documents housed in Singapore. Compare that to the work that was required to uncover the pre-colonial period: traveling to archives around Europe, learning to read multiple languages, the painstaking work of field archaeology, and the complex operation of salvaging maritime wreckages. The shift towards pre-colonial Singapore can thus also be read as a shift towards an entirely new form of writing history—one where a greater diversity of sources is respected and outside-the-box thinking is encouraged. These are qualities that we should continue to promote.

Chapter 1

Sources for the Study of Singapore before 1800

Peter Borschberg

This chapter addresses sources touching on Singapore and its surrounding region, broadly interpreting 'sources' to comprise written documents and visual materials. The focus is placed on sources produced by European authors, whether the creators may have been based in Europe or Asia. The sources, written in Latin and the main European vernaculars, represent the vast majority of surviving documents related to Singapore during the three centuries from approximately 1500 to 1819.

It should be recognized, however, that certain written sources—chiefly texts and maps—have also survived in Asian languages, including Malay, Arabic, Persian, Thai, and Chinese. Though numerically fewer, these Asian sources offer unique and valuable information for reconstructing Singapore's and the region's history before 1800. Due to my specific language skills set, however, the present chapter focuses almost exclusively on the European sources.

Over the past three decades, I have spent much time identifying, transcribing, and evaluating text and graphic sources that touch on Singapore and its surrounding region. In this chapter, I have drawn on that extensive experience and structured it around three sections.

The first explains the pre-1800 history-scape in Singapore up until the mid-1990s. In this context, I highlight that the retrieval and study of non-English European sources relating to Singapore and its region is a relatively recent endeavour, with significant progress only made in the last two to three decades.

The second section addresses the pre-1800 European texts and graphic materials touching on Singapore. Through a series of questions and answers, I discuss the types of sources that have been retrieved, their quantity, and some of the unique challenges presented in evaluating them.

The third section reflects on specific challenges of raising public awareness about these early modern European sources and concludes with some reflections on the opportunities that lie ahead in this long-term journey of discovery.

With this agenda in mind, we now turn to explore the state of the pre-1800 Singapore history-scape at the end of the twentieth century.

Pre-1800 Singaporean History Before the Mid-1990s

When I began to work on pre-1800 sources touching on Singapore and the region in the first half of the 1990s, I was met with well-intentioned cautions that my search would likely be futile and yield little of value. Despite significant advances in Singapore's archaeology since the mid-1980s (which are discussed in another chapter of this book), the prevailing view of Singapore's historical trajectory had remained largely unchanged since the end of the colonial era. This held that Singapore, a port city that had flourished in the fourteenth century, was destroyed and abandoned in the late-1300s, after which it became fallow land and remained in a state of neglect until around the time the British established a trading post on the island. This portrayal framed Singapore as little more than a sleepy seaside kampung during the fallow period.[1] The state of knowledge and the prevailing views on Singapore's pre-1800 history were encapsulated in a chapter by Arthur J.J. Lim in *The History of Singapore*, published in 1991— just a year before I assumed my teaching duties at the National University of Singapore (NUS).[2]

At that time, research in the NUS History Department was still rooted in a tradition that had been established during the colonial era. Three assumptions had underpinned the study of Singapore history generally since the 1950s and 1960s, all of which are now deemed problematic.

First, the long trajectory of Singapore's history, as conceptualized during the colonial era, was grounded in the belief that Singapore had been destroyed and depopulated after the late 1300s and then revived by the British after 1819. This narrative postulated that the arrival of the British heralded a new era for Singapore. Any settlement that may have existed centuries earlier on the island was simply irrelevant to the post-1819 developments.

Second, central to this narrative was the idea that Singapore was historically known either as Temasek or Singapura. Researchers thought that any reference to Singapore would be found by trawling the sources for these names.

Third, historians emphasized the value of British administrative documentation in the reconstruction of Singapore's history. Non-conventional sources, including the non-English language materials, were largely neglected or simply ignored. Young and aspiring researchers were discouraged from consulting or introducing non-English language sources.

---

[1] See esp. John Crawfurd, *Descriptive Dictionary of the Indian Islands and Adjacent Countries* (London: Bradbury and Evans, 1856), 401; C. Mary Turnbull, *A History of Singapore, 1819–1975* (Kuala Lumpur: Oxford University Press, 1977); and the relevant chapters in Ernest C.T. Chew and E. Lee, eds., *A History of Singapore* (Singapore: Oxford University Press, 1991).

[2] Arthur J.J. Lim, "The Geography and Early History of Singapore", in *A History of Singapore*, ed. E.C.T. Chew and E. Lee (Singapore: Oxford University Press, 1991), 1–14.

Given these assumptions and preferences, the historical narratives assumed predictable contours. A cursory glance at the different theses on Singapore's history that were completed in the University of Malaya and later University of Singapore's history departments reveals a clear preference for topics discussing institutions, policies, and individuals. These studies were Anglocentric (rather than Eurocentric) and thus generally focused on social elites.[3]

The colonial narrative remained the prevailing template for Singapore's historiography well beyond the city state's independence from Malaysia in 1965. This maintained a clear and temporally wide chasm between Singapore's remote past as Temasek and its present as an independent post-colonial city state, a perspective Kwa Chong Guan has explored in his 'Introduction' to the essay collection *Studying Singapore before 1800*.[4] He highlights that no connection was seen between the pre-1800 era of Singapore's history and the modern port city, and for this reason Singapore's deeper past was simply dismissed as a matter of mere antiquarian interest, a view infamously echoed in the 1960s by the Raffles Chair of History at National University of Singapore (NUS) (then University of Malaya), Kennedy Gordon Tregonning.[5]

Despite the long echo of the British colonial narrative, there were admittedly researchers in Singapore who took a different vantage point and showed interest in developing a new narrative by tapping into a greater variety of sources, including European non-English language texts and documentation. Harry Marks, for

---

[3] See also Matthew Oey's 'Introduction' in this volume.

[4] Kwa Chong Guan, "Introduction", in Kwa and Borschberg, eds., *Studying Singapore Before 1800* (Singapore: NUS Press, 2018; hereafter KBSS), 1–26. For another discussion on the problems of starting Singapore's history in 1819, see also Kwa et al., *Seven Hundred Years: A History of Singapore* (Singapore: National Library Board and Marshall Cavendish Editions, 2019), 1–17.

[5] Tregonning, "The Historical Background", 14. See also the 'Introduction' by Matthew Oey and the chapter 'Colonial Rule and the Power of History Making' by Christopher Hale in this volume.

instance, examined the first years following the founding of British Singapore up to about the year 1824 by consulting Dutch materials that had been transcribed and published in the Netherlands over the course of the nineteenth and early twentieth centuries.[6] Similarly, members of Singapore's South Seas Society together with public intellectuals—like Hsü Yün-ts'iao (Xu Yunqiao) and Han Wai Toon (Han Huaizhan)—adduced Chinese-language sources for their study of local Singaporean and peninsular history between the 1940s and 1970s.[7] During the final years of colonial rule, researchers—including Carl-Alexander Gibson-Hill, Ian MacGregor, Gerard Tibbetts, and Paul Wheatley—began to cite both unconventional as well as non-English language materials in order to broaden the established narrative.[8]

One of the most critical early voices to target the distortions created by Singapore's colonial narrative was the Dutch-trained sociologist Syed Hussein Alatas.[9] In 1971, he published a short but

---

[6] Harry Marks, *The First Contest for Singapore* (The Hague: Martinus Nijhoff, 1959).

[7] Hsü Yün-T'siao, "Singapore in the Remote Past", *Journal of the Malaysian Branch of the Royal Asiatic Society (JMBRAS)* 45, no. 1 (1972): 1–9, or its reprint in KBSS, 38–52; Han Wai Toon, "A Study on Johore Lama", *Journal of the South Seas Society (JSSS)* 5 (1948): 17–35 (in English) and ibid., 5–25 (in Chinese); more ideas in Hsü Yün-Ts'iao, "Notes on the Malay Peninsula in Ancient Voyages", *JSSS* 5 (1948): 1–16 (in English) and ibid., 25–39 (in Chinese).

[8] C.A. Gibson-Hill, "Singapore: Notes on the History of the Old Strait, 1580–1850", *JMBRAS* 27, 1: 175–176; C.A. Gibson-Hill, "Singapore Old Strait and New Harbour, 1300–1870", *Memoirs of the Raffles Museum*, no. 3 (1956): 11–115, and its reproduction in KBSS, 211–308; Ian A. MacGregor, "Johore Lama in the Sixteenth Century", *JMBRAS* 28, 2 (1955): 48–125; Ian A. MacGregor, "Notes on the Portuguese in Malaya", *JMBRAS* 28, 2 (1955): 4–47; Gerard R. Tibbetts, *A Study of the Arabic Texts Containing Material on South-East Asia* (London and Leiden: E.J. Brill, 1979); Paul Wheatley, *The Golden Khersonese: Studies in the Historical Geography of the Malay Peninsula before A.D. 1500* (Kuala Lumpur: University of Malaya Press, 1961); Paul Wheatley, *Impressions of the Malay Peninsula in Ancient Times* (Singapore: Eastern Universities Press, 1964).

[9] Peter Borschberg, "Alatas' Raffles. A Review of Syed Hussein Alatas' Thomas Stamford Raffles", *Singapore Journal of Tropical Geography*, 43, 1 (2022): 111.

seminal study entitled *Thomas Stamford Raffles: Schemer or Reformer?*, in which he openly questioned the views surrounding Sir Thomas Stamford Raffles' alleged reputation as a humanitarian and social reformer.[10] Alatas' open criticism led to a lively exchange with Ernest Chew of the University of Singapore's history department that was also published in *Suara University* in 1972.[11]

Wong Lin Ken, who served as the head of the history department and authored some important studies on the colonial port of Singapore,[12] did not so much challenge the foundations, but rather sought to clarify certain aspects of the British colonial narrative. He challenged historians to answer the question of why Singapore was only founded by the British in the early nineteenth century, and why nobody seems to have recognized the locational value of Singapore before that date. Wong himself did not venture to answer this question but surmised that investigations into the Anglo-French rivalry in India during the long eighteenth century might yield the necessary evidence.[13]

As seen from the investigations into Singapore's history-scape so far, there were clearly researchers in the 1950s and 1960s who were actively engaged in the study of pre-1800 Singapore history, and they were basing their research on a range of both Asian and European sources. The question now emerges: Why were these

---

[10] Syed Hussein Alatas, *Thomas Stamford Raffles: Schemer or Reformer?* (Singapore: NUS Press, 2020).

[11] Ernest Chew and Syed Hussein Alatas, "A Controversy on Raffles", *Suara University* 3 (1972): 49–61. More context about this exchange and its role in setting the agenda for the writing of Asian-centric history, see Kwa Chong Guan, "Raffles and the Writing of Asia-Centric History. A Review of Syed Hussein Alatas, Thomas Stamford Raffles", *Singapore Journal of Tropical Geography*, 43, 1 (2022): 116–119.

[12] L.K. Wong, "The Trade of Singapore, 1819–1869", *JMBRAS* 33, 4 (1960): 4–315; L.K. Wong, "Singapore: Its Growth as an Entrepot Port, 1819–1941", *JSEAS* 9, 1 (1978): 50–84.

[13] Won Lin Ken, "A View of Our Past", in *Singapore in Pictures, 1819–1945*, ed. Lee Yik and C.C. Chang (Singapore: Sin Chew Jit Poh and Ministry of Culture, 1981), 15.

efforts abruptly discontinued or abandoned? A clear answer is not immediately forthcoming, as multiple developments appear to have been in play. Two such developments, however, stand out.

First, Singapore's sudden independence from Malaysia in 1965 would also impact Singapore's historical narrative in two distinct ways. On the one hand Singapore's reorientation saw it look outward to the global stage. This reorientation was accompanied by a recalibration of the nation's economy, transforming it from colonial port with a hinterland into a city state that would develop global ambitions.

Second, before 1965, Singapore had always been seen as being part of something larger—whether it was Siam, the Melaka Sultanate, Johor, the British Empire, or Malaysia. Independence, however, abruptly changed this perspective. Singapore's birth as a sovereign nation spurred demands for a different historical framework and narrative. Seen in this way, independence not only generated fresh challenges, but also a new set of priorities. The focus of the nation now shifted to a narrative of growth and survival in the present. 'Singapore history', it was said in 1965, 'begins now.'[14] As a result of its independence and new priorities, the study of pre-1800 Singapore was viewed as irrelevant, meaningless, and disconnected from the challenges facing the island and its peoples in the present. Mary Turnbull's narrative of the British free port emerged as the dominant narrative precisely because it focused on Singapore, its port and its economic connectivity with the wider world. For a young nation severed from its sprawling roots across the region, Turnbull's narrative offered a practical and forward-looking perspective, one that was better suited to explaining the island's survival against many odds and its growth trajectory in an ever-changing world.

To wrap up these observations regarding the evolving pre-1800 Singapore history-scape, it's important to be very clear on one specific point: The use of non-British European sources in the study of Singapore's history is certainly not a long-established tradition.

---

[14] C.M. Turnbull, *A History of Modern Singapore, 1819–2005* (Singapore: NUS Press, 2009), 1.

It is only in the past two decades or so that historians have been systematically trawling these sources for insights and information. British sources and colonial texts were clearly given a priority, while other records—Asian and European—were neglected or even dismissed as fictitious, ill-informed, contradictory, misleading, or polemical.[15] It was long assumed that any search for meaningful information in non-British records would yield few concrete results and ultimately prove to be a waste of time.[16] This was the history-scape that still prevailed when I first launched my investigations into the sixteenth and seventeenth-century history of Singapore and Johor sometime in the first half of the 1990s.

In the following section we turn to explore the ongoing task of identifying and processing pre-1800 sources touching on Singapore. The different issues and challenges will be addressed through a series of questions and answers about the types, quantity, and quality of these sources.

Some Key Questions and Answers Regarding the Pre-1800 Source Materials Touching on Singapore and Its Region

Earlier, we examined the study of Singapore's history before 1800 by singling out and discussing some key assumptions that shaped the Singaporean history-scape before around the mid-1990s. Among these were some deep-seated biases against non-English language texts, both of Asian and European origin. We also plotted how initiatives to study Singapore's longer and deeper past were upended after 1965.

In this section, we explore the developments in the history-scape of pre-1800 Singapore since the mid-1990s. Discussions about archaeology and material culture generally will

---

[15] Richard Carnac Temple, "Some Discursive Comments on Barbosa", *The Indian Antiquary: A Journal of Oriental Research, etc*, 52 (1923): 137.

[16] C.M. Turnbull, *A History of Modern Singapore, 1819–2005*, 20; Arthur J.J. Lim, "The Geography and Early History of Singapore", 3.

be set aside, as these are the subject of Kwa Chong Guan's chapter in this volume. Special attention has been paid to non-English language sources of European origin (including Europeans living in or travelling through Southeast Asia). These arguably constitute the majority of texts that survive from the three centuries between 1500 and 1800. Evaluating the different Asian-language texts requires a distinct skills set that I, unfortunately, do not possess, so Asian sources have not been covered in this chapter in meaningful depth.

The following discussion is structured around a series of questions and answers. The questions focus on the types, number and quality of sources that have been identified. Organizing the chapter in this way helps understand the scopes, strengths, and limitations of these texts. Toward the end, this chapter identifies and addresses some of the principal challenges faced in presenting the different research findings to the Singaporean public. The concluding thoughts finally take stock of where research on pre-1800 Singapore history currently stands and offer some reflections on the difficulties ahead.

What types of European sources are there?

Engaging with pre-1800 materials is not for everyone. It is not because there is a lack of interest in them, but rather because there are comparatively few researchers who are equipped with the necessary skills. To successfully study and evaluate texts from this era, some highly specialized skills are required, including languages in their modern and pre-modern forms. Another essential skill is palaeography—the skill of reading and evaluating old handwriting. It takes years of dedicated study to master old languages and old handwritings.[17]

---

[17] More on the challenges of working with early modern texts, see Peter Borschberg, *Reconstructing Singapore before 1800* (Singapore: NUS Press, forthcoming), Chapter 1; Peter Borschberg, "Portuguese and Dutch Records for Singapore before 1819: An Overview", in *1819 & Before: Singapore's Pasts*, ed. Kwa Chong Guan (Singapore: ISEAS Publishing, 2021), 88–99.

Extant European sources related to pre-1800 Singapore can be divided into four basic subgroups:

- conventional sources,
- unconventional sources,
- literary texts,
- graphic materials.

Conventional sources are those that historians traditionally draw on when researching and constructing their narratives. These comprise travelogues, letters, missionary documents, legal documents, or confidential reports by early colonial authorities and the East India companies. Official documents, meanwhile, encompass treaties, administrative records, and diplomatic correspondence. Some source materials, like published travelogues, were written with an eye for the book markets of Europe and public consumption, offering vivid, and admittedly often embellished, accounts meant to captivate readers.[18] Others, such as confidential commercial and political reports, were meant to be read by high-ranking officials, offering more guarded, strategic assessments of the region.

Unconventional texts, meanwhile, considerably expand the scope of possible source materials on the region and include reference books, glossaries, and even literary works. These materials often contain important linguistic or cultural information as well. European merchants, missionaries, colonial officials, and scholars of the early modern period compiled glossaries, dictionaries, and handbooks as handy reference guides to local languages, customs, resources, commodities, flora and fauna, and geography. These additional sources can help researchers today in grasping how Europeans understood the various regions they were visiting or operating in, even if these interpretations were skewed, flawed, and biased. These types of printed reference works, collectively

---

[18] Benjamin J. Q. Khoo and Peter Borschberg, *Knowing Singapore: The Evolution of Published Information in Europe, c.1500–1819* (Malaysian Branch of the Royal Asiatic Society, 2023), 15.

dubbed compendia, were characterized by a number of problems, including repetition. They often copied from one another, and in so doing, perpetuated outdated or misleading information.[19] Anachronisms and decontextualization were sometimes the result. Some dictionaries, for example, continued to refer to a 'great city' by the name of 'Sincapura', which was located at the tip of the Malay Peninsula.[20] In other cases, reference works like the eighteenth-century German *Zedler Universal-Lexikon* (Universal Lexicon or 'Encyclopaedia'), contains several entries relating to Singapore but placed under different spellings: 'Sincapor(e)', 'Sincapur', 'Sincapura', 'Sincapurum Promontorium' (Singapore Promontory), and 'Singapour'.[21] The multiple entries under different spellings has something to say not just about the confusion over the name Sincapura and what it might all refer to, but the different entries reveal how the editors collected and compiled information for their compendia entries.

Literary works have also found their place and value in historical research. While they are primarily creative works of fiction, they reveal much about the time and societies that wrote them, expressing values and concerns of their era. Literary criticism has increasingly informed historical writing over the past few decades, including the historiography of Singapore. For instance, Daniel Defoe's *Adventures and Piracies of the Famous Captain Singleton* published in 1720 paints a grim picture of the Singapore region and portrays it as one of the most challenging

---

[19] Pre-1800 compendia touching on Singapore and its region have been discussed in Benjamin J. Q. Khoo and Peter Borschberg, *Knowing Singapore: The Evolution of Published Information in Europe, c.1500–1819* (Malaysian Branch of the Royal Asiatic Society, 2023).

[20] Peter Borschberg, *Mapping Singapore Before 1819* (Singapore, NUS Press, forthcoming); Benjamin J. Q. Khoo and Peter Borschberg, *Knowing Singapore*, 88–89.

[21] J.H. Zedler, *Grosses vollständiges Universal-Lexicon aller Wissenschafften und Künste*, 64 vols. (Leipzig and Halle: Verlag Heinrich Zedler, 1732–54), vol. XXXVII, col. 1596, 811. This publication is freely accessible at www.zedler-lexikon.de (Accessed on 17 Aug. 2024).

and dangerous maritime straits worldwide.[22] Though Captain Singleton may be a fictional character, the book reflects common fears about the Singapore Straits in Defoe's time—namely the early-eighteenth century. When mariners and Europeans thus heard the name 'Singapura' in the pre-1800 era, it evoked images of peril and doom.[23]

Bringing the different sets of conventional and unconventional sources into dialogue with each other can thus yield penetrating glimpses into the past. Conventional texts help to establish foundational narratives, but unconventional materials, such as glossaries or literary works, yield insights into the way Singapore and its region were painted in Europe's collective imagination.

The next category of sources, namely graphic materials, offers more than just snapshots in time. Maps and charts—whether printed or remaining in manuscript form—fall into this category.[24] In my forthcoming book on the historical cartography of Singapore before 1819, I explain that maps transcend their function as mere visualizations of geographic space.[25] They can act as repositories of cumulative knowledge and expressions of the human imagination. They tell stories in their own right, offering valuable insights into how a particular region or geographic feature was understood at different points in time.[26]

---

[22] Daniel Defoe, *The Life, Adventures, and Pyracies, of the Famous Captain Singleton* (London: Printed for J. Brotherton, 1720), 231; Benjamin J. Q. Khoo and Peter Borschberg, *Knowing Singapore*, 17–18.

[23] Benjamin J. Q. Khoo and Peter Borschberg, *Knowing Singapore*, 26–31.

[24] See Peter Borschberg, "Singapura in Early Modern Cartography: A Sea of Challenges", in *Visualising Space: Maps of Singapore and the Region. Collections from the National Archives and National Library of Singapore* (Singapore: National Library Board), 6–33.

[25] Peter Borschberg, *Mapping Singapore Before 1819* (Singapore: NUS Press, forthcoming).

[26] For more ideas, see also Peter Barber, "'Context is everything…' Ruminations on Developments in the History of Cartography since the 1970s and Their Consequences", *Imago Mundi*, 72, 2: 131–147, esp. 138–140; Matthew H. Edney, "Theory and the History of Cartography", *Imago Mundi* 48 (1996): 185–191;

With reference to Singapore, the majority of detailed maps and charts of the region were created to serve a specific purpose: to guide mariners through the perilous waters of the Singapore Straits. When examined alongside texts of the era, these maps and charts contain information that clearly transcend the different navigational routes. They mark dangers lurking beneath the water surface, highlight where crews could find fresh water, and identify visual markers above the waterline. Sometimes, they provide a list of the commodities available at a given port or plot the trade routes—by sea, river, or overland—that connected them.[27] In this way, maps and charts capture not just the geographic features of the region but also share how Europeans saw the economic dynamics and opportunities across the region.

Among the graphic materials are also sketches and images that prove helpful for writing historical narratives in a number of ways. They not only record local flora and fauna but also provide glimpses into places, spaces, and peoples. Sketchbooks drawn by mariners, soldiers, and travellers have been adduced to reconstruct and illustrate the histories of port cities like Melaka, Batavia, Banten, and Ayutthaya. For Singapore, much of what survives stems from a later period, such as the early nineteenth-century sketches by Étienne Eugène Cicéri. As an official artist aboard the French corvette *Astrolabe*, Cicéri was a member of the 1837–1840 expedition to the South Pacific and Antarctica that sailed under the command of Jules-Sébastian-César Dumont d'Urville. During a stopover in Singapore between June and July 1839, Cicéri sketched a number of scenes of Singapore's town, port, and peoples that would later be published with the written accounts describing the journey.[28]

---

and Christian Jacob, "Cultural History of Cartography", *Imago Mundi* 48 (1996): 191–198.

[27] Peter Borschberg, *Mapping Singapore Before 1819*; Peter Borschberg, "Singapura in Early Modern Cartography".

[28] J.S.C. Dumont d'Urville and C.A. Vicendo-Dumoulin, *Voyage au Pôle Sud et dans l'Océanie sur les corvettes Astrolabe et La Zélée par ordre du roi pendant les années*

Illustrations such as those by Cicéri, the mid-seventeenth century sketchbook of Wouter Schouten depicting scenes of daily life in Batavia, or the coloured eighteenth-century sketchbook by Jan Brandes, are rare and clearly exceptional.[29] They capture snapshots of their time and prove invaluable to historians today.

European sketches relating to Singapore dating from the pre-1800 period are very rare. Two of them, both dating from the early seventeenth century, were published by Theodore de Bry and his sons as part of a book series narrating the first Dutch voyages to the East Indies. One sketch represents a crude map that schematically illustrates a series of skirmishes between the Dutch and the Portuguese in October 1603. These naval battles took place in the Johor River, around Pedra Branca and off the northern coast of Batam. Though this printed image likely derives from a now-lost original, its significance lies in its identification and naming of certain geographic features around Singapore.[30]

The second sketch depicts Johor's junior ruler, Raja Bongsu, sailing toward the ships of Dutch Vice-Admiral Jacob Pietersz, a scene also connected to the skirmishes of October 1603. Whether based on a lost or forgotten original or drawn purely from imagination, the printed sketch was almost certainly embellished by artists working in Theodore de Bry's studio in Germany. Raja Bongsu, is shown dressed in what appears to be

---

1837, 1839, 1840, 10 vols. (Paris: Gids & C.ie, 1841–1846). Two companion volumes contain the maps and illustrations.

[29] The sketchbooks of Wouter Schouten and Jan Brandes are preserved in the Rijksmuseum Amsterdam.

[30] For a brief discussion of this schematic sketch, see Peter Borschberg, "Map Showing Battles in the Johor River and the Singapore Straits", in *On Paper: Singapore Before 1867* (Singapore: National Library Board, 2019), 34–39; and more extensively in Peter Borschberg, "A Luso-Dutch Naval Confrontation in the Johor River Delta, 1603", *Zeitschrift der Deutschen Morgenländischen Gesellschaft* 153, no.1 (2003): 157–175, or its reprint in KBSS, 309–324.

Turkish garb, and a European-style city is depicted on what is evidently Singapore Island.[31]

To sum up this section, historians today have broadened the range of sources that they are willing to draw on, covering a far wider array of forms and languages. These are additionally enriched by surviving material culture, including archaeological finds that have been omitted in this chapter. The days have thankfully passed when researchers of Singapore's history confined themselves almost exclusively to official English-language documents produced by the British East India Company (EIC) and its colonial successor institutions. As a result, researchers now engage with different types of sources across different languages—Asian and European. When these different sources are not studied in isolation but are brought into conversation with each other, they yield the most intellectually stimulating and rewarding results.

Having discussed the broadening of the different types of sources that researchers today draw on for reconstructing Singapore's history before 1800, we now turn to the next question: How many of these sources have been identified so far? At this juncture, I am reminded of the advice I had received in the 1990s: I would likely find few, if any.

How many sources are there?

After three decades of research on the early modern history of Singapore and its region, it is not possible to reliably estimate the number of pre-1800 European sources that have been uncovered. A few years ago, I conservatively estimated that researchers had gained access to between one and two thousand accounts and

---

[31] The original is found in J.T. de Bry, *Icones seu gennuinae et expressae delineationes omnium memorabilium, etc.* (Frankfurt am Main: De Bry, 1607), plate VII. For contemporary reproductions of this sketch, see Peter Borschberg, "Map Showing Battles in the Johor River and the Singapore Straits", 38; Peter Borschberg, *The Singapore and Melaka Straits. Violence, Security and Diplomacy in the 17th Century* (Singapore and Leiden: NUS Press and KITLV Press, 2010), 91.

references of varying length and depth, and I presently see no grounds to revise that appraisal.[32] The core issue at hand, however, is not really about the number of sources that have been made available but rather the expanse and quality of insights that they can offer.

The vast majority of references retrieved are brief—often just a few words or a sentence or two. As a consequence, they only hold limited value as sources for the reconstruction of Singapore's pre-1800 history. Substantial passages comprising more detailed observations are the exception rather than the norm. To illustrate this point, let me highlight two examples that both relate to Singapore in the sixteenth and seventeenth centuries.

The first concerns the more substantive records. One of the most important European sources touching on Singapore dating from the early modern period are the writings of the independent Flemish trader Jacques de Coutre who was based at Melaka at the turn of the 1590s and early 1600s.[33] When his various passages regarding Singapore are taken collectively, they form what is doubtlessly the most substantive European record available. Coutre's writings provide valuable insights into a range of topics, including the 'Orang Laut' who were active around the island, key geographical features such as the Old and New Straits of Singapore, Siloso Spring, and, importantly, also the 'Shahbandaria'. He further touches on political and strategic considerations, while offering observations on the local flora and fauna—particularly the fruits harvested by the Orang Laut, which were offered for barter to passing ships.[34]

While most sources from the early modern period offer only fleeting mentions of Singapore, Coutre's observations stand out

---

[32] Peter Borschberg, "Portuguese and Dutch Records for Singapore Before 1819: An Overview".

[33] Peter Borschberg, *Jacques de Coutre's Singapore and Johor (c.1594–1625)* (Singapore: NUS Press, 2015).

[34] See also Peter Borschberg, "Jacques de Coutre as a Source for the Early 17th Century History of Singapore, the Johor River, and the Straits", JMBRAS, 81, 2 (2008): 71–97.

as unusual contributions. His observations can not only help frame our understanding of Singapore's role and position within in the regional trading networks but also provide a rare glimpse into the daily lives of the Orang Laut, of the environment as well as the island's strategic importance as seen from a European vantage point.

The second example relates to the Jesuit missionary and Roman Catholic Saint, Francis Xavier. He travelled through the Old Strait of Singapore, a narrow body of water that is located between present-day Sentosa and Harbourfront. His handful of letters, marked with the location '*ex freto Syncapurano* (from the strait of Singapore)', otherwise offer no details about the strait, the island, or its peoples.[35] Their value lies simply in confirming that the celebrated missionary passed Singapore at a particular point in time. In his letters, he expressed concern that he might miss the westward sailing season from Melaka to India. For this reason, he despatched several letters to his Jesuit brethren in Melaka to inform him of his imminent arrival. These letters and their content suggest the existence of a service—likely an oared vessel or a fast sampan—capable of delivering messages from the Singapore Straits to Melaka in a short time span.[36] As for yielding insights into Singapore and its surroundings, however, Francis Xavier's letters take us no further.

Are we likely to find much more?

When viewed in terms of probability, it's highly likely that hitherto unknown sources and references touching on Singapore

---

[35] The letters of Francis Xavier are found in Henry J. Coleridge, ed., *The Life and Letters of St. Francis Xavier*, 2 vols. (London: Burns and Oates, 1872–76), II, 363–364, 528–529; Georg Schürhammer, ed., *Francisco Javier: su vida y su tiempo*, 4 vols. (Pamplona: Gobierno de Navarra, 1992), vol. IV, 41. The historical context of these letters was earlier discussed in Ian. A. Macgregor, "Notes on the Portuguese in Malaya", *JMBRAS* 28, no. 2 (1955): 4–47.

[36] Kwa et al., *Seven Hundred Years*, 81.

will continue to surface in archives worldwide. The number of such sources, however, is probably secondary to length and quality of such new sources or even the location where they may be found. When new sources come to light, they will probably not be found in the standard depository institutions such as the British Library in London, the Torre do Tombo Archives in Lisbon, or the Dutch National Archives in The Hague. Instead, they could be retrieved in smaller or unexpected places or even in collections of private persons. Let me elaborate on this point via a few examples.

One such unexpected find came during my recent research into the historical cartography of Singapore before 1800. I retrieved some new specimens in places I hadn't expected, such as the Bayerische Staatsbibliothek (State Library of Bavaria) in Munich. This institution owns a manuscript copy of Robert Dudley's *Arcano del Mare* that contains several manuscript maps of the Malay Peninsula and the Singapore and Melaka Straits region.[37] One particular specimen caught my attention—it named several geographical features as 'Singapura', namely a settlement, river, bay, bar, strait, and cape. It is highly unusual to have so many features named Singapura marked up on a single map.

Moving from cartography to texts and private collections, my attention was drawn a few years ago to a seventeenth-century book of rutters (navigational instructions), known as the *Codex Castelo Melhor*. While the contents of this privately owned collection of rutters had been earlier described by the French scholar Pierre-Yves Manguin, a transcription of the Portuguese rutters was recently made available thanks to the recent doctoral dissertation by Jorge Semedo de Matos. This collection contains a short set of instructions for sailing the so-called 'New Strait of Singapore'.[38]

---

[37] Robert Dudley, *Dell'Arcano del Mare* Vol. I. (Munich, Bayerische Staatsbibliothek, Ms. Cod. Icon. 138, 1636), 182.

[38] The instructions for sailing the New Strait of Singapore are found in the *Codex Castelo Melhor*, fols. 63v–64r. The *Codex* is owned by Francisco Vasconcelos e Sousa in Lisbon. For a description and study of this collection of rutters, see

While several accounts describe the course through the Old Strait of Singapore, such as the Dutchman Jan Huyghen van Linschoten's *Itinerario* (1595), instructions for sailing the New Strait are rare.[39] The text contained in the *Codex Castelo Melhor* describing the New Strait may veer to the short side at just over a thousand words, but it is unique and thus offers a valuable addition to the historical sources documenting the maritime routes around Singapore Island.

Another example comes from a source that has made headlines in recent months, namely the journal or diary of a ship's surgeon named Bremond, who sailed aboard the French warship *Oiseau* as part of some well-publicized diplomatic exchanges between King Louis XIV of France and King Narai of Siam.[40] In 2023, the National Library of Australia acquired Bremond's diary from Christie's.[41] This manuscript stirred a great deal of attention because it includes one of the earliest recorded European sightings of the western Australian coast, predating Captain Cook by almost a century. Bremond's account of the *Oiseau*'s passage through the Singapore Straits came during the ship's return

---

P.Y. Manguin, "A mid-17th Century Collection of Roteiros for Asian Waters", *Studia*, 48 (1989): 187–212; L.J. Matos, "Roteiros e rotas portuguesas do oriente nos séculos XVI e XVII", doctoral thesis, University of Lisbon, 2016, 333–335, for a transcript of the Portuguese text.

[39] Jan Huyghen van Linschoten, *Voyage ofte schipvaert van Jan Huygen van Linschoten naer Oost ofte Portugaels Indiën, 1579–1592, vierde deel: Reys-Gheschrift vande Navigatiën der Portugaloysers*, ed. J.C.M. Warnsinck, Linschoten Vereeniging (The Hague: Martinus Nijhoff, 1939), vol. IV, 97–99. For a translation into English from the late Elizabethan era (turn of the sixteenth and seventeenth centuries) see J.H. van Linschoten, *The Voyage of John Huyghen van Linschoten to the East Indies: From the Old English Translation of 1598*, ed. A.C. Burnell and P.A. Tiele, 2 vols. (London: Hakluyt Society, 1874, reprint 1885), II, 119.

[40] Dirk van der Cruysse, *Louis XIV et le Siam* (Paris: Fayard, 1991); Dirk van der Cruysse, *Siam and the West, 1500–1700* (Chiang Mai: Silkworm Books, 2002).

[41] Bremond, "Journal of a voyage from Brest to Siam in L'Oiseau, 1687-1688", National Library of Australia, accessed April 30, 2025, https://catalogue.nla.gov.au/catalog/8819817.

journey from Siam to France, via Melaka and the French colony of Pondicherry in India. The diary's description of the Singapore Strait appears on folio 70 verso, but, disappointingly, Bremond offers little detail. He simply notes that the ship entered the strait on 13 December 1687 and that the crew had to wait for the wind to pick up before continuing the onward voyage. The *Oiseau's* course past Singapore was marked up in several French maps of dating from the late-seventeenth and early-eighteenth centuries.[42] The observations made and the data collected by the *Oiseau's* officers and crew while passing through the Singapore Strait found their way into subsequent French charts of the Singapore and Melaka Straits region, as can be evidenced, for example, by map of the southern Malay Peninsula and its surroundings by the French navy hydrographer Jaques Nicolas Bellin dating from 1760.[43]

What kind of information do these sources contain?

Researchers with little or no experience working with early modern materials often approach sources from this period with undue preconceptions or unrealistic expectations. They hope to retrieve detailed answers to questions that the pre-1800 documents on Singapore and the region simply cannot provide. Sources from this era are qualitatively uneven and frequently incomplete—they are what they are, warts and all. It is simply futile to wish the authors had written something different or to try and extract meaning from a given text that simply isn't there.

One need bear in mind that the authors of these documents differed greatly in terms of their education, vocabulary, and

---

[42] "Carte de l'isle Thimon en Malacca [Document cartographique manuscrit]: corrigée sur les lieux en passant sur le vaisseau du roi l'oyseau ou la trace dudit vaisseau est marquée par des points rouges et les mouillages comme cy après", Paris, Bibliothèque Nationale de France (BnF) Catalogue Général, 1687, accessed April 30, 2025, https://catalogue.bnf.fr/ark:/12148/cb470063074.

[43] "Carte du Detroit de Malacca [Map of the Malacca Strait]", Paris, Bibliothèque Nationale de France (BnF) Collection d'Anville, 1760, accessed April 30, 2025, https://gallica.bnf.fr/ark:/12148/btv1b7200809v.

command of their written language. It is not exactly common to come across original sources, such as letters, that are lucidly written and grammatically coherent. Such texts generally mirror the linguistic and educational shortcomings of their writer, resulting in inconsistencies and ambiguities that researchers today must carefully evaluate.[44]

Additionally, many of these printed texts and manuscripts were altered by editors and publishers seeking to fire the imagination of Europe's growing reading public. Stories were 'spiced up' by inserting entire passages lifted from other works, all without clearly divulging the source of these additions. Copying was also common, so statements found in the early modern printed texts are not always original, accurate, or even helpful.[45] The researcher today has to navigate what is authentic about an account and what has been added by later editors—a challenge that demands a sharp eye and years of experience.

The interplay between personal experience and imagination is also tricky. The accounts that have survived were rarely written in real-time. Authors were not hurriedly jotting down diary entries as events unfolded. Instead, their observations were often recorded years or even decades after the actual events. By the time they set their thoughts to paper, their memories had been filtered through the lens of time, shaped by hindsight and influenced by later experiences. What may appear to be straightforward recollections are coloured, moreover, by the evolving perspectives of the writer. Authors recording their memories may have also adapted their storyline to suit the literary style and taste of the day, an observation that has also been made regarding the autobiography of Jacques de Coutre.[46]

---

[44] More ideas on this problem in Peter Borschberg, "Portuguese and Dutch Records for Singapore before 1819".

[45] On this issue see for example the essay collection in Daniel Carey and Claire Jowitt, eds., *Richard Hakluyt and Travel Writing in Early Modern Europe* (Abingdon: Routledge, 2016).

[46] "Introduction" to J. de Coutre, *Journal, Memorials and Letters of Cornelis Matelieff de Jonge: Security, Diplomacy and Commerce in 17th-century Southeast Asia*, ed.

The convergence of all these factors—linguistic and educational limitations, editorial interference, and the passage of time—certainly make the analysis of pre-1800 sources a complex undertaking. The philosophy of language, with its focus on how meaning is constructed, distorted, and conveyed, offers some help in closing the gaps between what was intended, what was recorded, and what can be reasonably interpreted today.

What does the name 'Singapura' (and all its variant spellings) refer to?

Researchers who scan texts for references to the names Temasek or 'Tumasik' and Singapura will find limited results. So far, no references to Temasek or Tumasik have been found in the European sources. Singapura, by contrast, registers several issues: There are many different spelling variants of the name, some of which are almost beyond immediate recognition. Then, there are the different ways in which its meaning of the name Singapura was understood over time with the 'Lion City' being only one of several explanations. And then, there is the question of what the name actually refers to in any given instance.

Over the course of reviewing and studying the early modern European sources for well over three decades, I have been able to identify about eleven different geographical features that at some time were named Singapura (with one of its many variant spellings). These include a settlement, a river, a river bar, a bay, an island, a kingdom or polity, at least two separate straits, a mountain ridge, a cape or promontory, as well as an entire hinterland

---

P. Borschberg and tr. R. Roy (Singapore: NUS Press, 2014). Concerning the adaptation to literary tastes, see: George D. Winius and C.C. Chorba, "Literary Invasions in 'La Vida de Jaques de Coutre': Do They Prejudice Its Value as an Historical Source?", *A Carreira da Índia e as Rotas dos Estreitos: Actas do VIII Seminário Internacional de História Indo Portuguesa,* ed. Arturo Teodoro de Matos and Luís Filipe Reis Thomaz (Angra do Heroísmo: Barbosa & Javier, 1998), 709–719.

stretching from Singapore and northwards as far as the Pahang and Muar rivers.[47]

Occasionally, I receive emails written by members of the general public who inform me that they have 'found' a reference to the name 'Singapura' in some text or document dating from before 1800. On closer examination, the majority of these mentions are so vague that it is not clear from the text exactly what feature is being mentioned, but as a rule, it is most probably the Old or New Strait of Singapore. Here is an example: When encountering a sentence like, 'We passed a ship that arrived from Singapura,' what does that even mean? It would be problematic to argue that the name Singapura here refers to a port or city by that name, but the possibility cannot be entirely excluded. As the sentence stands, the wording is not sufficiently clear. Perhaps, the larger context provided by the text would justify such a conclusion, but that is not usually the case. The name could also reference one, or a combination, of the other geographical features known historically as Singapura, such as a strait, bay, river, or a cape.

The historic elasticity of a given place-name is by no means limited to Singapura; similar questions and ambiguities arise, for example, with the name Malaca, which could refer to a type city, port, river, kingdom or polity, region or hinterland, strait, or the entire Malay Peninsula. 'Melaka' is also a type of tree that, according to the *Malay Annals*, lent its name to the city. 'Malaca' was frequently used in early modern sources to refer to the Spanish city of Malaga (simply by switching the soft guttural sound 'g' for the hard 'c'). So, a casual reference reading along the lines of: 'Among the many merchants present was one from Malaca' may in the end have nothing to do with a merchant from Melaka on the Malay Peninsula.

And yes, there was more than one Singapura. As John Miksic explains in his study *Singapore and the Silk Road of the Sea*, '[t]he island now known as "Singapore" is one of several locations in Southeast Asia that bears this name; "Singapura" was a fairly

---

[47] Peter Borschberg, *Mapping Singapore Before 1819*.

common name for a city in early Southeast Asia'.[48] Miksic identifies three settlements, all in Southeast Asia: one established in the fifth century by the Cham people located 'at Tra Kieu near Hoi An, central Vietnam'. A second settlement is located in central Thailand corresponding to present-day Sing Buri and dates back to the Angkorean period around the twelfth century. A third 'Singapura' dating from around the fifteenth century is located in West Java. Additional, mentions are found in the Indian texts such as the *Ramayana*.[49] In my forthcoming volume *Mapping Singapore before 1800*, I have identified a few more possible candidates based on early modern European cartography.[50] So, when it comes to reading these pre-1800 European (and Asian) sources, due caution is advised.

What about inaccurate information?

The information that scholars can glean from early modern sources is not always accurate, and one must mind the pitfalls inherent in these historical documents. Factual errors, misunderstandings of key terms, and misinterpretations of geographical names abound. In this section, I shall focus on two problem areas that have implications for research on pre-1800 Singapore: anachronisms and decontextualization.[51]

Anachronisms occur when something is mistakenly placed outside or beyond its temporal lifespan. An excellent example taken from Singapore and its surrounding region involves the former capital of Johor named Batu Sawar that was located about thirty-odd kilometres upriver. This settlement served as the royal administrative centre of Johor after 1587, following

---

[48] J.N. Miksic, *Singapore and the Silk Road of the Sea* (Singapore: NUS Press, 2013), 151.

[49] Ibid.

[50] See the section "How Many Singapores" in Peter Borschberg, *Mapping Singapore Before 1819*.

[51] More on these problems in Khoo and Borschberg, *Knowing Singapore*, 83.

the destruction of Johor Lama by the Portuguese that year. Batu Sawar flourished as an important trade centre until 1613–1615 when it was burned to the ground in the wake of two Acehnese attacks on Johor.[52] The settlement then briefly regained its status as the capital of Johor in the third quarter of the seventeenth century, only to be destroyed yet again in 1673, this time during an attack on Johor by Jambi.[53] By the early 1700s, Johor's administrative centre had relocated out of the Johor River region to the Riau Islands, specifically Bintan (the seat of the Raja Muda) and Lingga (the seat of the Lingga Sultan). This is what we know in broad brush strokes. European compendia and geographical dictionaries, however, continued to describe Batu Sawar as Johor's capital well into the 1700s. They copied and repeated outdated information—mainly based on information provided in the published travelogue of Dutch admiral Cornelis Matelieff, who visited Batu Sawar in 1606. In this travelogue, the admiral portrayed Johor's capital as a city with houses built on stilts, spanning both sides of the Johor River.[54] This eyewitness information, though accurate at the time of Matelieff's visit in the early 1600s, was hopelessly outdated by the end of the century. Yet, echoes of Matelieff's description of Batu Sawar found entry into the European sources well into the latter 1700s, copied and

---

[52] Concerning these events, see Ian MacGregor, "Johore Lama in the Sixteenth Century", *JMBRAS* 28, 2 (1955): 48–125, and its reprint in *KBSS*, 206–220; Peter Borschberg, *The Singapore and Melaka Straits*, appendix II; Kwa Chong Guan, Derek T.S. Heng, and Tan Tai Yong, *Singapore, a 700-Year History from Early Emporium to World City* (Singapore: National Archives of Singapore, 2009).

[53] E. Netscher, *De Nederlanders in Djohor en Siak, 1602–1867* (Batavia: Bruining & Wijt, 1870), 33–34; L.Y. Andaya, *The Kingdom of Johor 1641–1728: Economic and Political Developments* (Kuala Lumpur: Oxford University Press, 1975); Kwa Chong Guan, *Precolonial Singapore* (Singapore: Straits Times Press, 2017); Kwa et al., *Seven Hundred Years,* 147.

[54] Peter Borschberg, *Admiral Matelieff's Singapore and Johor (1606–1616)* (Singapore: NUS Press, 2016), 108–109; Peter Borschberg, "Urban Impermanence on the Southern Malay Peninsula: The Case of Batu Sawar Johor (c.1587–1615)", *Journal of East Asian Urban History* 3, 1 (2021): 57–82.

repeated long after the city had ceased to serve as the capital and most probably no longer even existed.

This problem of outdated information surviving historical realities also introduces another problem that characterizes these early modern printed reference works, namely decontextualization. This occurs when information, once recorded, becomes severed and completely detached from its original source and temporal context, only to be reprinted or mentioned in successive publications without any reference to the origin of this information. The problem of decontextualization grew as different bits of information about the region were increasingly ordered alphabetically and incorporated into glossaries and geographical reference works.[55] With an eye on Singapore, a case in point can be made with the entry on 'Singapore' found in Johann Georg Heinrich Hassel's *Geographisch-Statistisches Handwörterbuch* (Geographical-Statistical Pocket Dictionary), published in 1817. In his entry under the spelling 'Sincapur', Hassel explains that the name referred to an 'Asian city on a small island at the southern tip of the Melaka Peninsula, subject to its own prince and inhabited by immigrants from Sumatra.'[56] He then adds the observation that the city is surrounded by numerous forested islets, which make voyage through the Singapore Strait particularly dangerous. In the end, he points out that the rock Pedra Branca lies at the Singapore Strait's eastern entrance.

Though the Johor *temenggong* had taken up residence in Singapore with some of his followers around 1811, Hassel's 1817 portrayal of an independent kingdom with a city inhabited by immigrants from Sumatra stands in stark contrast to British observations, made two years later, that painted Singapore as a sleepy, sparsely populated, and long-neglected seaside kampung. So, how can we explain this contradiction? Hassel's description is representative of both an anachronism as well as decontextualized

---

[55] On this problem see also Khoo and Borschberg, *Knowing Singapore*, 77–80.

[56] J.G.H. Hassel, *Geographisch-Statistisches Handwörterbuch: nach den neuesten Quellen und Hülfsmitteln*, 2 vols. (Weimar: Im Verlage des geographischen Instituts, 1817), vol. II, 406.

information. Thinking about the possible printed sources readily available for researching and writing his glossary entry, Hassel and his research team are not describing here the conditions prevailing in early nineteenth century Singapore. This entry, rather, echoes a much older narrative—one tied to Parameswara, the exiled prince of Palembang, who fled to Singapore in the late 1300s. Parameswara overthrew the local ruler and was soon joined by more of his followers from Sumatra—those very 'settlers' mentioned by Hassel.

The story of Parameswara had long circulated in European texts, appearing most notably in the sixteenth-century Portuguese chronicles of João de Barros and Brás de Albuquerque.[57] Translations of both Albuquerque's *Comentarios* and Barros' *Décadas da Ásia* (Decades of Asia) were made accessible in translations published in the course of the 1700s, such as those printed in Holland by Pieter van der Aa in 1706.[58] The origin of Hassel's claim that Singapore had been settled by 'immigrants from Sumatra' may be traced back to the following statement in Albuquerque's *Comentarios:*

> As soon as it was known in the kingdom of Palembang how prosperous Parameswara had become [after his coup d'état at Singapore], 3,000 natives of this kingdom made their way to the king, and these he kept with him, and he lived in the city of Singapore for five years, robbing everyone who

---

[57] For modern editions of these texts see J. de Barros, *Décadas da Ásia* (Lisbon: Sá da Costa Editora, 1945–1946); B. de Albuquerque, *Comentarios de Afonso d'Albuqerque*, ed. J.V. Serrão, text of the second edition of 1576, 2 vols. (Lisbon: Imprensa Nacional–Casa de Moeda, 1973); for an English translation see *Commentaries of the Great Afonso Dalboquerque, Second Viceroy of India: Translated from the Portuguese Edition of 1774*, ed. and tr. W. de Gray Birch, 4 vols. (London: Hakluyt Society, 1875–1884).

[58] J. de Barros, *Held-dadige scheeps-togt van Alfonso d'Albuquerque, na de Roode-Zee, in het jaar 1506, etc.* (Leiden: Pieter van der Aa, 1706).

passed through, for he had a numerous fleet of launches on the sea.[59]

It is presently unclear, however, whether Hassel and his research team had access to printed copies in the original Portuguese or in Dutch or French translation, or whether they were extracting this information from other intermediary sources, such as François Valentyn's *Oud en Nieuw Oost-Indiën*.[60] But it is certainly clear that the information he repeated was well out of date. His entry is both an anachronism, because it is historically misplaced, and decontextualized, as it has been decoupled from its original source and historical context.

In the following, we turn to the third and final section of this chapter, which addresses the challenges in presenting the pre-1800 sources to the general public as well as the tasks and obstacles on the road ahead.

What Are the Challenges Associated with the Pre-1800 Sources?

The most useful contributions to public history are those that build upon what the public is already familiar with. Historians typically work with established narratives, broadening or extending the conversation where earlier scholars left off. In the case of pre-1800 Singapore, however, there had been little to expand or build upon. As has been mentioned in this chapter and also in Matthew Oey's 'Introduction', there remains a deeply entrenched belief that there is little to say about Singapore's history between the fall of ancient Temasek and the arrival of the British in 1819.

---

[59] B. de Albuquerque, *Commentaries of the Great Afonso Dalboquerque*, vol. III, 71.

[60] F. Valentyn (sometimes Valentijn): *Oud en Nieuw Oost-Indiën, Vervattende Een Naauwkeurige en Uitvoerige Verhandelinge van Nederlands Mogentheyd in die Gewesten, etc.*, 5 parts in 8 vols. (Dordrecht and Amsterdam: Johannes van Braam and Gerard Onder de Linden, 1724–1726).

Historians researching the early modern history of Singapore, therefore, face several formidable challenges in crafting a narrative: The first has been to construct a rudimentary scaffolding of historical developments that connects the late 1300s and the early 1800s. A comparison of the two *Seven Hundred Years* volumes published in 2009 and 2019 clearly shows that reaching a more or less seamless narrative covering all seven centuries from the 1290s to the late twentieth century was only achieved less than a decade ago.[61] Some of the larger gaps relating to Singapore's history in the fifteenth and eighteenth centuries promise to be filled with the forthcoming revised edition of the book to be published in 2026. But, clearly, some significant research gaps remain.

To address these remaining gaps, some historians have turned to models and analytical frameworks to guide their ongoing studies. These research tools provide structured questions that help interrogate sources and organize the different findings. However, when applied to Singapore before 1800, these tools tend to prove inadequate. This is because the primary sources dating from the latter Middle Ages and early modern period are fragmentary, incomplete, uneven in quality, and hardly plentiful—all factors that render these sources less suited to the research questions and rigorous interrogations demanded by such analytical frameworks.

Researchers experience frustration when they begin to fully appreciate that the authors of early modern texts grappled with different concerns than those presupposed by the analytical frameworks. This disconnect can tempt researchers to either ignore information that doesn't fit or distort the evidence to reach conclusions that are stipulated by a given model or framework. Researchers may find themselves metaphorically 'shaking the texts', hoping that if they apply enough pressure, something

---

[61] Kwa Chong Guan, Derek S.T. Heng, and Tan Tai Yong, *Singapore, a 700-Year History. From Early Emporium to World City* (Singapore: National Archives of Singapore, 2009); Kwa et al., *Seven Hundred Years*. In 2013, John Miksic's *Singapore and the Silk Road of the Sea* still assumed a hiatus or fallow period in Singapore's history, though he had admittedly narrowed that period from the early seventeenth and the early nineteenth centuries.

meaningful will emerge—even when the sources themselves clearly resist such manipulation.

In my own experience, the philosophy of language offers a more effective alternative to models and analytical frameworks. This is done by focusing on how meaning is constructed, understood, and communicated through the use of language. Resisting the temptation to impose certain concepts onto the evidence to reach predefined results, this approach invites researchers to closely engage with the original texts and to examine their words, phrases, and ideas in their original context. This method allows for an exploration of how meaning is shaped, distorted, and transmitted through language, offering a range of insights that models and frameworks would generally overlook. This is what I mean when, in some of my past publications, I say that I let the texts 'speak for themselves'.[62]

Because Singapore was always part of 'something else' between the fall of Temasek and the arrival of the British in 1819, any history of this period must, at least initially, rely on broader global histories or regional narratives. These yield crucial points of reference—key events and developments that are also shared with Singapore's neighbours in the region. With an appreciation of shared experiences in place, researchers can then begin to 'connect the dots' as more evidence surfaces.

While this approach to research makes a lot of sense within academic circles, I am less optimistic about how it resonates with the average reader. Successfully engaging members of the public requires more than filling in gaps within the historical record. It invites us to craft a narrative that is relevant, accessible, and connects to the stories people are already familiar with. In my experience, this is the most formidable challenge in crafting a history of Singapore before the British colonial era.

---

[62] Peter Borschberg, *The Singapore and Melaka Straits*, 15; more background and ideas in Peter Borschberg, *Reconstructing Singapore, c.1500–1800* (Singapore: NUS Press, forthcoming), Chapter 1.

How do we create awareness and get the message out?

To some extent, professional historians are public intellectuals. Their research is not solely for the benefit of the historical fraternity, they also engage the general public through different channels, ranging from newspaper articles to full-length books. The task at hand is to engage the public and effectively communicate their research findings to a wider audience. There is a difficult balancing act between advancing the field through scholarly publications and repackaging ideas for the public. This has serious career implications for professional historians based at institutions of higher learning, requiring them to carefully navigate their obligation to produce rigorous peer-reviewed academic research and meaningfully engage the public. This meaningful engagement, in my experience, is the toughest challenge of all. Based on my own time in the field and the subject of pre-1800 Singapore history, I single out three scenarios to illustrate what this challenge entails:

- 'I found a reference': As mentioned earlier, enthusiastic members of the public sometimes contact and share with me that they have discovered a reference to 'Singapore' in some old text or document. Upon closer investigation, however, such references are mostly too vague to yield any new or tangible insights. In such cases, expectation management is warranted: How does one explain that not all references are equally valuable without dousing enthusiasm or the excitement of having found a proverbial 'needle in the haystack'? Providing an answer in such a scenario is neither easy nor straightforward.
- 'You are making this up': The entrenched and lingering belief among members of the public that there are only a handful of references to Singapore from the period between c.1400 and 1800 often leads to scepticism. In some cases, I have even been accused of fabricating evidence. Such episodes serve as a reminder that researchers not

only have to discover and analyse new materials but also communicate one's research findings persuasively. Constructing a narrative that resonates with the public while remaining firmly grounded in the primary materials can be a daunting task, requiring a blend of creativity, persuasiveness, and verbal clarity.[63]

- 'I can't read this!': After a public lecture well over a decade ago, a member of the public came up to me and angrily vented his frustration that he couldn't read and verify the historical sources I had used to prepare my lecture. With hindsight, this incident marked a turning point in my research and in sharpening my research priorities. It is simply not enough to identify, evaluate, and incorporate new findings on Singapore before 1800 into an emerging narrative. The new texts and materials that have been identified must also be made accessible to the non-expert reader. In practice, this means making them available for public consumption in the form of annotated transcriptions and translations.[64] While these additional tasks of making the primary sources available to the public doubtlessly slow the pace of research output, my own experience shows that they certainly enhance their impact. So, when I get emails from members of the public along the lines of: 'I had no idea! This raises so many more questions!' I can confidently say to myself: 'Mission accomplished.'

The lesson here, especially for those working on the history of Singapore before 1800, is that historians, particularly those members of the fraternity conducting original research, have a responsibility to make their findings accessible to members of the public. This can involve the preparation of transcriptions

---

[63] Ibid.
[64] Ibid.

and annotated translations of the different types of new materials retrieved, but by the term 'accessible', I also mean that new research is made readily available and especially affordable to the average reader. There is little point in publishing one's research findings in prohibitively priced outlets that are also poorly distributed in Singapore and the region at large. In the end, historians as public intellectuals must find ways of sharing their work with the general public and not restrict their published research to the historical fraternity or publication outlets that are locked behind expensive paywalls.

Where do we go from here?

In his *Descriptive Dictionary of the Indian Islands and Adjacent Countries*, John Crawfurd claimed that 'for a period of about five centuries and a half [*sic*], there is no record of Singapore having been occupied, and it was only the occasional resort of pirates'.[65] This assertion, as seen, long formed the cornerstone of Singapore's pre-1800 historical canon, deeply entrenching the idea of a long temporal gap separating the fall of ancient Temasek and the arrival of the British in 1819. The centuries in-between represent a long pause or a void that remained virtually unrecorded and undescribed.

Today, however, we know that Crawfurd and British colonial historiography, generally, were wrong to assume that the centuries in-between represented a 'fallow space'. Over the past two decades, researchers in Singapore have begun to fill in this assumed temporal void with insights, events, and some colourful individuals. While good progress has been made in establishing a seamless timeline of key events, some significant gaps remain. But ongoing research is steadily illuminating Singapore's pre-1800 history-scape. Singapore's historiography has come a long way

---

[65] John Crawfurd, *Descriptive Dictionary*, 401.

since the early 1990s or even since the publication of *Singapore, a 700-Year History: From Early Emporium to World City* in 2009.

While some centuries before 1800 have admittedly been better researched than others, good progress has been made in recent years with respect to the eighteenth century, which covers the period between the assassination of Sultan Mahmud of Johor in 1699 and the founding of the British trading post in 1819. Noteworthy research has been completed by Benjamin Khoo, who has relied on Dutch and Malay sources. Separately, Jeff Khoo has trawled French-language materials touching on Singapore and the region dating back to the seventeenth century.[66]

In the British colonial tradition of documenting Singapore's history, emphasis was overwhelmingly placed on English-language written sources, while materials in other European languages were almost entirely disregarded. Only in the past two to three decades have researchers more systematically sought, examined, and evaluated a broader range of both conventional and unconventional sources, including those written in other European vernaculars as well as Asian languages. As a result, when commentators sometimes critique 'Eurocentric' perspectives in Singapore's historiography, they are generally referring to the 'Anglocentric' reconstructions from the era of high imperialism and early independence. It must be emphasized that these two concepts are by no means synonymous, and it has only been in recent years that the study of non-English European sources has contributed very considerably to enriching our understanding of Singapore's pre-1819 past.

Authors and editors of recent studies fully appreciate that their work does not represent the last word on the subject. The good news for aspiring researchers is that there are still ample opportunities to contribute to the ongoing historical explorations.

---

[66] Benjamin J.Q. Khoo, "The Changing Fortunes of the Raja Negara and the Orang Laut of Singapore in the 18th Century", *Temasek Working Papers Series*, no. 7 (2024): 1–32; Jeff Khoo Chun Yok, "French Encounters with the Straits Entrepot, 1680–1787", unpublished doctoral thesis, Department of History, National University of Singapore, 2024.

While historians are not in the business of predicting the future, they can nonetheless identify the direction in which current developments are trending. With that in mind, I will conclude this chapter with three key observations:

- Prospective researchers of pre-1800 Singapore's history need to be aware of the various skill sets that are required to successfully study and evaluate the different types of primary sources available to them. This means they need to learn languages (Asian, European, or both) and palaeography, among other ancillary skills.
- Thanks to the greater variety of sources and perspectives today, the Singaporean history-scape is also becoming more pluralistic. History is driven by the different questions we ask, and when we ask different questions, we will get different answers. In this spirit, it seems likely that Singapore's historical narrative, both before and after the nineteenth century, will grow more complex. In the future, we will be speaking increasingly of the histories of Singapore in the plural.[67]
- The extension of Singapore's historical timeline back to the 1290s and the construction of a seamless narrative spanning the thirteenth to the twenty-first centuries has also reframed the role and significance of Singapore's colonial experience. This augmented timeline relativizes both the role of Singapore in the British Empire as well as the significance researchers afford to Sir Thomas Stamford Raffles. It is entirely appropriate that each generation reexamines Raffles anew and reassesses the role, if any, they continue to assign to him.[68]

---

[67] See the concluding thoughts in Peter Borschberg, *Reconstructing Singapore*, Chapter 1.

[68] Peter Borschberg, "Alatas' Raffles. A Review of Syed Hussein Alatas' Thomas Stamford Raffles", *Singapore Journal of Tropical Geography*, 43, 1 (2022): 112.

Chapter 2

Archaeology in the Writing of Singapore's History

Kwa Chong Guan

For John Miksic
Who Pioneered the Development of Archaeology in Singapore

Introduction

Archaeology has profoundly reshaped our understanding of Singapore's history by offering insights that written records alone cannot provide. A series of groundbreaking excavations—from the 1984 Fort Canning digs to more recent maritime archaeological work—have provided crucial information into Singapore before its colonial foundations in 1819. These discoveries challenge earlier assumptions about Singapore's historical trajectory, placing the island within a broader regional and global context that long predates the arrival of the British in the nineteenth century.

The essay argues that archaeology complements and expands upon traditional documentary records, offering an alternative lens to reconstruct Singapore's history. Excavations of prehistoric sites and shipwrecks, along with artefacts such as Chinese ceramics and metal tools, reveal intricate networks of trade and cultural exchange. These findings not only deepen our understanding of

Singapore's place in regional and global histories but also challenge linear narratives of colonial dominance by highlighting the island's historical agency. By tracing the movement of people, goods, and ideas, archaeology situates Singapore within a connected world. This underlines its enduring role as a key node in international trade before the age of 'globalization'.

The Importance of the 1984 Excavations

In January 1984, the first archaeological investigations at Fort Canning were conducted by the Old National Museum. The goal was to seek confirmation of a pre-1819 settlement on the hill, which was first reported by Stamford Raffles and Dr John Crawfurd over a century ago. Professor John N. Miksic, then lecturer at Gadjah Mada University in Jogjakarta, was invited to undertake the investigations and, against all odds, recovered in situ artefacts confirming what Raffles and Crawfurd saw. The former Directors of the old Raffles Museum, Michel Tweedie and Dr C. A. Gibson-Hill, did not think to investigate the hill—ironic given that it was located right behind the museum. Instead, they turned their attention to excavating prehistoric sites on the Malay peninsula, focusing on the areas of the seventeenth-century capitals of the Johor Sultanate further up the Johor River. They might have assumed that any 'antiquities' on the hill were destroyed by the artillery fort constructed there in 1859 and the subsequent digging of the reservoir in 1926. It thus came as a huge surprise when, in 1984, Professor Miksic recovered in situ fourteenth-century artefacts there. This stimulated public interest in the potential for archaeology to reveal more about Singapore's deep past—interest that would facilitate further digs around Fort Canning over the next thirty years. Prior to 1984, there was little interest in local archaeology within Singapore. Today, promoting archaeology and caring for its treasures has become a more mainstream concern, demonstrated by its inclusion in the National Heritage Board's 'Our Heritage Plan 2.0'.

Prehistoric Archaeology of Cave Settlements

Why was there more interest in archaeology on the Malay peninsula than in Singapore? The Raffles Museum has been interested in the prehistorical archaeology of this area since the beginning of the twentieth century. At the time, they mounted the first small-scale exhibition of archaeological and historical artefacts, including some neolithic tools from Pahang, in 1925. When F.N. Chasen joined the museum in 1921 and was later appointed director in 1932, the museum became more actively engaged in prehistorical archaeology.[69] With the support of M.W.F. Tweedie and H.D. Collins, who joined the museum in 1932 and 1934 respectively, the museum was able to excavate three cave settlements around Ipoh in Perak and around Guar Kepah in Province Wellesley. They also worked with the Dutch prehistorian P.V. van Stein Callenfels who convened the first Congress of Prehistorians in Hanoi in 1932 and the second in Manila in 1935. Chasen and Collins attended both and reported on their work in Perak. The Congress was so impressed that they designated the Raffles Museum as the repository for centralising typological and comparative collections of prehistoric objects from the whole of the further East. This decision by the Congress enabled the Raffles Museum to grow its prehistoric collection through donations of artefacts from around the region.

This interest in the paleo-archaeology of the Malay peninsula was part of a wider, global interest in human origins that burgeoned in the early twentieth century. It started with the recovery of

---

[69] B. Luyt, "Collectors and Collecting for the Raffles Museum in Singapore 1920–1940," *Library & History* 26, no. 3 (2013): 183–195, DOI: 10.1179/175834810X12731358995235 on how Chasen built a network of social relationships that enabled him to expand the collections of the Raffles Museum. Highlights of the archaeological collections deposited or donated to the Raffles Museum between 1930 and 1940 are in Alexandra Avieropoulou Choo, *Archaeology; A Guide to the Collections, National Museum Singapore* (Singapore: National Museum of Singapore, 1987).

Australopithecus africanus in 1924, followed by Robert Broome's 1930 work at Sterkfontein and later Louis and Mary Leakey's 1930 recovery of Oldowan tools in their excavations at Olduvai Gorge. In Asia, the 1921 recovery of *Homo erectus* remains in the Zhoukoudian cave in China and on Java spurred interest in paleo-archaeology on the Malay peninsula. In fact, both Raffles Museum digs in 1934 and 1938, including Collin's and Tweedie's excavations in Perak, Pahang, and Kelantan, were funded by a grant from the Carnegie Corporation of New York. These archaeological investigations into the prehistory of the Malay peninsula by Tweedie and his colleagues apparently impressed the colonial government so much that it prompted them to host the Third Congress of Prehistorians of the Far East in January 1938.[70]

Tweedie resumed his research into prehistoric Malaya after Second World War with an account of 'The Stone Age in Malaya', published in 1953, and a more popular introduction, *Prehistoric Malaya*, in 1953, which went through two further editions in the following decade.[71] Tweedie's reconstruction of Malayan prehistory borrowed from the prevailing conventional European framework of the Palaeolithic era. This was represented by the Kota Tampan stone industry, first excavated by Collins in 1938 and further excavated by G. de G Sieveking and D. Walker in 1954. The Palaeolithic was followed by a Mesolithic, represented by the 'Hoabinhian' sites Collins and Tweedie excavated. These

---

[70] *Proceedings of the Third Congress of Prehistorians of the Far East, Singapore, 24th January–30 January 1938*, ed. F.N. Chasen and M.W.F. Tweedie (Singapore: Government Printers/Washington D.C.: U.S. Government Printing Office, 1940). See Foo Shu Teng, "Hoabinhian Rocks: An Examination of Guar Kepah Artifacts from the Heritage Conservation Centre in Jurong," MA Thesis, National University of Singapore, January 2010. DOI: 10.13140/ RG.2.2.28005.29929) for an examination of the relevance of these colonial-era excavations for research today.

[71] M.W.F. Tweedie, "The Stone Age in Malaya," *Journal of the Malayan Branch of the Royal Asiatic Society (JMBRAS)* 26, part 2 (1953): 4–87. M.W.F. Tweedie, *Prehistoric Malaya* (Singapore: Donald Moore for Eastern Universities Press, 1955, 2nd edn. 1957, 3rd edn. 1965).

sites were named 'Hoabinhian' after the Mesolithic assemblages excavated by M. Colani in 1927 in the north Vietnamese province of Hòa Binh. The First Congress of Prehistorians accepted them as indicative of a prehistoric culture dated to the Holocene. The Neolithic is well represented in the findings from the rock shelter at Gua Cha in Kelantan, started by H.D. Noone in 1935 and systematically excavated by Sieveking and Tweedie in 1954.[72] They not only recovered polished stone tools but also pottery and human skeletons. Tweedie was aware of the limitations of imposing a European framework on Malayan prehistory. However, this cultural framework has proved robust and continues to structure much of the ongoing prehistoric research in Malaysia up to today.[73]

Between 1952 and 1957, the Raffles Museum engaged Prince John Lowenstein, a colleague of Tweedie, along with G. de G. Sieveking to investigate the post-Neolithic Metal Age in Malaya. Lowenstein authored a long essay on the origins of the Malayan metal age, in which he stated that bronze artefacts—drums, bells, and celts—were introduced into the peninsula from Dong Son in Vietnam. The problem in investigating the Metal Age in Malaya is

---

[72] G. de Sieveking, "Excavations at Gua Cha, Kelantan, 1954, Part 1," *Federation Museums Journal* 1–2 (1954–1955): 75–138.

[73] See for example, *Arkeologie di Malaysia dahulu dan kini*, ed. Asyaari Muhamazd (Bangi: Penerbit Universiti Kebangsaan Malaysia, 2018); *Arkeologi di Malaysia; Sejarah, Warisan dan Kebudayaan*, ed. Stephen Chia and Velat Bueng (Kuala Lumpur: Dewan Bahasa dan Pustaka, 2020); *Prasejarah dan Protosejarah Tanah Melayu: Sejarah Nasional Malaysia*, ed. Nik Hassan Shuhaimi Nik Abdul Rahman and Zuliskandar Ramli (Kuala Lumpur: Dewan Bahasa dan Pustaka, 2021); *Tamadun Prasejarah Malaysia/ Prehistoric Civilization of Malaysia*, ed. Adi Haji Tahan, revised edition (Kuala Lumpur: Muzium Negara, 2022). See also Nik Hassan Shuhaimi Nik Abdul Rahman, "Current Issues on Prehistory and Protohistory in Malaysian Archaeology," *JMBRAS* 80, no. 1 (2007): 41–57; Adi Haji Taha, "Archaeology in Peninsula Malaysia: Past, Present and Future," *Journal of Southeast Asian Studies* 18, issue 2 (1987): 205–211; Stephen Chia, "A History of Archaeology in Malaysia," in *Handbook of East & Southeast Asian Archaeology*, ed. Junko Habu, Peter V. Lape, and John W. Olsen (New York: Springer, 2017), 125–141.

that all the metal artefacts and associated items were chance finds devoid of any archaeological context. Consequently, the best Lowenstein and Sieveking could do was an inventory of the metal artefacts and related pottery in the Raffles Museum, the Taiping, and the Kuala Lumpur museums. Otherwise, the Metal Age in the Malay Peninsula is usually associated with slab-lined graves and its related artefacts of glass and carnelian beads and pottery found by Collins in Southern Perak and northern Selangor in 1937.[74]

Collins resumed his fieldwork in 1948 using the remnants of the 1938 funds from the Carnegie Corporation. He investigated the site of Tanjong Bunga on the southwest coast of Johor where a flake tool culture had been found to be more widespread than was originally suspected and may have extended to the northern coast of Singapore island. In 1949, Collins and anthropologist P.D.R. Williams-Hung investigated the shoreline of Ubin Island, where casual finds of Neolithic tools had been reported but did not find any identifiable stone artefacts.[75]

Tweedie's and Collins' field notes were re-examined by Durham University's prehistoric archaeologist David Clinnick in 2017 as part of a George Lyndon Hicks Fellowship awarded by the National Library. Clinnick and National Museum's Assistant Curator Sharon Lim were able to work out from the field notes left by Collins and Tweedie that the site they investigated had been on the far western end of Pulau Ubin. Clinnick and Lim then embarked on a field trip to the area where they identified and collected several pieces of cracked angular basalt eroding out of the ground. On examining them, they found that the artefacts had been chipped and flaked by humans.[76]

---

[74] H.D. Collins, "Recent Finds of Iron Age Sites in Southern Perak and Selangor," *Bulletin of the Raffles Museum* series B, 1 pt. 2 (1937): 75–92.

[75] P.D.R. Williams-Hunt, "Recent Archaeological Discoveries in Malaya (1845–1950)," *JMBRAS* 24, no. 1 (1951): 191.

[76] D. Clinnick and S. Lim, "In Search of Prehistoric Singapore," *MuseSG* 10 no. 36, issue 2 (Singapore: National Heritage Board, 2018): 40–42.

In summary, the pioneering forays of Tweedie, Collins, and other Raffles Museum curators into the prehistory of the Malay Peninsula secured for the peninsula, including Singapore, a place within the wider regional prehistory of Asia. The renowned Harvard University prehistorian Hallam Movius recognized the work of Collins and Tweedie at Kota Tampan as a reconstruction of the connections between the lower Palaeolithic cultures of Southern and Eastern Asia.[77] Today, we recognize that the archipelago of Southeast Asia was an integrated maritime space, possibly even assimilated 'into broader socio-spatial spheres of interaction throughout the Holocene. Namely, it was part of a broader, yet weakly connected and piecemeal, proto-globalised world'.[78] For Singapore, further archaeological investigations on Pulau Ubin may confirm a 3,000-year or older settlement on the island, which may have been a part of this 'proto-globalization'.

Surveying and Excavating Johor Lama in 1953

Between 1948 and 1954, Gibson-Hill, along with the anthropologist P.D.R Williams-Hunt, H.D. Collins, and the entrepreneur-turned-scholar Han Wai Toon, had been collecting ceramic shards from sites on the Johor River, principally Kota Tinggi and Johor Lama. The archaeological survey and excavation of the fortified village of Johor Lama in 1953, which

---

[77] Hallam L. Movius, Jr (1907–1987) in his seminal overview essay "Palaeolithic Archaeology in Southern and Eastern Asia, Exclusive of India," *Cahiers d'histoire Mondiale* 2/iii (1955): 511–512.

[78] Tim Denham, "Domestic Dispersal, Human Agency and Connectivity in Island Southeast Asia during the Holocene," in *Globalization in Prehistory: Contact, Exchange and the "People Without History,"* ed. N. Boivin and M.D. Frachetti (Cambridge: Cambridge University Press, 2018), 81; B. Bellina, "Was There a Late Prehistoric Integrated Southeast Asia Maritime Space? Insight from Settlements and Industries," in *Spirits and Ships: Cultural Transfers in Early Monsoon Asia*, ed. A. Acri R. Blench and Alexandra Landmann (Singapore: ISEAS–Yusof Ishak Institute, 2017), 239–272.

Gibson-Hill, Sieveking, and University of Malaya's historical geographer Paul Wheatley undertook was an extension of this surface collection of ceramic sherds.[79] It was also a continuation of the work of the British orientalist H.G. Quaritch who had been invited by the Government of Johor to extend his field work on the early historic site of Bujang Valley in Kedah between 1937 and 1940. More specifically, the survey and excavation of Johor Lama was to obtain archaeological evidence of the shifting settlements of the Johor sultans, on which there is a paucity of documentary evidence.[80] The Portuguese records referring to Johor and their rivalry with the Johor sultans were being researched for the first time by Ian A. MacGregor at the history department of the University of Malaya[81] and provided Gibson-Hill with new materials for his detail reconstruction of 'Johore Lama and Other Ancient Sites on the Johor River'.[82]

The ceramic shards collected by Gibson-Hill are now housed at the National Heritage Board's Heritage Conservation Centre, along with his detailed reconstruction of Johor Lama's history— supported by MacGregor's study, 'Johor Lama in the Sixteenth Century'. They received little attention from the University of Malaya's history department. At the time, the department was more focused on the modern history of Singapore and Malaya, leaving these earlier historical insights largely overlooked.

---

[79] G. de G. Sieveking, Peter Wheatley, C.A. Gibson-Hill, "Archaeological Discoveries in Malaya (1953); The Excavations at Johore Lama," *JMBRAS* 27, part 2 (1954): 224–233. A more recent archaeological investigation of the Johor River sites is Asyaari Masihi, *Seramik empayar Johor; Abad 11–19* (Kuala Lumpur: Jabatan Muzium Malaysia, 2012).

[80] G. de G. Sieveking, "The Fortified City of Johore Lama, and the Use of Archaeological Evidence," *JMBRAS* 28, part 2 (1955): 198–199.

[81] I. A. MacGregor, "Johore Lama in the Sixteenth Century," *JMBRAS* 28, part 2 (1955): 48–125.

[82] C.A. Gibson-Hill, "Johore Lama and Other Ancient Sites on the Johore River," *JMBRAS* 28, part 2 (1955): 126–197.

It was only in 1986 that the relevance of these ceramic shards, especially the under-glazed blue porcelain, became relevant to the reconstruction of Singapore's early modern history after the 1984 Fort Canning excavations.

In early 1986, The Oral History Department and the National Archives organized an exhibition on 'Singapore Before Raffles', which drew on the deep social memories of the Malay community around settlements in the Kallang River estuary. At the time, I was the director of the Oral History Department. I persuaded an old friend, Ms Lee Geok Boi, to lend the exhibition a collection of nine under-glazed blue porcelain sherds that she had received as a gift from an Australian friend, the late Mr Geoffrey Ovens. He operated a dredge to clear the Kallang estuary in the late 1960s, part of the construction project of the Benjamin Sheares Bridge, and collected these nine under-glazed shards as part of a sack of ceramic fragments. Ovens was sufficiently sharp-eyed to notice unusual objects being dredged from the river bed. He stopped the dredge and collected a sack of Chinese ceramic shards from the mud and called the old National Museum to come and check the significance of what he had been dredging up. As Ovens recounted to his friends in Singapore, including myself, the museum curators he spoke to were uninterested in what he had found. The bag of shards were thus distributed among his friends or thrown away. Only nine shards were kept by one of them, Ms Lee Geok Boi, whom I persuaded to loan to the 1986 Oral History and Archives exhibition. They were eventually donated to the National Museum, where they are now displayed as evidence of an early seventeenth-century port settlement in the Kallang River estuary.[83]

The early seventeenth-century dating of the port settlement in the Kallang River estuary is inferred from the style of the motifs painted on shards. They can be precisely traced to the era

---

[83] Kwa Chong Guan, "A Seventeenth-Century Port Settlement in the Kallang Estuary," in *Shipwrecks and the Maritime History of Singapore*, ed. Kwa Chong Guan (Singapore: ISEAS–Yusof-Ishak Institute, 2023), 70–79.

of the Ming emperor Wanli (1573–1620),[84] the same as that of the shards Gibson-Hill collected from Johor Lama and other sites on the Johor River. These shards confirm seventeenth-century Portuguese cartographic references to a harbour of sorts in the Kallang River estuary. The Portuguese–Malayan explorer and cartographer Manoel Godinho de Eredia marked a *xabandaria* (the Portuguese transcription of the Persian 'Shabandar', literally, the 'Lord of the Haven') on the east coast of Singapore in his map 'Chorographic Description of the Straits of Sincapura and Sabban, 1604 A.D'. Another map of the Singapore and Melaka Straits and the Riaus by Andé Pereira dos Reis, c. 1654, also marks a xabandaria on Singapore's east coast. The shards dredged by Ovens from the Kallang River estuary were likely remnants of a cargo of porcelain that cracked or broke during its journey from China. These damaged pieces were probably thrown overboard when the ship was anchored in the estuary to replenish fresh water and other supplies. The shards also suggest that—supported by similar shard findings along the Johor River sites—Singapore was the gateway harbour to a trading network that extended up the Johor River.

Excavations on the Forbidden Hill, 1984

The 1984 archaeological investigations were 'rescue' or 'salvage' archaeology undertaken in advance of construction or land development that could have permanently damaged or destroyed potential surviving artefacts on the historic site. This was in part a response to the Singapore Tourism Board's proposals to redevelop the hill into a high-activity tourism centre, which may have further destroyed any remaining in situ

---

[84] Kwa Chong Guan, "16th century underglazed Blue Porcelain Sherds from the Kallang Estuary," in *Early Singapore 1300s-1819: Evidence in Maps, Text and Artefacts*, ed. J.N. Miksic and Cheryl-Ann Low Mei Gek (Singapore: Singapore History Museum, 2004), 86–94.

fourteenth-century artefacts.[85] Miksic had ten days approved by the museum to search for any archaeological evidence of early settlement on Fort Canning or Bukit Larangan, meaning the Forbidden Hill, as it was earlier known to the Malay community in Singapore when Raffles arrived in 1819. Most of the subsequent archaeological investigations and excavations around the environs of Fort Canning were also rescue or salvage archaeology undertaken ahead of the development of the site—for example the new Parliament House Complex in November 1994 or the lawn at Empress Place before its redevelopment for the celebration of Singapore's fiftieth anniversary in 2015.

Against the odds, the excavations from 18 to 28 January 1984 recovered 1,346 pottery shards weighing a total of 14.31 kilograms, which confirmed Crawfurd's observation in 1822 of antiquities pointing to an earlier settlement on Fort Canning.[86] National Museum consultant A. Choo-Avieropoulou undertook a follow-up excavation in June 1984 and January 1985.[87] The next advance in the excavation on Fort Canning was in November 1987, when the National Museum hosted the Fourth Archaeological and Conservation Workshop, convened by the ASEAN Committee

---

[85] Fort Canning has since been developed into a history and nature park exhibiting Temasek history in a preserved archaeology excavation trench and a recreated fourteenth-century royal orchard and bathing pool. The nineteenth-century history of the hill is preserved in the tombstones of the old cemetery embedded in its perimeter walls. The military history of the hill is preserved in the gates of the old fort and the twentieth-century military command centre.

[86] John N. Miksic, *Archaeological Research on the "Forbidden Hill" of Singapore: Excavations at Fort Canning, 1984* (Singapore: National Museum, 1986) sets the standards for archaeological investigation and reporting. Miksic provides a summary of his 1984 investigations in: John N. Miksic, *Singapore & the Silk Road of the Sea, 1300–1800* (Singapore: NUS Press, 2013 and reprints), 222–229.

[87] A. Choo-Avieropoulou, *Report on the Excavation at Fort Canning Hill* (Singapore: National Museum, 1986). Miksic notes that 'the report of those excavations is somewhat difficult to interpret' on 229–231 of his *Singapore & the Silk Road of the Sea*.

on Culture and Information.[88] One conclusion emerging from the Intra-ASEAN Archaeological and Conservation Workshop was that the area between the *keramat*, which Crawfurd recorded on Fort Canning, and the old cemetery wall warranted further investigation. Miksic thus turned to this location in 1988 for a major excavation that recovered further large quantities of fourteenth century artefacts. All of these digs confirmed that the location of Fort Canning was a high activity area seven hundred years ago.

The excavations on Fort Canning in the 1980s raised public awareness and interest in archaeology, increasing support for archaeological investigations into other potential locations along the Singapore River before major redevelopments. Miksic was involved in these excavations at the site of the new Parliament House Complex before its construction in late 1994, at Empress Place in 1998 before its restoration as the Asian Civilisations Museum, and at Colombo Court in 2000 before it became the site of the new Supreme Court. In early 2003, the Singapore Cricket Club even allowed Miksic to excavate a corner of its cricket pitch. The artefacts recovered in the original two-week excavation confirmed the Padang as a potentially large archaeological site. The St. Andrew's Cathedral also allowed Miksic to excavate its grounds in late 2003 before the construction of an extension to the cathedral. A longer lead time provided by the cathedral allowed Miksic to plan a more careful excavation, which recovered artefacts weighing almost a tonne in total.

Salvage archaeology of possible historical sites scheduled for development continued into the 2000s. They were helmed by Lim Chen Sien, a postgraduate student of Miksic, who was then leading the Archaeological Unit established at the ISEAS-Yusof Ishak Institute in 2010. Lim excavated a segment of the old Parliament Lane behind the Victoria Concert before its

---

[88] Fourth Intra–ASEAN Archaeological and Conservation Workshop Singapore, 1–21 November 1987, *Report* deposited in https://eservice.nlb.gov.sg/item_holding.aspx?bid=5295851.

repair and recovered some 600 kilograms of artefacts. Lim and his team also recovered over 300 kilograms of artefacts in the space between the old Supreme Court and the old City Hall before its redevelopment into a National Gallery in November 2010. The Archaeological Unit also participated in a 2010 investigation led by Dr Goh Geok Yian of an area on Fort Canning near the keramat, which was then planned for development as part of a 'Spice Garden'. The investigation recovered a significant quantity of in situ fourteenth century artefacts. However, the largest excavation undertaken by the Archaeological Unit was at Empress Place, in front of the Victoria Concert Hall in early 2015. Lim Chen Sien and his team recovered some two and a half tonnes of artefacts from their two-month excavations.

Thanks to the several tons of artefacts excavated on and around Fort Canning, fourteenth-century Temasek is now one of the best archaeologically documented port sites on the Melaka Straits. Most of the artefacts were ceramics. Local earthenware for everyday use, such as pots and utensils, constituted some 50 per cent of the ceramics recovered.[89] Coarse stoneware jars for storage and transportation of various foodstuffs constituted the next largest category of ceramics finds. Also excavated in large numbers were what are now called 'small mouth jars', coarse stoneware used to store various liquids from wine to sauces.[90] The bulk of the high-fired ceramics recovered is green-glazed celadons produced in quantity for export at Southeast China provincial kilns and the Longquan kilns at Zhejian province. High-quality Qingbai and Shufu white wares for everyday use were also recovered in notable quantities. But what is most significant is the large quantity of underglaze blue-and-white porcelains found on Fort Canning. These underglaze blue-and-white porcelains

---

[89] Miksic, *Singapore and the Silk Road of the Sea*, 266–280 for a typology and analysis of fourteenth-century Singapore earthenware.

[90] Sharon Wai-yee Wong, "A Case Report on the Function(s) of the 'Mercury Jar': Fort Canning, Singapore, in the 14th Century," *Archaeological Research in Asia* 7 (2016): 10–17.

were produced for the first time at the Jingdezhen kilns when their potters started experimenting with brush painting underglaze and cobalt pigments to produce the brilliant blue decorations on their wares during the Yuan dynasty.[91] The notable quantities of these highly valued porcelains found on Fort Canning thus singles out fourteenth century Temasek as a significant import market for this particular category of Chinese ceramics. This archaeological documentation of Fort Canning and its environs has enabled Miksic to locate Temasek in its regional context from the fourteenth to the eighteenth centuries, which he summarized and published in his reflective overview *Singapore & The Silk Road of the Sea 1300–1800*. More specifically, this documentation has also enabled Derek Heng to attempt a reconstruction of the layout of the port settlement on and around Fort Canning along with locating that port settlement as an international and regional trading port in the thirteenth and fourteenth centuries.[92] More recently, Heng has explored how small archaeological finds can help identify the social status, demographic differences, and cultural identity traits not only in Temasek but also in other contemporaneous port cities in the region.[93]

---

[91] Ann Gerritsen, *The City of Blue and White: Chinese Porcelain and the Early Modern World* (Cambridge: University Press, 2020), 103–113.

[92] D. Heng, "Reconstructing Banzu: A Fourteenth Century Port Settlement in Singapore," *JMBRAS* 75, no. 1 (2002): 69–90; D. Heng, "Temasik as an International and Regional Trading Port in the Thirteenth and Fourteenth Centuries: A Reconstruction Based on Recent Archaeological Data," *JMBRAS* 72, no. 1 (1999): 113–124.

[93] D. Heng, "Urban Demographics along the Asian Maritime Silk Road," in *The Maritime Silk Road: Global Connectivities, Regional Nodes, Localities*, ed. Franck Billé, Sanjyot Mehendale, and James W. Lankton (Amsterdam: AUP, 2022): 215–241; D. Heng, "Regional Influences, Economic Adaption and Cultural Articulation: Diversity and Cosmopolitism in Fourteenth-century Singapore," *Journal of Southeast Asian Studies* 50, no. 4 (2019): 476–488, DOI: https://doi.org/10.1017/S0022463420000016; Shah Alam Zaini, "Metal Production and Social Organization in Fourteenth Century Singapore," *Journal of Southeast Asian Studies* 50, no. 4 (2019): 489–506, DOI: https://doi.org/10.1017/S0022463420000028.

Maritime Archaeology

In 2005, The Singapore Tourism Board acquired the cargo of a ninth century ship that was shipwrecked off the Indonesian island of Belitung. It was turned into a display as a tourist attraction, sparking interest in what the wreck could illuminate about earlier cycles of global trade.[94] The Belitung shipwreck was part of a large wave of historical shipwrecks recovered in the Riau, the Java Sea, Vietnam, and the East Coast of Malaysia. Together, they provided a regionally wider and chronologically longer context of global trade in the South China Sea and Indian Ocean, which helped frame the emergence of Temasek as a port settlement in the fourteenth century and explain its historical development since then. It was only in 2016 that a shipwreck was accidentally discovered near the rock outcrop of Pedra Branca or Batu Putih on the eastern approach to the Singapore Strait. Its excavation over the next three years identified it as a fourteenth century ship headed for Temasek.[95]

In 2019, further surveys of the sea around Pedra Branca found a second wreck, which was excavated over the next two years. This second wreck has been identified from archival records as an eighteenth merchant ship, the *Shah Muncher,* which was commissioned and owned by the Bombay trader and shipowner Sorabjee Muncherjee Readymoney. The *Shah Muncher* was built in India in 1789 and sank on its return voyage from China to India in 1796 while carrying a diverse cargo of Chinese ceramics and other goods ranging from glass to copper alloy. These two shipwrecks challenge our understanding of the maritime trade that underpinned Temasek in the fourteenth century and Singapore in the nineteenth century.

---

[94] See Natali Pearson, *Belitung: The Afterlives of a Shipwreck* (Honolulu: University of Hawai'I Press, 2023) for a critical heritage study of the Belitung shipwreck.

[95] Kwa Chong Guan, ed., *Shipwrecks and the Maritime History of Singapore* (Singapore: ISEAS–Yusof Ishak Institute, 2023) is a series of essays on the archaeological and historical context of these two historic shipwrecks.

The first issue is the large volume of under-glazed blue-and-white porcelain that was recovered from the wreck. This was pointed out by Michael Flecker, who led the excavation of both wrecks. He noted that he had not seen such quantities of blue-and-white porcelains on any other historic shipwrecks he had previously worked on. That the porcelains were identical to what had been excavated on and around Fort Canning suggests that the cargo was destined for Temasek. But the sheer volume of porcelains suggests that, while some of it was for local consumption, much of it would have been re-exported to other port cities in the Indian Ocean. Chinese porcelains have been found at some 123 archaeological sites in India, from the peninsula to Delhi. The most interesting and significant was the accidental find of a hoard of broken Yuan blue-and-white ceramics, which came from the royal kitchen of the Tughlaqs ruler Feroze Shah of the Delhi sultanate.[96] These findings suggest that Temasek was a major entrepôt for the trade in Chinese ceramics.

Second, the volume of ceramics recovered from the Temasek wreck—not to mention earlier wrecks from the Belitung/Tang cargo to the Ming wrecks in Malaysia and Vietnam—has revised our understanding of Asian premodern trade. An earlier generation of economic historians, led by Dutch socioeconomic historian J.C. van Leur, characterized premodern Asian trade as a form of itinerant commerce, where traders would load their ships with jars or bundles of goods and sail from port to port, engaging in exchange along the way. It was a system like that of medieval Europe, where traders in their caravans moved from town to town between a circuit of markets and trade fairs. However, the large number of bundled and stacked plates and bowls found from the excavations suggests otherwise. Asian trade was not built

---

[96] *Hoard of Chinese Porcelain (A Rare Discovery from Firoz Shah Kotla)* (New Delhi: Archaeological Survey of India, 2017) was an exhibition catalogue of these chance finds of Yuan blue-and-white wares discovered some fifty years ago in Firoz Shah Kotla, Delhi.

on peddling. Rather, it was wholesale trade of mass-produced ceramics involving large-scale financing. These historic shipwrecks thus raise new questions about how this large-scale trade of mass-produced ceramics was organized. Who provided the funding for such large-scale orders of ceramics and their shipping? How were Temasek and other post-settlements organized for the marketing of such a large volume of ceramics? These are questions that remain open as of now.

Third, the shipping records show that the *Shah Muncher* was registered as a private merchant ship. This is significant because it suggests that it was not an official British East India Company (EIC) ship. The EIC had a monopoly over the Cape of Good Hope, which means that the *Shah Muncher* was registered to sail in the Indian Ocean and South China Sea but not around the tip of Africa. These 'country ships', as they were called, engaged in the profitable but risky trade at the small ports of the Indian Ocean, the East Indies, and China, places that the EIC had withdrawn from by the eighteenth century. The cargo recovered from the *Shah Muncher* tallies with its manifest and indicates the wide range of goods it carried not only for its owners but also for other countries or private traders operating outside the EIC's jurisdictions. It was these country traders—like A.L. Johnston, David Napier, his partner David Scott, and Alexander Gutherie— who decided to base themselves in Singapore, the new EIC 'station' established by Stamford Raffles as a free port in 1819. Together with other country traders, they formed a community that actively lobbied the EIC and the British Government to hold on to Singapore in the face of Dutch opposition to the settlement. The *Shah Muncher* wreck thus gives us insights into the structure and contents of the country trade that underpinned Singapore's survival and prosperity as a port city during its earlier colonial years. This was particularly important because of the EIC's declining interest in Singapore after it lost its royal monopoly on trade with China in 1833.

Conclusion

The archaeological evidence reviewed here is more than a complement to the archived textual record and its lacunae. As Sieveking argued, '[I]n view of the paucity of documentary evidence for the movement of the Malay sultans and their followers during the 16th and 17th centuries, it is of interest to review the possibilities of obtaining such evidence by archaeological methods.'[97] The artefacts recovered by archaeologists, whether they are prehistoric lithic tools or Wan-li blue-and-white porcelains, are evidence of an alternative history embedded in objects—a history of production that traces their creation, functional use, and the social significance reflected in their form, style, and decorations. These objects, once presented as gifts, preserved as heirlooms, or traded, are evidence of a connected history that cannot be fully captured by documentary evidence.[98] The brilliant blue underglaze-decorated vase was a local object at its point of manufacture in Jingezhen but transformed into a global object once it was shipped to Temasek and onwards to the Feroze Shah Kotla complex in Delhi or the Ardebil Shrine in Iran.[99] Archaeological evidence is, therefore, a reluctant yet powerful witness to our interconnected histories before the age of globalization.

---

[97] G. de S. Sieveking, "The Fortified City of Johore Lama and the Use of Archaeological Evidence," *JMBRAS* part 2 (1955): 198.

[98] Chris Caple, *Objects: Reluctant Witnesses to the Past* (London: Routledge, 2006); E.S. Cooke, Jr, *Global Objects: Toward a Connected Art History* (Princeton: Princeton University Press, 2022).

[99] J.A. Pope, *Chinese Porcelains from the Ardebil Shrine* (London: Sotheby Parke Bernet, 2nd edn. 1981).

Part II

The Reassessments:
New Perspectives on the 1819 Paradigm

Preface to Part II

The Reassessments: New Perspectives on the 1819 Paradigm

Behind any origin story are kernels of truth shrouded in myth. 1819 has been traditionally identified as the official and unambiguous start date of Singapore's history. It was the year that Sir Stamford Raffles landed ashore near today's Boat Quay, which, we are told, forever transformed Singapore's future. However, Singapore's future was arguably most shaped by two later treaties that were separately and independently signed in 1824, both of which sought solutions to unresolved disputes arising from the original 1819 Singapore Treaty.

When Raffles first arrived in 1819, he found that Singapore was a fiefdom of Malaysia's Johor Sultanate, which was a proxy of the Dutch East India Company. In short, the Dutch had claims to the land already. Recognizing this predicament, Raffles bypassed the Johor Sultan by signing the treaty with his semi-illegitimate half-brother. The 1819 treaty thus came with many shortcomings and was heavily disputed. First, administrative control over Singapore would be split between the Sultan's brother and the British. The British did not immediately acquire *sovereignty* over the island, meaning that they could not enact legislation or undertake extensive planning and construction. Instead, they leased a small parcel of land on its southern shores to set up a trading post. This angered the Dutch, who felt that Raffles illegally bypassed their territorial claims by signing the treaty with the Sultan's brother.

Immediately in 1820, the British and Dutch governments began negotiating how to peacefully resolve their overlapping claims to Singapore. Discussions were finally concluded in 1824 with the Anglo-Dutch Treaty, signed in London between the United Kingdom and the Netherlands. The treaty traded British and Dutch colonial holdings, such that the regions around Malaya, Java, Sumatra, Borneo were divided between British-Malaya (including Singapore) and the Dutch East Indies. One of the most consequential treaties for modern Southeast Asia, it laid the borders that today define modern Singapore, Malaysia, and Indonesia. Ironically, not a single representative of Southeast Asia was present.

A second treaty was simultaneously and independently signed in Singapore between John Crawfurd of the British East India Company and the Johor Sultanate. This second Treaty of Friendship and Alliance replaced Raffles' 1819 treaty by ceding to the British full control over the island. In one year, these dual treaties resolved all the faults of Raffles' original agreement and firmly established Singapore—in its entirety—as a British colony. Raffles himself took no part in either development.

Singapore's origins story is thus much more complicated—and interesting!—than often appreciated. Even though 1819 is considered a turning point in its history, it was really 1824 that established British control and secured Singapore's future. During the five years in between, Singapore was caught in the middle of territorial disputes between the British and the Dutch, and the British EIC saw it as more of a liability than an asset. Traditional narratives on Singapore's founding often glaze over this critical five year interim in favour of the much simpler story of Raffles' discovery. One potential conclusion is that 1824 should be seen instead as the 'start date' of Singapore's modern history. But the larger point is that history is much more complex than the narratives that we create to retell it. There is much more to

Singapore's founding than just Raffles and 1819. Chris Hale and Benjamin Khoo will expand on these issues further.

Hale's essay shows how the 1819 paradigm was itself a historical construction that was pursued by the colonial administration in Singapore in the late nineteenth century. What he means is that, during Singapore's founding, it was not clear that the date 1819 and the 'discovery' of Raffles would become so important in retrospect. In fact, Raffles left Singapore forever in 1824, the same critical year that its ownership was being decided. For about sixty years thereafter, he was all but forgotten. It was only in the 1880s that the Straits Settlement, the colonial governing body in Singapore, decided to erect a Raffles statue and turn his 1819 'discovery' into a foundational narrative for the colonial administration. The use of history as a political tool and its focus on great men was part of a British intellectual tradition called 'Whiggish' history, which traces to historians such as Edward Gibbon, James Mill, and Thomas Macaulay. Hale argues that the 1819 paradigm of Singaporean history was a product of this milieu. Raffles himself was an avid reader of these histories and an admirer of 'greats' such as Napoleon. To understand the traditional narratives on Singapore's founding thus requires that we study how British elites perceived themselves and the world in the late nineteenth century.

Benjamin Khoo tackles a separate complication in Singapore's 1819 origin story. Because both of the major 1824 treaties were signed separately and independently between four parties about the nature of Singapore's ownership, the situation naturally led to confusion. While the Dutch relinquished claims to Singapore, the British bought Singapore from the Malay Sultans. The colonial perspectives on this tripartite arrangement are well documented. However, there is no direct record of what the Malay sultans were considering when they signed away Singapore. Khoo traces a recently rediscovered Dutch copy of the 1824 Treaty of Friendship and Alliance that arose from confusion between the overlapping treaties. The scribe's notes about the Malay princes are currently the only evidence we have of what they might have been thinking at the time, and Khoo uses them to offer insight into the unspoken Malay perspective on this watershed in Singapore's past.

This shows how moving beyond a colonial-centric perspective does not mean disregarding colonial sources altogether. European sources, particularly in the non-English speaking world, can yield valuable insights about local and indigenous perspectives when there are no better alternatives. Khoo's essay is thus evidence that there is still much to discover about Singapore's colonial origins in the nineteenth century and serves as an interesting model for future research into forgotten perspectives on this episode.

Chapter 3

Confronting 'The Singapore Story': Colonial Rule and the Power of History-making

Christopher Hale

Introduction

In 2019, visitors to Fort Canning Park, in downtown Singapore, ascended Bukit Larangan, the 'Forbidden Hill' as it is known in Malay culture, to enter the subterranean chambers of the 'Battle Box' museum before joining the long queues outside the special exhibition put on to celebrate the Bicentennial. That year, the park was saturated in contested memory. It was here, two centuries earlier, that Sir Stamford Raffles and his successors, long regarded as the founders of Singapore, had strolled among the ruins of a long vanished Malay settlement while claiming the island for the British East India Company. A hundred and twenty years later, the British surrender of Singapore to the Japanese in 1942, which was decided inside the Battle Box, exposed the fragility of British rule in Asia and signalled its eventual demise. A short walk from the Battle Box, the Bicentennial exhibition, with its lavish budget and spectacular multimedia dioramas, unfolded another Singapore story: A shiny revamp of the past that embraced a much deeper history firmly embedded in a regional 'longue durée'. The Bicentennial Exhibition relativized the foundational narrative of 1819 and, of course, its leading actor. Not far from Fort Canning Park, the statue of Raffles on Boat Quay, which somehow withstood both the shocks of Japanese occupation and independence, had now been joined by effigies of Asian notables that included, in pride of place, the legendary medieval founder of the 'Lion City', Sang Nila Utama. Inadvertently, the exhibitors had reinforced the foundational trope, since Sang Nila Utama was, according to the *Sulalatas Saladin* (the *Malay Annals*), a refugee prince of Palembang—in other words, a kind of proto-colonizer. Notably, all he discovered on the island was the mythical lion rather than signs of human activity.[100]

This essay will address two questions. First, why was Singapore's foundational myth so enduring? Second, to what extent has the new longue durée version of the 'Singapore story' genuinely reshaped national memory? The second question is by far the most difficult to answer, since there is very little available data about popular memory in Singapore and whether (or not) this longue durée now has deeper roots in local soil.[101] A Google search for the terms 'founder' and 'Singapore' generates a long list of sites focused either on Raffles and/or the supposedly controversial assertion that his rival William Farquhar should instead be regarded as the 'true founder' of Singapore.[102] In other words, the Raffles 'myth' may be proving more durable than the architects of the Bicentennial assumed or hoped. The question

---

[100] "Sang Nila Utama, Pioneers Join Stamford Raffles Along Singapore River," *CNA International*, January 4, 2019, https://web.archive.org/web/20190104121919/https://www.channelnewsasia.com/news/singapore/singapore-bicentennial-river-statues-raffles-history-pioneers-11086338.

[101] Kwa Chong Guan, Derek Heng, Peter Borschberg, and Tan Tai Yong, *Seven Hundred Years: A History of Singapore* (Singapore: Marshall Cavendish and National Library of Singapore, 2019), 13.

[102] "William Farquhar: The First Resident," *Roots*, n.d., https://www.roots.gov.sg/en/stories-landing/stories/the-first-resident/the-first-resident.

is, why? In this essay, I will attempt to answer that question by looking at the role and power of the discourse of history itself— or to be more precise, the act of history-making. I contend that whoever owns the tools of history-making can own the world.

Debating History in Singapore

At first sight, the Bicentennial Exhibition of 2019 reflected a historiographical gear change. As part of the event, the Prime Minister's Office released the publication of *Seven Hundred Years: A History of Singapore* authored by a number of historians, including contributors to this volume—Kwa Chong Guan and Peter Borschberg.[103] It is telling, however, that when *Seven Hundred Years* was first published in 2009, without the involvement of Borschberg, the authors' original message seemed to have fallen on less fertile soil. A decade later, *Seven Hundred Years* more confidently proclaimed a sea change in national memory: The history of Singapore should be reconceived with an Asian founder and a deeper, regionally interconnected history as a Medieval trading emporium.

What exactly had changed? Earlier generations of historians did not, of course, deny that Singapore had a history before 1819. It was simply seen as *irrelevant to the development of modern Singapore*. Raffles Professor of History K.G. Tregonning asserted, 'Modern Singapore began in 1819. Nothing that occurred on the island prior to this particular relevance to an understanding of the contemporary scene . . .'[104] This 'conventional and dominant' view was further armour-plated in the work of British historian Mary Turnbull, who insisted that the rise of Singapore as a

---

[103] Kenneth R. Hall, "Singapore. Studying Singapore before 1800 Edited by Kwa Chong Guan and Peter Borschberg Singapore: NUS Press, 2018. Pp. 408. Maps, Illustrations, Index," *Journal of Southeast Asian Studies* 50, no. 3 (2019): 458–59. https://doi.org/10.1017/S0022463419000456.

[104] K.G. Tregonning, *The British in Malaya: the First Forty Years, 1786-1826* (Tucson: University of Arizona Press, 1965).

modern city state could only be interpreted through the lens of British colonial history.[105] Thus, taking issue with the Tregonning–Turnbull version of the past meant not only demonstrating that Singapore before 1819 had not been an historical vacuum or *terra nullius* but also revealing connections to what happened afterwards, i.e. the emergence of a modern city state in a globalized economy.

From a historiographical point of view, the Bicentennial brought together in a public space, several streams of academic inquiry into archival, textual, and cartographic accounts as well as the archaeological discoveries of pre-colonial relics that redressed the 'truncated imagination' that Singapore was a 'modern colonial entity without a past'.[106] A broad consensus emerged that 'Singapura', 'Sincapura', or 'Temasek', the Malay settlement on the island, was a 'relevant' precursor to the modern nation state:

> The island as it was 700 years ago in fact *shares a number of similarities with today's cosmopolitan city-state*. In the 14th century, Singapore was already a centre for a vast trading network and actively engaged in commerce with neighbouring ports and regions. Commodities such as hornbill casques and lakawood (a type of aromatic wood used as incense) were exported from Singapore, or Temasek, as it was known then. [author's emphasis][107]

This account of the 2019 Bicentennial as a pivotal moment of historiographical revision is misleading. The history of Singapore

---

[105] C.M. Turnbull, *A History of Modern Singapore, 1819–2005* (Singapore: NUS Press, various editions starting in 1977; the final edition was published in 2009 in a new format).

[106] Geok Yian Goh and John N. Miksic, *Ancient Southeast Asia* (1st ed.) (Routledge, 2016); J.N. Miksic, *Singapore and the Silk Road of the Sea, 1300–1800* (Singapore: NUS Press, 2016).

[107] Tan Tai Yong, "Looking Back at 700 Years of Singapore," Biblioasia, National Library Singapore, January 31, 2019, https://biblioasia.nlb.gov.sg/vol-14/issue-4/jan-mar-2019/looking-back-at-sg/.

and how it should be taught to Singaporeans has been frequently debated and revised since the late 1950s. Furthermore, was significantly shaped after independence from the top down by the Singaporean government, in particular the Ministry of Education (MoE), rather than historians. Defining and redefining history was a vital and contested ingredient of nation building after 1965. As Michael Barr stressed: 'Classroom history is a natural vehicle for transmitting national identity.'[108]

By 1965, Singapore had discordantly split from the Federation of Malaysia and become an independent state. The source of discord was the commitment of the ruling United Malays National Organisation (UMNO) to a Malay centred (*bangsa Melayu*) national policy, which openly favoured Malay Muslims. Lee Kuan Yew and other leaders of the People's Action Party (PAP) had never disguised a commitment to a 'Malaysian Malaysia', which was meritocratic and multicultural. The PAP's renunciation of Malay dominance ran counter to anti-colonial, nationalist movements sustained by ethnic identity and difference. To neutralize the perils of identity politics, the PAP government clearly understood that the same issue had to be expurgated from the new nation's history and how it was taught. Singapore's pre-colonial history, which highlighted the significance of Malays as powerbrokers and former owners of the territory, would be expunged. Singapore's first Minister of Culture, S. Rajaratnam, deplored what he pungently called 'political archaeologists' who were fomenting ethnic strife by 'rummaging among ancient myths, doubtful legends and historical records'. By legends, myths, and records, he meant, of course, Malay writings.[109] The consequence of such rummaging, the Minister insisted, would be the reinforcement of separate identities that would subvert

---

[108] Michael D. Barr, "Singapore Comes to Terms with its Malay Past: The Politics of Crafting a National History," *Asian Studies Review* 46, no. 2 (2022): 350.

[109] Rajaratnam's remarks are reproduced in *S. Rajaratnam on Singapore: From Ideas to Reality*, ed. Kwa Chong Guan (Singapore: World Scientific/Institute of Defence and Strategic Studies, 2006), 252–253.

the PAP project of a singular 'Singaporean' one, albeit shaded by diversity of cultural origin. Rajaratnam further pointed out that looking deeper into the well of history and tracing 'our ancestry' back to Malay kingdoms, India, China, the Middle East, or Sri Lanka might create the conditions for 'endless racial and communal conflicts by some of the more powerful and bigger nations from which Singaporeans emigrated'.[110] Lee put the PAP case even more directly: 'This is not a Malay nation; this is not a Chinese nation; this is not an Indian nation. Everybody will have his place. Equal.'[111]

For the PAP, turning back the national clock back to 1819 and no further meant that the identities of modern Singaporean citizens were, at a stroke, severed from the roots of any conflicting ethnic identities. An important symbolic consequence was that the statue of Singapore's colonial 'founder' Sir Stamford Raffles could stay put as a kind of guardian of the PAP's origin story, frequently celebrated by Lee: 'We have left Stamford Raffles outside the Victoria Memorial Hall,' he declaimed in 1977. 'But for him, [Singapore] would still be a mudflat. Let us not pretend it was anything else . . .'[112] Since the history of Singapore before 1819 was 'lost in the mists of time', Lee argued, the narrative of the past could be taught as a collaboration between British wisdom and Chinese enterprise. Thus, Malay history was brutally evacuated from the narrative of the past.[113]

The response of the Malay minority in Singapore to such historical slights was muted by allegiances to the PAP. But, in 1970,

---

[110] Quoted in Terence Chong, "The Bicentennial Commemoration: Imagining and Re-Imagining Singapore's History," in *Southeast Asian Affairs 2020*, ed. Malcolm Cook and Daljit Singh (ISEAS–Yusof Ishak Institute, 2020): 326.

[111] Ibid. 327; Lee Kuan Yew, "Transcript of a Press Conference Given by the Prime Minister of Singapore, Mr. Lee Kuan Yew, at Broadcasting House, Singapore, at 1200 hours on Monday 9th August, 1965."

[112] Lee, 1967, quoted in: Michael D. Barr, "Singapore Comes to Terms with its Malay Past": 354.

[113] L. Z. Rahim, *The Singapore Dilemma: The Political and Educational Marginality of the Malay Community* (Oxford University Press, 1995).

the MOE published a new set of history textbooks that reinforced the government's narrative by excluding any pre-colonial history. This proved to be a revision too far: Members of the youth wing of a Malay political party the Singapore Malay National Organisation (PKMS) publicly burned copies of the textbooks, declaring that teaching this history 'humiliates the Malays [. . .] idolizes Raffles [. . .] makes fun of the history of Temasek [. . .] by treating it as a mere legend and deals with Singapore's history as though it commenced from the time of Raffles.'[114]

Not long after the book burning incident dramatically brought to the surface fractious and divisive dimensions of history education in Singapore, the MOE scaled down the space allocated to history in the curriculum ostensibly to favour 'useful' core subjects like English, mathematics, science, and a second mother tongue language.[115] Yet, despite the squeeze on history in the curriculum, a number of developments signalled its resilience and, as it would transpire, laid the ground for a resurgence.

The squeeze on the space allotted to history in the curriculum dampened down the protests. It would seem, however, that Lee and his government were finding other uses for history. At the end of the 1970s, the government stepped up support for the National Archives of Singapore, increasing the number of staff, and in 1979, founded the Oral History Unit, which invited ordinary Singaporeans to record their own histories.[116] In 1980, Lee insisted that 'to understand the present and anticipate the future, one must know enough of the past . . .'[117] Lee had come to realize that the downside of the '1819 horizon' was that Singaporeans might

---

[114] Mirror of Opinion, 3 March 1970, quoted in: Michael D. Barr, "Singapore Comes to Terms with its Malay Past."

[115] Quoted in Michael D. Barr, "Singapore Comes to Terms with its Malay Past": 355.

[116] "Oral History Centre (Singapore)," National Archives of Singapore, accessed 3 April, 2025, https://www.nas.gov.sg/archivesonline/government_records/agency-details/97.

[117] K.Y. Lee, "History Is Not Made the Way It Is Written," *Speeches: A Monthly Collection of Ministerial Speeches* 3, no. 8 (1980): 3–12.

become deracinated citizens in awe of western colonial values. The new Singaporean citizen should not be ignorant of the rich Asian cultures from which their ancestors had sprung and, just as important, be forgetful of the more recent achievements of the PAP leaders, the 'men in white' who had built Singapore after the traumas of separation and independence.

This reinvestment in the social value of transnational history, however, had little impact on the foundational status of Stamford Raffles, and it was a British historian who decisively shaped the contours of the history that was now firmly back on the national agenda. Constance Mary Turnbull was a former member of the National University of Singapore's history department who, in 1971, was driven out of her university position during a period of 'academic decolonisation'.[118] In her history, Turnbull unequivocally asserted:

> Modern Singapore is unique in that she was founded in 1819 on the initiative of one individual, Sir Stamford Raffles, despite almost universal opposition. An unwanted child, foisted upon the English East India Company, Singapore managed to survive and flourish, but her story was not one of steady and unchecked progress. Her prosperity and sometimes even her existence were threatened many times...[119]

Turnbull not only devalues any pre-colonial contribution to the development of Singapore but reiterates a model of history-making that was defined by Herbert Butterfield in 1931 as the Whig interpretation of history. According to Butterfield, Whig historians 'stud[y] the past with reference to the present'; they judge 'historical personages' by classing them according to

---

[118] Karl Hack, "Framing Singapore's History," in *Studying Singapore's Past: C.M. Turnbull and the History of Modern Singapore*, ed. Nicholas Tarling (Singapore: NUS Press, 2012), 17–64; Kevin Blackburn, "Mary Turnbull's History Textbook for the Singapore Nation," in *Studying Singapore's Past*, 65–86.

[119] C.M. Turnbull, *History of Singapore* (1977), xi.

whether they 'furthered progress . . . or tried to hinder it'.[120] The proper study of the historian, then, was the progressive ascent of societies shaped by individual actors. According to Thomas Carlyle, the most eloquent of Whig historians:

> Universal History, the history of what man has accomplished in this world, is at bottom the History of the Great Men who have worked here [. . .] all things that we see standing accomplished in the world are properly the outer material result, the practical realization and embodiment, of Thoughts that dwelt in the Great Men sent into the world.[121]

In 'On Heroes, Hero-Worship, and the Heroic in History' Carlyle argued in full spate that the 'great men' of history were driven by a God-given mission and were thus deserving of universal 'hero worship'. Turnbull's meticulously researched narrative rests firmly on the Whig footing of a single visionary individual—Raffles—who triumphed over corporate short-termism and a multitude of other adversities so that an 'unwanted child' would flourish and prosper.

Let us not forget that, in 1819, Raffles was no nation builder. He merely established an EIC factory on the banks of the Singapore River to serve the interests of the Chinese trade on land rented from its Malay owners Temenggong Abdul Rahman and Sultan Hussein Mohamad Shah. Furthermore, as Gareth Knapman points out 'Raffles was a self-serving colonial official [who] reneged on most of the important agreements he made and only supported reforming ideas if politically convenient.'[122]

---

[120] Herbert Butterfield, *The Whig Interpretation of History* (New York: Norton, 1931), 11.

[121] Thomas Carlyle, "Lecture I. The Hero As Divinity. Odin. Paganism: Scandinavian Mythology.[May 5, 1840.]," in *On Heroes, Hero-Worship and the Heroic in History* (Estes and Lauriat, 1885). Available at: https://www.gutenberg.org/files/1091/1091-h/1091-h.htm.

[122] C.M. Turnbull, *A History of Modern Singapore: 1819-1988* (Oxford University Press and National Library Board Singapore, 1989).

Turnbull's idolatry of a heroic Raffles marginalized Asian agency both in diplomatic and narrative terms.

In the 1980s, Turnbull's heroic history had a powerful allure for the MoE who were once again focused on redeveloping the national curriculum. They took very little interest in the very different narrative published just two years after Turnbull's *A History of Singapore, 1819-1975*. In 'Prince of Pirates: The Temenggongs and the Development of Johor and Singapore, 1784–1885' Carl Trocki emphasizes that the British and Dutch colonialists were just one set of political actors shaping the development of Singapore in the early nineteenth century. Trocki used indigenous records, written in Jawi or Rumi script, to develop a multi-agency history that highlighted the decisive roles played by Malay rulers and merchants. He reinserted Malays in the 'foundation narrative' and the later prosperity of the settlement.[123] Trocki and his colleague Michael Barr began advocating this very different narrative of Singapore, Malaysia, and Southeast Asian history that cleared away the 'mists of time' to expose the lineaments of a Malay-orientated history.

The tide was turning: A new generation of Malay historians began challenging the 'heroic' narrative.[124] It was the hard scabble science of archaeology, however, that most decisively unsettled the mythology of 1819 by unearthing the relics of what may have sounded like an oxymoron: medieval Singapore. John Miksic's

---

[123] For a detailed study of the role of the rulers of Johor in the development of Singapore see: Michael D. Barr, "Background Figures in a British Portrait: The Johor Royal Family in Nineteenth-Century Singapore," *History Australia* 18, no. 2 (2021): 283–301.

[124] Notably, R. Abdul Azeez, *Negotiating Malay Identities in Singapore: The Role of Modern Islam* (Sussex Academic Press, 2016); H.I. Abdul Rahman and H.S. Badriyah, "History Through the Eyes of the Malays: Changing Perspectives of Malaysia's Past," in *New Terrains in Southeast Asian History*, ed. A.T. Ahmad and L.E. Tan (Singapore: Singapore University Press, 2003); W.J. Abdullah, "Selective History and Hegemony-Making: The Case of Singapore," *International Political Science Review* 39, no. 4 (2018): 473–486; S.H. Alatas, *Myth of the Lazy Native: A Study of the Image of the Malays, Filipinos and Javanese from the 16th to the 20th Century and Its Function in the Ideology of Colonial Capitalism* (Frank Cass, 1997).

excavations on Fort Canning Hill, then threatened by development, provided incontestable evidence exposing the existence of ancient Singapore/Temasek as a Malay trading port with connections to India, China, as well as regional empires Majapahit and Srivijya/Palembang. By the end of the twentieth century, scholarship and 'archaeological rummaging' was snapping at the heels of PAP's guardians of Singapore's past.[125]

As Terence Chong stresses, this third phase of reimagining and *reenergizing* Singapore's history decisively fixed it as a Southeast Asian city with 'deep roots in local soil'. Singaporeans would frequently separate their national home from countries in the surrounding neighbourhood, but now they were unavoidably members of a regional community with a deep history. Rajaratnam might have been turning in his grave. Even after retirement in the 1990s, he persistently harangued Singaporeans to exorcise 'ancestral ghosts' and 'different histories'.[126]

To sum up, since independence, the historiography of Singapore has been characterized by considerable contestation and complexity. The fluidity of historical interpretation is a fundamental characteristic of all societies, and the nations of Southeast Asia are no exception to this rule. Historical memory functions not merely as a passive repository of past events but as an active instrument of meaning-making, subject to continuous reinterpretation and reconstruction. History is for as well as of. This raises a critical question: How has the foundational narrative elevating Stamford Raffles—manifested both physically through

---

[125] John N. Miksic, *Singapore & the Silk Road of the Sea, 1300-1800* (Singapore: NUS Press, 2013); John Miksic, "The Singapore Cricket Club Excavation Site Report, April 2003," Southeast Asian Archaeological Site Reports: The Singapore Cricket Club Excavation Site Report, April 2003, National Heritage Board, Singapore, accessed on April 4, 2025, https://doi.org/10.25717/7w0e-3n3c; John N. Miksic and Cheryl-Ann Low Mei Gek, *Early Singapore 1300s–1819: Evidence in Maps, Text and Artefacts* (Singapore: Singapore History Museum, 2004).

[126] Terence Chong, "The Bicentennial Commemoration: Imagining and Re-Imagining Singapore's History," in *Southeast Asian Affairs 2020*, ed. Malcolm Cook and Daljit Singh (ISEAS–Yusof Ishak Institute, 2020), 323–334.

his statue on Boat Quay and discursively through pervasive public narratives that position him as the heroic genius behind Singapore's establishment—demonstrated such remarkable persistence?

I suggest that the answer lies in the history-making process itself, the history of history. Drawing upon Prita Satia's *Time's Monster*, I argue that history served as a crucial mechanism in the construction and maintenance of colonial and imperial power. As Satia argues, 'evolving ideas about history shaped the unfolding of the British Empire'.[127]

The History Makers

The men who joined the Dutch, French, and English East India companies naturally focused on commerce and the exercise of power that facilitated profits for their shareholders.[128] As the example of Raffles shows, however, some of the administrative ranks of the companies fancied themselves not merely as merchants and administrators but also as reformers and historians. Like any modern corporation, the EIC devoted considerable energies to the accumulation and recording of

---

[127] P. Satia, *Time's Monster: History, Conscience and Britain's Empire* (London: Penguin UK, 2020), 15.

[128] There is a substantive literature on the East India Company, for example: Robert Brenner, *Merchants and Revolution: Commercial Change, Political Conflict, and London's Overseas Traders, 1550–1653* (Princeton: Princeton University Press, 1993); Kenneth R. Andrews, *Trade, Plunder, and Settlement: Maritime Enterprise and the Genesis of the British Empire, 1480–1630* (Cambridge: Cambridge University Press, 1985); K.N. Chaudhuri, *The English East India Company: The Study of an Early Joint-Stock Company, 1600–1640* (London: Cass, 1965); K.N. Chaudhuri, *The Trading World of Asia and the English East India Company, 1660–1760* (Cambridge, UK: Cambridge University Press, 1978); William Dalrymple, *The Anarchy: The Relentless Rise of the East India Company* (London: Bloomsbury, 2019).

commercial data.¹²⁹ Raffles launched his career as a clerk in East India House in London; he later supported the work of the scholar and translator John Leyden and self-published his book *The History of Java*.¹³⁰

The impact of an historical consciousness on the British colonial elite is well established. It was the consequence of the reverence for Classics or 'Greats' in prestigious English schools and universities, which educated the administrative elite of the colonial enterprise. Symonds points out that, in 1938, six of the eight provincial governors of India had read Greats at Oxford.¹³¹ Much earlier, many of the British agents of the EIC were saturated in the Classics and some imagined they were following in the footsteps of Alexander the Great or Julius Caeser. Classical education taught generations of English colonialists that the logic of history was imperial conquest.¹³²

Edward Gibbon, the most eminent historian of the late-eighteenth century, provided a model of history-making for many aspiring colonialists who consciously sought to avoid the errors that had doomed an ancient empire. Gibbon's six volume *The Decline and fall of the Roman Empire* provided both a narrative model and a guide to avoid the pitfalls of imperial ambition.¹³³ Its impact cannot be overstated. It was said that 'King George

---

¹²⁹ The evidence is collected here: "Digitised East India Company ships' journals and related records," Asian and African studies blog, British Library, 13 May 2020, https://blogs.bl.uk/asian-and-african/2020/05/digitised-east-india-company-ships-journals-and-related-records.html.

¹³⁰ J. Bastin, *Sir Stamford Raffles and Some of His Friends and Contemporaries: A Memoir of the Founder of Singapore* (World Scientific, 2019).

¹³¹ R. Symonds, *Oxford and Empire: the Last Lost Cause* (Oxford: Clarendon Press, 1986).

¹³² P. Vasunia, *Classics and Colonial India: Classical Presences* (Oxford: Oxford University Press, 2013).

¹³³ Edward Gibbon, *The Decline and Fall of the Roman Empire: a Modern Abridgment* (New York: Fawcett Premier, 1987).

in a fright—lest Gibbon should write—the story of Britain's disgrace.'[134] In other words, Gibbon's account of the decline and fall of Rome might foreshadow the decline of the British Empire, which in the late eighteenth century looked increasingly fragile. The 'disgrace', of course, was the catastrophic loss of the American colonies. The colonial intelligentsia thus sought in Gibbon any lessons that might avert their own 'decline and fall'.

When Gibbon was writing and publishing, moral questioning of the nation and its empire was loud and insistent. The hereditary aristocracy resented the rising power of the EIC's *nabobs* (from the Indian word nawab or prince) who returned from service overseas flaunting loot from their colonial conquests. In 1784, the government passed Pitt's India Act to regulate the EIC and its activities and when Warren Hastings, the former governor general of Bengal, returned to England, he was impeached on corruption charges.[135] Prosecuted by the liberal member of parliament (MP) and political philosopher Edmund Burke, Hastings' trial ground for six years between 1788 and 1795. Gibbon was often in the public gallery.[136] Burke's opening speech was a resounding plea for universal ethical standards: 'The laws of morality,' he argued, are 'the same everywhere,' and should not be abandoned by colonial agents when they left British shores 'as if, when you have crossed the equinoctial line all the virtues die . . .'[137]

Burke's rhetoric resonated with the implicit admonition of Gibbons' history. His record of the Roman past was read by

---

[134] A. Momigliano, "After Gibbon's 'Decline and Fall'," *Annali della Scuola Normale Superiore di Pisa. Classe di Lettere e Filosofia* 8, no. 2 (1978): 435–454. https://www.jstor.org/stable/24304986.

[135] Mithi Mukherjee, "Justice, War, and the Imperium: India and Britain in Edmund Burke's Prosecutorial Speeches in the Impeachment Trial of Warren Hastings," *Law and History Review* 23, no. 3 (2005): 589–630.

[136] P. Satia, *Time's Monster: History, Conscience and Britain's Empire* (London: Penguin UK, 2020): 39ff.

[137] Edmund Burke, *The Project Gutenberg EBook of The Works of the Right Honourable Edmund Burke*, Vol. X. (of 12) (Project Gutenberg, 2006).

many as a warning against the dangers of corruption that he blamed on imperial overreach. History, according to Gibbon, might become a narrative of progress if the right lessons would be learned in the present—as his friend Burke sought to do when he assailed Hastings and the EIC. It was at the margins of empire that Gibbon provided his British readers with another echo of the fate of Rome. It was weakened and eventually brought down by 'barbarian hordes'. Gibbon described barbarians as warlike, migrant, and fluid, a primeval force that initiated a 'primitive convulsion of nature, which had agitated and altered the surface of the globe'.[138] He warned that 'new enemies and unknown dangers may possibly arise from some obscure people, scarcely visible in the map of the world'. He noted that the 'Arabs and Saracens' had languished in poverty 'till Mahomet breathed into those savage bodies that soul of enthusiasm'.[139] Gibbon looked forward to the triumph of European reason over barbarism on a global scale—at the edge of the]'civilizational' map.[140]

Gibbons' *Decline and Fall*, as its title implies, was not a Whig history: He examined how Rome advanced as a republic and declined as it became corrupted by religion and exposure to 'barbarian' savagery. In short, the arc of history was not progressive. As Satia shows in *Time's Monster*, by the early nineteenth century the success of the Abolitionist movement and the founding of the Aboriginal Protection Society signalled the emergence of a liberal and paternalistic imperialism that would 'compensate for the original sin of conquest'. The trauma of the loss of the American colonies, the years long Hastings trial and the excesses of the nabobs would be expiated by acts of

---

[138] Edward Gibbon, *The Decline and Fall of the Roman Empire: A Modern Abridgment* (New York: Fawcett Premier, 1987).

[139] Ibid.

[140] Tim Stuart-Buttle, "Gibbon and Enlightenment History in Eighteenth-Century Britain," in *The Cambridge Companion to Edward Gibbon*, ed. Karen O'Brien and Brian Young (Cambridge: Cambridge University Press, 2018), 110–127.

civilizing minds and territories.[141] And those indigenous minds would indeed require civilizing. According to Hastings' successor Lord Cornwallis, 'Every native of Hindustan is corrupt.'[142]

Liberal imperialism would soon discover its history-maker in the political radical and devotee of Jeremy Bentham's utilitarian philosophy James Mill. He began writing his *History of British India* during the Napoleonic Wars in 1808, eventually publishing its many volumes in 1817. Mill never travelled to India and claimed, 'A duly qualified man can obtain more knowledge of India in one year in his closet in England than he could obtain during the course of the longest life, by the use of his eyes and ears in India.'[143] Like Burke, Mill criticized the EIC and deplored the corruption of its officials. But he equally despised Orientalists like William Jones who esteemed and studied Indian languages and cultures. Instead, the historian's task was to write a 'judging history' that excoriated the 'rude and barbarous nature' of Indians and their culture. The role of the EIC and its agents was to free India of barbarity and elevate Indians on the 'scale of civilisation'. For Mill, the premise of history was no longer about decline and fall but ascent:

> [E]very society may progress if it chooses, or can be shown how to do so, but it will then follow the same road which more advanced societies have taken before it and acquire the same features which everywhere distinguish barbarism from civilisation.[144]

---

[141] P. Satia, *Time's Monster: History, Conscience and Britain's Empire* (London: Penguin UK, 2020), 70.

[142] T.R. Metcalf, *Ideologies of the Raj* (University of California, Berkeley, 1995), 24.

[143] Quoted in Javed Majeed, "James Mill's The History of British India," in *Ungoverned Imaginings: James Mill's The History of British India and Orientalism* (Oxford: Oxford English Monographs, 1992).

[144] Quoted in Catherine Hall, *Macaulay and Son: Architects of Imperial Britain* (New Haven: Yale University Press, 2012), 208.

Mill's *The History of British India* proved immensely influential. It was widely read by British officials in India and became a textbook for Indian Civil Service examinations.[145] After Mill, imperial government would become reformatory and transformative. Mill was writing and publishing when Raffles was busy occupying Java and then settling Singapore. *The History of Java* authored by Raffles was published in the interregnum between the governorship of Java and his posting to Bencoolen in Sumatra from where he launched his quest for an EIC factory in the Melaka Straits. Mill's *The History of British India* and Raffles' activities as a self-appointed custodian/historian of Javanese culture are not only contemporaneous but, as we will see shortly, fit the same liberal-imperial model.

Long after Raffles seized Singapore, Thomas Babington Macaulay authored *The History of England from the Accession of James the Second* (aka *History of England*) in December 1848 to, in the words of Catharine Hall, 'rapturous applause and unprecedented sales'.[146] Macaulay had served as second-in-command to the Governor General of India in the 1830s and his *History of England* provided Victorians with the epic narrative of themselves as an imperial people, makers of both nation and empire.

Macaulay had been deeply impressed by Mill's *The History of British India* and the way it presented India as a benighted, backward society requiring rescue by a superior, civilizing power. He spent years in India trying to do just that but as Hall writes, he was himself repelled 'by the black bodies, the fruit and vegetables, the strange flora and fauna, the heat and insect life, the excesses of religious fanaticism'.[147] In moments of pessimism, Macaulay doubted that even with an English education, the 'Musselman',

---

[145] Quoted in Javed Majeed, "James Mill's The History of British India," in *Ungoverned Imaginings: James Mill's The History of British India and Orientalism* (Oxford: Oxford English Monographs, 1992), 128.

[146] Catherine Hall, *Macaulay and Son: Architects of Imperial Britain* (New Haven: Yale University Press, 2012), 71.

[147] Ibid.

the 'Parsee', and the 'Hindoo who worships a lump of stone with seven heads' could ever become civilized 'brown Englishmen'. Instead, he devoted the rest of his life to providing a historical narrative for the Englishmen who would have to civilize the barbarians.

Macaulay's two volume *History of England* marked the high noon of Whig history-making. The English, he proclaimed, were the 'acknowledged leaders of the human race' and that he would celebrate in passionate, ringing language 'the empire of our arts and morals, our literature and our laws'. Macaulay's *History of England* told a heroic story of a great people—a narrative that 'stirred the blood of Englishmen'. Macaulay's history was rooted in binaries—nation and empire, English and Other. In one of his 'Minutes on Education' written in India, Macaulay had diagnosed the weakness of indigenous couture:

> It is, I believe, no exaggeration to say that all the historical information which has been collected from all the books written in the Sanskrit language is less valuable than what may be found in the most paltry abridgments used at preparatory schools in England.[148]

The English had reached the summit of civilization; the peoples they ruled had barely begun to ascend from rude and backward barbarism.

Raffles as a Historian

In his bestselling defence of imperialism, *Colonialism: A Moral Reckoning*, theologian and self-appointed 'culture warrior' Nigel Biggar eulogizes Raffles as the founder of a trading post at

---

[148] Thomas Babington Macaulay, "Minute on Education (1835) by Thomas Babington Macaulay," Internet Archive, 1835, accessed on 4 April 2025, https://archive.org/details/1-macaulays-minute-pages-from-selections-from-educational-records-part-i-1781-1839-1919-pg-107-117/.

Singapore and as historian of 'the value and beauty of Java's pre-Islamic Hindu heritage . . .' Defending the morality of empire, Biggar also cites Raffles' campaign against slavery on the island of Penang, his banning of slave importation to Java, and prohibition of slavery in Bencoolen. Raffles, in short, becomes not merely an agent of the EIC but an imperial exemplar, a humanitarian hero.[149] This is, of course, a vital ingredient of the founding myth. Who would want an unscrupulous colonial opportunist as the nation's founder?

In his 'Note on the Founding of Singapore', Richard Winstedt sums up the account in the *Sejarah Melayu* (*Malay Annals*) as 'a jumble of legend and history mixed up with the story of Alexander the Great'. He concludes that the Annals are a 'hotchpotch of Chola and Palembang folklore [out of which] little can be made'.[150] It would be simplistic to compare this example of an indigenous narrative with the historiography of the British settlement of Singapore after 1819. But any historian who proposes reconstructing a narrative of events will have at her disposal a profusion of verifiable personal and eyewitness accounts as well as diplomatic and archival records. The EIC that employed Raffles and his colleagues was a corporate data gathering machine. Raffles began his career as a company clerk compiling 'histories' for the company managers alongside scores of other young men.

Throughout the long history of the 'Honourable Company', accounting and writing generated a rich loom of corporate narrative, the raw material of history. History-making was thus closely entwined with territorial and market acquisition. As Nicholas Dirks argues, knowledge simultaneously enabled colonial conquest and was its outcome.[151] Colley has documented

---

[149] N. Biggar, *Colonialism: A Moral Reckoning* (London: Collins, 2023), 2.

[150] Kwa Chong Guan and Peter Borschberg, eds., *Studying Singapore Before 1800* (Singapore: National University of Singapore Press, 2018), 9.

[151] Nicholas B. Dirks, *Colonialism and Culture* (Ann Arbor: The University of Michigan Press, 1992).

the way that the sword has closely aligned with the pen in modern world history: treaties and written constitutions proliferated as European powers reached out across the Americas, Africa, and Asia under the shielding canopy of an emerging discourse of international law. The career of Hugo Grotius, the 'father of international law', fused lawmaking and commerce in the early seventeenth century when he acted as a lawyer on behalf of the directors of the Dutch East India Company (VOC).[152] Colonial warfare and conquest provoked treaty- and constitution-making, which bound trade and conquest in a tightly woven lexical web.

Colonial history can be understood as combining acts of territorial conquest with associated acts of writing—an extensive apparatus of accounts, reports, testimonies, diplomatic correspondence, and treaties that drew on the sanctity of both the word and the law. The EIC was an armed corporation equipped with formidable powers of documentation and the production of commercial narratives. That command of history-making ensured that the chronicle of the EIC's settlement of Singapore in 1819 would push aside any indigenous history. That narrative, of course, was that, in 1819, the island was in the words of Raffles' associate John Crawfurd virtually *terra nullius*:

> With the exception of a single village of poor and predatory Malay fishermen and that only formed in 1811 was covered with a primeval forest down to the 6th day of February 1819 [. . .] For a period of about five centuries and a half, there is no record of Singapore having been occupied, and that it was only the resort of pirates.[153]

---

[152] P. Borschberg, *Hugo Grotius, the Portuguese, and Free Trade in the East Indies* (Singapore: NUS Press, 2011); Martine Julia van Ittersum, "The Long Goodbye: Hugo Grotius' Justification of Dutch Expansion Overseas, 1615–1645," *History of European Ideas* 36, no. 4 (2010): 386–411.

[153] Quoted in J. Bastin, *Raffles and Hastings: Private Exchanges Behind the Founding of Singapore* (Singapore: National Library Board Singapore, Marshall Cavendish Editions, 2014).

According to the foundational myth, it was the 'genius' of Raffles to see beyond or behind the predatory fishermen, pirates, and primeval forest to imagine 'a British station commanding the southern entrance of the Straits of Malacca, and combining extraordinary local advantage with a peculiarly admirable Geographic position . . .'"[154]

The remarkable persistence of Singapore's foundational mythology, anchored on Raffles and his associates, warrants critical examination, as its central tenets dissipate when subjected to rigorous historical analysis, not unlike Bram Stoker's metaphorical vampire confronting daybreak. The establishment of Singapore as a distinct entity should be more accurately attributed not to Raffles but to legal practitioners and diplomatic emissaries whose contributions have been largely obscured until excavated by historian Peter Borschberg.[155]

Legalizing Narratives

Although the foundational narrative suggests otherwise, Singapore had not been Raffles first choice for a British post. As Borschberg puts it, he 'ogled' Semangka Bay near the Sunda Strait, Bintan, and the Karimun islands. His interest in Bintan was frustrated by the Dutch and the Karimun Island proved unsuitable for the kind of settlement the British envisaged. Only then did Raffles' eye fall on Singapore island. Raffles was aware that his actions would provoke the Dutch, who claimed the sultanate of Johor-Riau, where the island was situated, as a 'lawful and perpetual fief'. This is why he and his associate William Farquhar turned to Abdul Rahman, the temenggong, a vassal of Sultan Husain, who, for his own reasons, agreed to sign a provisional treaty. Once this sham legal gesture had been wrapped up, the British flag was

---

[154] Kwa Chong Guan and Peter Borschberg, eds., *Studying Singapore Before 1800*, 3.

[155] P. Borschberg, "Dutch Objections to British Singapore, 1819–1824: Law, Politics, Commerce and a Diplomatic Misstep," *Journal of Southeast Asian Studies* 50, no. 4 (2019): 540–561.

planted upon Singapore shores. Plans were made to build a fort on the elevation known as the Bukit Larangan (Forbidden Hill) among Malays when Sultan Hussein (Tunku Long) arrived on 1 February, whereupon the trio agreed to sign a second treaty on 6 February.

This infuriated the Dutch. When news of the 'English occupation' of the island reached the minister of colonies, Baron Falck, he despatched a furious letter to Lord Hastings, insisting that Raffles abandon Singapore. Recalling the treaty that he, as a representative of the Dutch government, had signed earlier with the Sultan of Johor-Riau, Falck insisted that Dutch proprietary rights must be respected. Hasting's reply was cunning. He alleged that Raffles had been ordered not take any step 'which should be a collision with the functionaries of the Netherlands government . . .' As a consequence, he claimed 'this government censured Stanford Raffles'.[156] This was almost certainly nonsense, for Hastings recognized that if Raffles was ordered to relinquish Singapore, this would, in effect, recognize Dutch rights over the island. This was anathema to the British—and so the dispute escalated. As a consequence, a cloud of uncertainty hung over Singapore for the next few years as the British and Dutch wrangled over its legal status.

The British government dragged its heels but by 1823, the matter of Singapore had become, as Baron Falck observed, 'a matter of special concern in London'.[157] Agents of business and trade, backed by London newspapers, lobbied the government to hold on to Singapore. Legality be damned! On the Dutch side, indignation about the upstart Raffles gave way to strategic recalculation. If they gave up the claim to Singapore, which now seemed to have a grip on British public opinion, they might barter for a more advantageous territorial swap. The upshot was that the British and Dutch negotiators agreed to a much broader division

---

[156] Ibid. 548.
[157] Ibid. 554.

of the territorial spoils that, on the one hand, allotted Singapore, Melaka, and the Malay Peninsula to the British, while Sumatra and the rest of the archipelago was taken by the Dutch.

So, it was only in March 1825—five years after Raffles had landed in Singapore and signed treaties with Abdul Rahman, the Temenggong, and Sultan Husain—that legal rights to the island were finally settled. Rights negotiated in London and the Netherlands that rode rough shod over any native ruler or agreement.

Why then did the Dutch relinquish Singapore? It is striking that nearly two decades earlier in 1809, the former Dutch governor of Melaka, Abraham Couperus, had lamented the disadvantages of Melaka and proposed founding a new emporium at the tip of the Peninsula either on Singapore or Bangka. By 1823, however, the Dutch negotiators had concluded that by giving up on Singapore they had little to lose.[158] In Falk's words, 'as a produce yielding territory, Singapore has no value'. Singapore's strategic value, he went on 'is appraised far too high'.[159]

The establishment of British control over Singapore presents a complex case study in colonial legitimacy and international law. From a juridical perspective, Raffles' acquisition of Singapore operated outside established legal frameworks of the period. This assessment is substantiated by contemporaneous objections from multiple parties: the Dutch administration's formal protest against what they termed 'illegal possession, and significantly, the British governor of Penang, John Bannerman's own admission that the settlement 'cannot be supported by reason or justice'.[160] Borschberg emphasises that Raffles' actions constituted an *ultra vires* (beyond the powers) exercise of authority: the treaties he secured with the Temenggong and Sultan Husain Shah had fundamental defects of legal capacity, as neither signatory

---

[158] Ibid. 560.

[159] Ibid. 548.

[160] Ibid. 559.

possessed the requisite authority to execute such agreements. By 1824, Britain's continued presence in Singapore lacked demonstrable legal foundation during Anglo-Dutch negotiations. The resolution ultimately emerged through pragmatic diplomacy rather than legal principles. The Dutch government recognized Singapore's strategic value as a negotiating instrument to secure their primary objective: hegemony over Sumatra. The subsequent territorial demarcation, while originating from extra-legal circumstances, proved strategically beneficial for both colonial powers. The spheres of influence established through these negotiations ultimately shaped the geopolitical boundaries of contemporary Southeast Asian nation-states—Indonesia, Malaysia, and Singapore—demonstrating how contested colonial acquisitions could evolve into recognized international borders.

Let us return to the main flow of our argument. Raffles was described by a Dutch observer as a 'word peddler'—he was a storyteller. He saw himself as the architect of a new state and was intrigued by Britain's former arch enemy, Napoleon Bonaparte. Raffles even visited the exiled emperor on the island of St Helena. Although Raffles spent little time in Singapore, he followed Napoleon's example by drawing up 'something like a constitution and a representative body'. Linda Colley, the historian of constitutional history, describes Raffles' vision as 'engineered, controlled and written into improvement and modernity . . .'[161] All religions and ethnicities would be tolerated; slavery and slave trading abolished along with drinking, gambling, and cockfighting. The future inhabitants of Singapore would be 'morally cleansed and improved human beings'.[162] Backed by the force of the EIC and the British government, Raffles was convinced that this faraway island could be reconfigured and regulated as an outpost of civilization.

---

[161] Quoted in L. Colley, *The Gun, the Ship and the Pen: Warfare, Constitutions and the Making of the Modern World* (Profile Books, 2021), 201.

[162] Ibid.

Traditional historians of colonial Singapore have shown little interest in the protracted if bloodless legal disputes that followed in the wake of the events of 1819. Raffles himself took no part in the London negotiations. The foundational myth *excludes* the legal-diplomatic manoeuvrings that took place after 1819 or represents the negotiations as merely 'tidying up'. However, the treaty allowed Raffles' successor John Crawfurd to further marginalize Abdul Rahman, the temenggong, and Sultan Husain.

Raffles was neither philosopher nor historian. But his legally transgressive actions and the eventual diplomatic solution of 1824 firmly placed Singapore in the flow of western teleological history. His 'word peddling' provided Singapore with both an *imminent* identity and *imaginary* future as some sort of utopian community of commercial equals. This was the vision that in the 1960s gripped the imaginations of the leaders of the PAP as they, following the example of Raffles, established the contours of an engineered future in the twenty-first century.

Seizing the Past

Raffles and his EIC associates William Farquhar and John Crawfurd had no doubt that Singapore had a history. They were scholar-conquerors. In his report of January 1819, Raffles referred to Singapore as 'the ancient capital of the Kings of Johor'.[163] When Farquhar climbed the Bukit Larangan, which would become the site of Fort Canning, he noted that 'the tombs of the old Rajahs were there and it was considered sacred, as it is to the present day'.[164] Not long after Farquhar's visit, parts of the hill were cleared and a road was built. Yet, Bukit Larangan continued to fascinate the EIC agents in Singapore. A few years

---

[163] Quoted in Kwa Chong Guan and Peter Borschberg, eds., *Studying Singapore Before 1800*, 3.

[164] Charles Burton Buckley, *Anecdotal History of Old Times in Singapore, vol. 1* (Singapore: Fraser & Neave, 1902), 53. See: https://archive.org/details/ananecdotalhist01buckgoog/page/n76/mode/2up.

later, in February 1822, John Crawfurd, who had also taken part in the conquest of Java, made his own ascent up the hill. 'I walked this morning round the walls and limits of the ancient town of Singapore . . .' his account began, and went on to describe the remains of various structures:

> Another terrace on the northern declivity of the hill, is said to have been the burying place of Iskandar Shah, King of Singapore. This is the prince whom tradition describes as having been driven from his throne by the Javanese in the year 1252 of the Christian era [. . .] Over the supposed tomb of Iskander, a rude structure has been raised, since the formation of the new settlement, to which Mohammedans, Hindus and Chinese, equally resort to do homage.[165]

Crawfurd was astonished to find that 'many of the fruit trees cultivated by the ancient inhabitants of Singapore are still existing [. . .] all so degenerated'. Between the trees, he discovered fragments of pottery, both 'Chinese and native', in great abundance.[166]

For Crawfurd and Raffles, then, Singapore was not merely a realm of primeval forest, predatory fisherman, and pirates. The Bukit Larangan inspired a daring imaginative identification with former Malay rulers of the island. Naturally, Raffles' rather morbid imaginings—so reminiscent of his literary contemporaries—acted, like his 'sort of constitution' and treaty making, to capture Singapore and bind it in a web of political, legal, and cultural ownership. For these EIC men, Singapore was not so much terra nullius as a decayed domain of relics and ruins severed from both the present and future. This capturing of Singapore did not dispose of history—instead, history-making served the purposes of the island's new legal owners.

---

[165] J. Crawfurd, *Journal of an Embassy to the Court of Siam and Cochin-China Exhibiting a View of the Actual State of Those Kingdoms* Vol 1 (London: Henry Colburn, 1830).
[166] Ibid.

From the beginning of his career, Raffles was thoroughly acquainted with the power of history-making. His long service as an EIC clerk at Company House in London had habituated him to industrious data accumulation and reporting, known to company clerks like himself as 'narratives'. When he was posted to Penang as assistant-secretary to the governor and escaped the 'dead tomes and mercantile transactions', he threw himself into both administrative duties and scholarly studies. His first published work *On the Maláyu Nation* proclaimed his knowledge of a wide range of indigenous Malay chronicles and other literary texts.[167] In the book, he made it clear that Malay historiography was not a 'blank slate'. Malays were history-makers too—even competitors. It was Raffles' partnership with the Scottish Orientalist John Leyden, who was translating the *Sulalatus Salatin* or *Sejarah Melayu*, which led him to formulate an Orientalist narrative of the Malay world—a contested world that the EIC was already drawing into its commercial orbit from its base in Penang.[168]

Along with Raffles, Leyden joined the British expeditionary forces led by Lord Minto that invaded Java in June 1811. In Batavia (Jakarta), Leyden began work inspecting a library that held a trove of indigenous manuscripts and subsequently caught 'Batavia fever' (malaria or dengue) and succumbed 'in Raffles' arms three days later'.[169] Raffles subsequently oversaw the publication of

---

[167] T.S. Raffles, "On the Maláyu Nation: With a Translation of Its Maritime Institutions," *Asiatick Research* 12 (Calcutta: Calcutta Gazette Office, 1816), 102–158.

[168] For Raffles' relationship and collaboration with Leyden see: J. Bastin, *Sir Stamford Raffles and Some of His Friends and Contemporaries*.

[169] Farish A. Noor points out that at the time of his death, Leyden was better known than Raffles and his passing was mourned in the Bombay Courier and the London Chronicle. See: Farish A. Noor, "Nothing Left to Know: Stamford Raffles' Map of Java and the Epistemology of Empire," *Working Paper No. 3 - November 2014*, ASEAN Studies Center, November 2014, 12; Stephen A. Murphy, ed., *Raffles in Southeast Asia: Revisiting the Scholar and Statesman* (Singapore: Asian Civilisations Museum, 2019).

the *Malay Annals* in 1821.[170] *Malay Annals* is a mistranslation, no doubt deliberate. The original title is *Sulalatus Salatin* (*Genealogy of Kings*) and its compilers did exactly that: trace the ancestry of the Melaka sultanate back to Alexander the Great. In Raffles' introduction to his late friend's translation, he tells us that Leyden 'espoused the cause of the Malayan race' because 'in the feudal notions and habits of this people, he found so much in accordance with his own feelings of honour'. Raffles contrasts the 'authentic history' of 'Mahometanism' with the 'wild traditions' of the Malays. Leyden's insight was that these 'wild traditions' contained 'glimmers of light' that could be decoded to provide insight into customs, traditions, and trade which had 'long collected at certain natural and advantageous emporia'. Raffles always claimed that it was from Leyen's translation of the *Malay Annals* that he first learned about Temasek, the island of Singapore, as one of those 'advantageous emporia'. [171]

At this point, Raffles turns his rhetorical guns on his commercial competitors whom he claims have corrupted the ancient mercantile culture of the Malays. He rebukes the Portuguese and Dutch for bringing 'ruin and desolation which ensued throughout a large portion of these islands'. The resources of the Archipelago, Raffles laments, were swallowed up by greedy policy and a 'narrow and rigid monopoly' that imposed 'arbitrary and restrictive regulations'. Raffles' rant against Dutch 'despoliation' of the Indies leads to his key argument:

> [T]he native states, deprived of their fair share of commerce, abandoned all attempts, and sunk into the comparative insignificance in which they were found at the period when our traders began to navigate these seas from Madras to Bengal. The destruction of the native trade of the

---

[170] The matter is discussed in detail in for example: O.W. Wolters, *The Fall of Srivijaya in Malay History* (Kuala Lumpur: Oxford University Press, 1970).

[171] *Malay Annals*, tr. John Leyden (London: Longman, Hurst, Rees, Orme, and Brown, 1821), 6, https://wellcomecollection.org/works/r9gx3qq5.

Archipelago by this withering policy, may be considered as the origin of many of the evils, and all of the piracies of which we now complain . . .[172]

Raffles' target here is, of course, the government of the Netherlands and the emerging threat of monopolistic Dutch trading practices in the Indies. Nevertheless, he uses this critique to establish a key and enduring colonial narrative: the decayed native state. While he fumes about the fate of the indigenous states and trading networks corroded by Dutch and Portuguese commercial monopolism, his depiction of the Malays is equally harsh; his rhetoric foreshadows later and pervasive colonial deprecations of 'lazy natives'.[173] According to Raffles, Malays had sunk into insignificance; they had fallen into apathy and indolence; they had resorted to piracy and plunder. Salvation, he argues, could come only through contact with British traders, anticipating the 'comprador' trading relationships that became so essential to the rise of Singapore as a globalizing emporium. For the Malays, history was over.

This historiography of decay and decline explains why Raffles and his associates so assiduously sought out and described the decayed city walls, orchards, and tombs of the medieval Malay rulers that lay scattered on Bukit Larangan. The indigenous peoples of the Peninsula and Archipelago were no longer agents of history but relics in a museum: objects of the past, not its makers and recorders.

Raffles: Historian of Java

Since the beginning of the seventeenth century, Europeans had been forced to confront the fact that non-Christian commercial

---

[172] Stephen A. Murphy, ed., *Raffles in Southeast Asia*.

[173] Syed Hussein Alatas, *The Myth of the Lazy Native: A Study of the Image of the Malays, Filipinos and Javanese from the 16th to the 20th Century and Its Function in the Ideology of Colonial Capitalism* (London: Frank Cass & Co., 1977).

civilizations had flourished outside Europe in the Indies. As Farish Noor has shown, Theodore de Bry's *Icones Indiae Orientalis*, published in 1601, shows in exquisite detail that Asians 'had developed their own system of commerce, governance, religious praxis, and culture to a level that rivalled Europe's'.[174] As European trading corporations like the English, Dutch, and French East India companies began to push their way into Asian territories armed with gunboat, musket, and rocket, this ecumenical generosity frayed. Asians now became competitors not merely objects of curiosity. Commercial competition demanded a new way of looking at and writing about Asians. Just as Malays were deprived of agency as historical relics, so too were Asian merchants and traders as 'pen and sword' conquered new monopolies. In short, by becoming historians of the territory they sought to control, European colonialists turned to history-making to explain and justify conquest.

Raffles' two volume *The History of Java* was published in 1817, a year or so after his return to England from Java. Raffles' meddlesome activities as lieutenant-governor had been widely reported and he was under personal attack from rivals in the EIC. During his six years in Java, he had written and published the immensely ambitious *Regulations for the More Effectual Administration of Justice in the Provincial Courts of Java* and *Revenue Instructions* (1814) to impose the EIC's yoke on this rich new possession. Raffles despatched cartographers, explorers, and engineers across Java, Sumatra, Sulawesi, and Borneo to accumulate a mass of data about this new colonial asset. However, to his intense disappointment, following the defeat of Napoleon at Waterloo, Java had to be turned over to its former colonial proprietors, the Dutch and Raffles set sail for England on 25 March 1816.

Raffles was under a dark corporate cloud when he arrived in London. His activities in Java had been widely criticized, and it was in these perturbing circumstances that he began work

---

[174] Farish A. Noor, *The Discursive Construction of Southeast Asia in 19th Century Colonial-Capitalist Discourse* (Amsterdam: AUP, 2016), 34.

writing a hugely ambitious *The History of Java*; he hoped that he might redeem his battered reputation as a scholar and in effect repossess the island and its cultures as historian. It was not an unrealistic ambition. As Bernard Cohn has shown, such high-minded activities were not unusual for elite functionaries of the EIC.[175] Scholarly research on the languages and artefacts of India demonstrated both India's antiquity and backwardness. This was, as we have seen, Mill's project in his *History of British India*. During the same period when Mill was preparing his monumental work for his publisher, Raffles rushed out his hefty two volume *The History of Java*, obsequiously dedicated to the Prince of Wales.

Raffles had a number of overlapping agendas. He used his history to fire broadsides on his Dutch rivals and the practices of the now defunct VOC. Dutch monopolistic evils and mismanagement had, he argued, ruined the Javanese economy. His main preoccupation, however, was cultural acquisition. By recording Java's indigenous history, he would retake ownership of the territory he had lost: history-making was repossession. Raffles omitted any significant references to the many Dutch scholars and explorers who had travelled all over the archipelago and written detailed accounts of the peoples and cultures they encountered: the great temples of Borobudur and Prambanan had long been shown on Dutch maps. Raffles claimed, 'The antiquities of Java have not, until recently, excited much notice.'[176]

Raffles' had lost possession of Java—but he sought to recapture it in his book. Java, he insisted, should have remained a Company possession: *The History of Java* signifies its implicit capture. How was this done? Raffles admits that the peoples of Java 'very early emerged from barbarism' but—and this is the

---

[175] Bernard S. Cohn, *Colonialism and Its Forms of Knowledge: The British in India* (Princeton: Princeton University Press, 1996).

[176] Farish A. Noor, *The Discursive Construction of Southeast Asia*, 77; John N. Miksic and Timbul Haryono, *Borobudur: Majestic Mysterious Magnificent* (BAB Publishing, 2010).

crucial point—their civilization had degenerated. It comprised magnificent but inert ruins and relics. He presents the Javanese as types, costumed performers, who are timid, incredulous, and infantile compared to the 'supple, venal and crafty' Chinese. What had happened to the builders of mighty Borobudur? What had led to their downfall? Naturally, the Dutch should shoulder much of the blame but his most venomous barbs targeted Muslim Arabs. Arab traders, he argued, have 'inculcated the most intolerant bigotry', so that the Javanese no longer know their own history.[177] He recommended cultural apartheid, so that Javanese communities would be segregated from the Chinese and Arabs and not contaminated by avarice or 'Mohametanism'. The reason for Raffles' animus is not hard to find: Arab traders, like the Dutch, remained a powerful mercantile force in the Indies.

As a self-appointed curator of ancient Javanese culture, Raffles wanted *The History of Java* to assert that he and the EIC, which employed him, had come to Java as both agents of modernity and curators of the past. The Javanese themselves were thus captured by his history as if in a museum constructed from words and images alongside antiquities that testified to a glorious Hindu–Buddhist past. The present and future belonged to Raffles and his employers.

As Noor shows, *The History of Java* reinforces this capture with its very impressive map. Engraved by John Walker, 'A Map of Java Chiefly from Surveys Made during the British Administration Constructed in Illustration of an Account of Java' includes nearly four hundred place names for villages, towns, ports, and ancient monuments as well as more than a hundred streams, rivers, valleys, and mountains of Java. Raffles' map is a cartographic masterpiece and a strategic masterplan for territorial appropriation. It meticulously traces the route of the British built road that connected Batavia to Cirebon and Raffles' exploratory expedition to the ruins of Borobudur and Mount Merapi. As Noor writes, the map adopts the position of a colonial gaze that has the

---

[177] Ibid. 57.

means to stand both above and below the material and human topographies of Java.[178] Noor highlights an inset mineralogical map—proclaiming the power of western science to expose a hidden, subterranean world unknown to the 'natives' and inviting exploitation. The message is loud and clear: We know more than you. For history-makers like Raffles, knowledge is ownership.[179]

To sum up, *The History of Java* and its cartography is a work of history-making that asserts ownership and power. It is simultaneously a valediction and a reclamation. As Benedict Anderson puts it in *Imagined Communities,* 'war by war, treaty by treaty, the alignment of map and power proceeded'.[180]

The publication of *The History of Java* restored Raffles' career and reputation. As noted, the two-volume work bears a dedication to the Prince Regent, later George IV, who Raffles had already wooed with gifts of several pieces of purloined Indonesian weaponry and Raffles was knighted by the Prince Regent in the same year. From the very beginning of his career, Raffles had been a data gatherer. In this, he was not in any way unusual. Data gathering was the life blood of the EIC—the cold matter that flowed through its mercantile arteries.

The Raw Matter of History-Making

Data, of course is not yet history but its enforced harvest is vital to lawmaking, taxation, and the appropriation of indigenous narrative. The EIC's rule in India and the contested domains of 'Lower India' in Burma, Malaya, and Singapore generated vast amounts of paper. Like other modern empires, the British wielded power, as Colley has shown, through the sword, the

---

[178] The idea of the colonial gaze is also explored in Martin Jay and Sumathi Ramaswamy, *Empires of Vision: A Reader* (New York: Duke University Press, 2014).

[179] Farish A. Noor, *The Discursive Construction of Southeast Asia*, 116.

[180] B. Anderson, *Imagined Communities* (Verso Books, 2016).

ship *and* the pen.¹⁸¹ The metanarrative that this unceasing recording and writing expressed was simple. The EIC and the colonial administrators who took over its role in the era of high imperialism after 1857 presented their task as redeeming native peoples from degeneration and misuses of power; the 'Asian despot' had top billing in the colonial narrative as an expressive focus of distrust and hostility. Here we have Gibbon's narrative paradigm of decline applied not to the colonial apparatus but to native states.

Data gathering thus went hand in hand with policing, pacification, and investment in compliant native rulers who would follow the blueprint of the colonial narrative. Policing would be partly entrusted to other native 'types' who displayed the appropriate 'martial' qualities. In the realm of history-making, these colonial narratives, such as the histories of India and Java we have discussed, followed in the paper wake of Gibbon, Mill, Macaulay, and Seeley—the high priesthood of history-making. Any anxiety that the British empire might follow its Roman ancestor into decline was countered by the ascent of a wise, pragmatic, and humane colonial governing class that would take the place of corrupted indigenous rulers.

Raffles was just one of many colonial data gathers and historical narrators deployed by the EIC in the first half of the nineteenth century. We have already met John Crawfurd toiling up Singapore's Forbidden Hill in search of the relics of the medieval Malay state that once occupied the island. Crawfurd was a Scottish surgeon who had served as an assistant surgeon in the EIC's Bengal medical service. As Gareth Knapman points out, '[L]ike many company officials, he believed that academic enquiry was part of his official duties.'¹⁸² His multifarious interests included

---

[181] L. Colley, *The Gun, the Ship and the Pen: Warfare, Constitutions and the Making of the Modern World* (Profile Books, 2021).

[182] Gareth Knapman, "Race, Empire and Liberalism: Interpreting John Crawfurd's History of the Indian Archipelago," in *17th Biennial Conference of the Asian Studies Association Proceedings (2008)* (bepress, 2008), available at: http://works.bepress.com/gareth_knapman/5/ (2008).

philology, ethnology, geology, biology, and political economy; he even spoke fluent Javanese. Along with Raffles, he took part in the invasion of Java and the sacking of the Kraton in Jogjakarta. The EIC then sent him to Siam (Thailand) and Cochinchina (southern Vietnam). In 1823, Crawfurd was appointed as the second British Resident of Singapore. With the Anglo-Dutch dispute resolved, on 19 November, 1824, Crawfurd inflicted 'A Treaty of Friendship and Alliance' on the Sultan and the Temenggong to replace the one they had signed with Raffles in 1819. Instead of a mere 'settlement', the Malay chiefs, vulnerable to a loss of pension rights, signed away 'in full Sovereignty and property to the Honourable the English EIC, their Heirs and Successors for ever, the Island of Singapore [...] together with the adjacent seas, straits, and islets to the extent of the ten geographical miles, from the coast of the said main island of Singapore.'[183] The colonial narrative of possession was now complete.

Crawfurd had secured Singapore with guile, bribery, and force sharpened by a shrewd appraisal of the vulnerabilities of the Malay rulers. He was, in modern terminology, an 'area specialist'. His rejoinder to Raffles' *The History of Java* was his own *History of the Indian Archipelago, Containing an Account of the Manners, Arts, Languages, Religions, Institutions and Commerce of Its Inhabitants*, which attempted to look at the cultures of the archipelago as a holistic system.[184] Once we locate Crawfurd's writings in the domain of ethnology, then his contribution to the capture of Southeast Asia

---

[183] This remarkable document can be read here: "The Crawfurd Treaty (1824): Treaty of Friendship and Alliance between the Honourable East India Company, and the Sultan and the Temenggong of Johore (1824)," Jus Mundi, 1824, https://jusmundi.com/en/document/treaty/en-treaty-of-friendship-and-alliance-between-the-honourable-east-india-company-and-the-sultan-and-the-temenggong-of-johore-1824-the-crawfurd-treaty-1824-monday-2nd-august-1824. For a legal analysis see: "Our Legal Heritage," Singapore Academy of Law, https://www.sal.org.sg/Resources-Tools/Legal-Heritage/Legal-and-Constitutional-History-of-Singapore.

[184] Crawfurd uses the term 'Indian Archipelago' to refer to all countries in modern Southeast Asia except Laos, Cambodia, Thailand, Burma, and Vietnam.

becomes clearer. He was a slippery and contradictory writer who, like Raffles, remonstrated against mercantile destruction of indigenous economies and, with unintended irony, the 'flagrant injustices' of treaties imposed on native states by European countries. But Crawfurd's main contribution to the historiography of empire was an emphasis on race.[185] He informed members of the Ethnological Society of London that the 'primordial distinctions of race' were fixed and hierarchical:

> The union of the highest and lowest species of the human race yields an intermediate progeny, inferior to the first, and superior to the last [. . .] The Mestizo is much inferior to the Spaniard, but much superior to the Red Indian. The result of the union of a Chinese and a Malay, one of frequent occurrence is a deterioration in the Chinese and an improvement in the Malay.[186]

Raffles, too, had represented the peoples of Java as types, but Crawfurd went much further. He was, after all, much better informed than Raffles about the emerging science of racial differences that insisted on the evolved status of western races and, in effect, their right to govern.[187]

Taken together, then, Raffles and Crawfurd complete the circuit of a racialized historical narrative that we can trace from Gibbon's 'Asiatic barbarians', Mill's 'backward Hindoos', and the noble nation building Britons of Macaulay's *The History of England*. Both Mill and Macauley present the Englishman as a natural ruler and the lead actor in a Whiggish drama of continuous

---

[185] Gareth Knapman, *Race and British Colonialism in Southeast Asia, 1770-1870: John Crawfurd and the Politics of Equality* (Routledge, 2017).

[186] John Crawfurd, "On the Classification of the Races of Man," *Transactions of the Ethnological Society of London* 1 (1861): 354–378, https://doi.org/10.2307/3014207.

[187] I. Hannaford, *Race: The History of an Idea in the West* (Woodrow Wilson Center Press, 1996).

advancement. History-making thus consumes the indigenous past in the glory of the colonial present and, by implication, the marvels of an imperial future. Non-European time is frozen; its narrative ritualized and static like a Wayang shadow play or Noh drama. European historiography aided and abetted the colonizer and possessed immense rhetorical power to reshape and capture the histories of the colonized. As Raffles and Crawfurd knew from scholarly research and everyday experience, the worlds they seized for King and Company had their own deep histories. But that history was locked up in past time like an artefact in a museum display case. It was a relic history of ruins and the tombs of kings. But in the historiographical gaze of the colonizer, time's arrow pointed only forward from 1819. What lay behind was the realm of ghosts.

Conclusions

This chapter began with questions. Why has the foundational myth of Singapore in 1819 proved so resilient? Why is Raffles still standing on Boat Quay? One explanation is that the tabula rasa version of Singaporean history, which closed off the colonial port city from its Malay antecedents had a political purpose after the separation of Singapore from Malaysia in 1965. The PAP leaders feared that digging too deep into the past would release the unpalatable genie of ethnic exclusivity and racial privileging. Later, fear of Americanization and cultural deracination led the Singaporean government to promote the recognition of ancestral Indian and Chinese cultures, but the door to Singapore's own past remained firmly shut.[188] Finally, in a new century, historians and archaeologists prised open that door to unveil the longue

---

[188] Michael D. Barr, "Singapore Comes to Terms with Its Malay Past: The Politics of Crafting a National History," *Asian Studies Review* 46, no. 2 (2021), 355–356.

durée of Singapore/Temasek as a Malay regional port city firmly entrenched in a regionalized history.

Throughout this evolution of re-imagined histories, however, the myth of 1819 and the singular foundation of Singapore as a colonial port state has proved oddly resilient. To explain this resilience, this essay highlighted the period after 1819 when the legal dispute between the British and Dutch government about the ownership of the island of Singapore led to a division of spoils in spheres of influence that laid down the territorial boundaries of future state-building. This colonial project took place under the aegis of the British EIC that, like its Dutch counterpart, promoted data gathering and scholarly history-making that aggressively captured the narrative of the Malay world. Both Raffles, his colleague Crawfurd, and (in the case of India) Mill authored lengthy histories and cartographies that locked up indigenous histories as relics. This teleological history-making assigned the future to the colonial powers; the past was decayed and degenerate.

Yet Sir Stamford Raffles was himself a creation of colonial history-making. In the mid-1880s, few in colonial Singapore remembered Raffles at all. The EIC he represented had lost all its administrative powers after 1857, the Straits Settlements had become a Crown Colony, and Singapore was embarking on a period of unprecedented economic growth as British and Chinese entrepreneurs began to tap into the resources of the Malay Archipelago.[189] In 1884, Sir Frederick Weld, the governor of the Straits Settlement, as Knapman puts it, 'plucked Raffles from obscurity'.[190] He lobbied for a statue of Raffles to be erected on the Padang and a few years later, in December 1887,

---

[189] Wong Lin Ken, "Singapore: Its Growth as an Entrepot Port, 1819–1941," *Journal of Southeast Asian Studies* 9, no. 1 (1978): 50–84.

[190] G. Knapman, "'Unencumbered by the Scruples of Justice and Good Faith': The Colonial Achievements of Raffles in Southeast Asia," *The Truth About Empire: Real Histories of British Colonialism*, ed. A. Lester (London: Hurst & Company), 143–144.

the Raffles Hotel was opened. Weld had a specific and illiberal reason for promoting the memory of Singapore's forgotten founder. The rapid growth of Singapore's Asian populations had led to demands from community leaders and Asian journalists for representative government. The British colonial administrators in London vigorously resisted all such demands and, in Singapore, Weld refused to grant self-government on the grounds that the British capacity for governing 'is a characteristic of our race': the Chinese were merely 'created to get rich and enjoy the good things in life'. Weld dragged Raffles out of obscurity as a visionary British governor-leader who embodied the rights of the white colonial master.[191] Weld's invention of the cult of Raffles, then, was colonial history-making in tooth and claw. Drawing on the Whig idea of predestination and Carlyle's adulation of the 'great man', Southeast Asian history was recast to enforce colonial power. Raffles as founder is a contingent construct of the final decades of the nineteenth century, disconnected from the events of 1819. We should be all the more impressed that since independence, Singaporean 'history-makers' have demonstrated a rare capacity to rethink the past and to challenge the ghosts of Raffles and Crawfurd, Gibbon, Mill, and Macaulay.

---

[191] Ibid. 143.

Chapter 4

Marginal Notes to a Treaty: The Quibble of the Malay Princes

Benjamin J.Q. Khoo

The Copy

The 1824 Treaty of Friendship and Alliance is one of the most important documents in Singapore's colonial history. It was signed on Government Hill (now Fort Canning Park) on 2 August 1824 between John Crawfurd, the second British resident of Singapore, and Sultan Hussein Shah and Temenggong Abdul Rahman. The written document effectively ceded to the English East India Company the full sovereignty of the island of Singapore, extending into the waters ten geographical miles from its coasts as well as the adjacent seas, straits, and surrounding islets in perpetuity.[192] For inking this treaty with their seals, Sultan Hussein Shah and Temenggong Abdul Rahman received for their labours a one-off sum of 33,200 and 26,800 Spanish

---

[192] A manuscript copy of the treaty can be found at the British Library, IOR/H/641, 547–556. Published copies of the treaty are otherwise available at C.U. Aitchison, *A Collection of Treaties, Engagements, and Sunnuds, relating to India and Neighbouring Countries*, vol. 1 (Calcutta: Foreign Office Press, 1876), 331–334; *Minutes of Evidence Taken Before the Select Committee on the Affairs of the East India Company*, vol. 14 (London: House of Commons, 1832), 502–504.

dollars, a princely payoff, as well as a monthly stipend of 1,300 Spanish dollars and 700 Spanish dollars for the rest of their lives, respectively. From this point on, Singapore was prised from its native hands and set on its unique path as a prized colonial port city. Previous studies have emphasized the duress that both Malay princes were under as well as the mix of threats and incentives offered to them by Stamford Raffles and John Crawfurd to compel them into signing away Singapore in the year preceding. Yet, despite Munshi Abdullah's imaginative description of that day and Crawfurd's own explications to Calcutta, we know little of their thoughts on the deal being offered to them and even lesser of whether they disputed any of the points in the treaty that they eventually signed.[193] Now, thanks to several lines written into the margins of a recently rediscovered copy of the 1824 treaty, and a close reading of the available evidence already in circulation, we are for the first time able to reconstruct in greater detail how the negotiations went and what exactly they were quibbling about.

To understand why the 1824 treaty is important and deemed expedient by Crawfurd, a better appreciation of the circumstances in which Singapore was founded is required. The 1824 treaty was, in effect, intended to replace the first treaty that had previously been agreed between the said Malay chiefs and Raffles in 1819. According to the initial arrangement, the 1819 treaty, the British were only allowed to establish a trading post on the island; it neither included any legal right for legislation nor allowed for extensive planning and construction on the settlement. In addition, the British, Sultan Hussein Shah, and Temenggong Abdul Rahman, shared equally in the island's administration, especially over the port, people, and market. In other words, the British did not have sovereignty over the territory. Sultan Hussein was still recognized as the true proprietor of the land, even within

---

[193] The Munshi Abdullah or Abdullah bin Abdul Kadir, was a teacher, scribe, and interpreter. He had worked as a copyist for Stamford Raffles and his autobiography, the *Hikayat Abdullah*, provides a valuable indigenous perspective of Singapore's early history. See Abdullah bin Abdul Kadir, *The Hikayat Abdullah*, tr. A.H. Hill (Kuala Lumpur: Oxford University Press, 1970).

the bounds wherein the Union Jack flew, and as the island's trade grew in size and consequence, it became of greater imperative to secure the land's sovereignty for Britain's own. The 1824 treaty negotiated by Crawfurd thus secured all that.

The Context

It must first be clarified that the document in question is in no way a facsimile of the original 1824 treaty. For a start, this is a scribal copy, made from a document first written in April 1825 that has likely not survived. Second, both the first and subsequent reproduction of the treaty were not written in English but in Dutch, with the remaining copy presently kept in the National Archives of the Netherlands in The Hague. So, what is this copy, how did it come about, and how did it end up in Dutch hands?

This curious rediscovery is readily explained by the conclusion of yet another treaty, one which was arguably more significant in the context of its time. A few months prior, on 17 March 1824, Dutch and British diplomats had shaken hands in London over the historic Anglo-Dutch Treaty. This international treaty not only withdrew Dutch objections to the British occupation of Singapore but it also led to a swapping of colonial holdings: Melaka for Benkulen and a division of the realm of Johor-Riau into two spheres of influence, each under the guardianship of a colonial power. However, in those days, when the flow and speed of information were determined by the progress of sailing ships, Crawfurd was unaware that negotiations to secure the island was already ratified in London and had resolved to complete the process of disentangling the British from the tenuous arrangements with the Malay princes and oust them from Singapore.[194] This meant that there were two treaties in existence and doubts arose as to whether the two treaties contravened each other, as both had been concluded independently and concerned

---

[194] Carl Trocki, *Prince of Pirates: The Temenggongs and the Development of Johor and Singapore, 1784–1885* (Singapore: NUS Press, 2007), 67.

the same piece of territory. Since the responsibility of ensuring that the Anglo-Dutch Treaty was implemented fell to the Dutch, the Dutch colonial government in Batavia decided to send its Malay translator, Christiaan van Angelbeek, to Singapore in early 1825 to ascertain on what footing the British now stood with Sultan Hussein and the Temenggong Abdul Rahman on Singapore.

Despite his tender twenty-three years of age, van Angelbeek came from a famous Dutch Indies family and was one of its most promising colonial officers. He was given his commission on 28 February 1825 and arrived in Singapore, a little more than a month later by boat, on 10 April 1825. Here, he passed four days with the more senior John Crawfurd and despite a difference of two decades, the two men got along agreeably. Crawfurd happily hosted him at Government Hill, providing courtesies of breakfast and lunch every day, and took van Angelbeek on a tour around the small settlement in his coach. Diplomatic goodwill between the two colonial governments was thus solidified by the friendship of the two men, and van Angelbeek seemed impressed by the sincerity and candour of Crawfurd. 'He is a very cultured and British gentleman,' wrote van Angelbeek, with further choicy lines about the marvel and progress of the settlement.[195] On his first visit after disembarking, Crawfurd was generous enough to inform his Dutch visitor that he had contracted a treaty with the two native chiefs, Sultan Hussein Shah and the Temenggong Abdul Rahman of Johor, and promised him a reading of the contract. The following day, Crawfurd proved good on his word, entertaining van Angelbeek on 11 April 1825 with a private showcase of the Treaty of Friendship and Alliance. Since the treaty was yet to be ratified by the British Parliament, a copy could regretfully not be made, but the ever-conscientious van Angelbeek, upon returning to his lodgings, conscious of its

---

[195] 2.21.007.57, Stukken betreffende Riouw en Malakka [Documents Concerning Riau and Melaka] (Oude inv., no. 24 Be.) 1818–1825, Nationaal Archief, The Hague, 144–145.

import to the Dutch government, proceeded to set what he remembered of the articles of the contract on paper, alongside his own comments therein.

The journey of this manuscript is, thereafter, eminently traceable. It was dispatched from Singapore and reached Batavia, where a copy was made by the one-time secretary of the then Governor-General of the Dutch East Indies Gerard J.C. Schneither. This copy of a copy was then kept in Schneither's private collection of government documents, which included other very sensitive information on Melaka, Riau, and Singapore between 1819 and 1826. The collection was later spirited away to the Netherlands upon Schneither's retirement and after the bureaucrat's death, the book-trading house Nijhoff procured these documents from his descendants. They later came to be reacquired by the Department of Colonies in 1878. This is how a loose echo of the 1824 treaty can now be found in the Dutch Archives almost two hundred years later.

The Comparison

Because it was written entirely from recollection and naturally subject to the occasional error of scribal hands, a comparison inevitably raises many discrepancies between the transcript copy as recorded by van Angelbeek for his superiors and the actual treaty signed between Crawfurd on one side and Sultan Hussein Shah and Temenggong Abdul Rahman on the other.

There are several issues at stake here. First, when looking at diplomatic agreements between two parties with different levels of linguistic competency, we can compare the fidelity of translation and whether it conveys an accurate understanding and interpretation. One such linguistic contestation can be made over the sentence, '*Het Eiland Singapoera met de daaronder eilanden, zeeën, straten en kanalen*' (The Island of Singapore with *its* [my emphasis] islands, seas, straits, and channels) which were given over to the EIC. Can these islands, seas, straits, and channels be said to *belong* to Singapore at this time, considering that they were all under the dominion of Johor-Riau, and what were the geographical entities or seascapes that he was possibly referring to? The English version delineating ten geographical miles from Singapore's coast already gave rise to much confusion and this translation muddles it even further. Another quibble concerns the word *belooft* or loosely understood as 'to promise' with regards to the payment made to the two Malay princes, which we can compare against the English word used, 'to engage'. Is this to be understood as a stronger binding sort of promise or merely a less strong commitment by the EIC to prevaricate on the dispensation of its payout? More such titbits abound in-text for us to split hairs about, but these are just a few standout examples.

Second, both differed significantly in content. Although the cession of Singapore is never in doubt, van Angelbeek's copy jumbles up the order of the articles of the treaty, leaving some points out while adding others, and is imperfect in communicating the exactitude of several details. For example, Article 3 and 4 of the 1824 treaty are very similar. Article 3 is the engagement of the EIC to pay the Malay princes the lump sum and the stipend, and Article 4 is the acknowledgment by the same of the said figures. In van Angelbeek's transcript, he records Article 3 as the sum payable to the Malay princes and Article 4 as the stipend that the EIC was obliged to pay out—an understandable error. Article 5 (to receive the Sultan and the Temenggong with dignity and respect when they visit Singapore) and Article 12 (regarding the upholding of free trade in Johor dominions) are left out entirely. However, it is the paraphrases from the actual ratified treaty that are the most interesting. In van Angelbeek's rendering of Article 13, both the Sultan and the Temenggong were said to be expressly forbidden from the purchase of new slaves while those that were already in their households had to be registered with their names by the Resident in a 'special book'. If their names were not found in this name register, they would be deemed to have been illegally acquired and would be set free. Besides the question of whether these were truly 'slaves' as we understand them today, the considerable difference raises the intriguing possibility that van Angelbeek, who was fluent in Malay, was possibly looking at a Jawi version of the treaty (which has not survived) that differed significantly in meaning from the English version.[196] Considering that Crawfurd had 'not permitted the present treaty to be polluted even by the mention of that subject', and yet so insistent on dealing thoroughly with this issue, this is not entirely out of the question.[197]

This brings us suitably to the third point—the faultiness of remembrance, especially when we consider van Angelbeek was influenced by further explanations Crawfurd provided in conversation. The reference to slavery in the context of this treaty was possibly not only altered by Crawfurd's strength of conviction about the subject but also tainted by his comparison with a copy of the public consultation in Singapore, which van Angelbeek had affixed as a copy to the Governor-General. There are other such mishaps as well: the date on which the treaty was concluded was fixed on 4 August 1824 instead of 2 August 1824, which seemed an error on van Angelbeek's or the scribe's part. Moreover, regarding Article 8 (cf. Point 6 of van Angelbeek's transcript), which prohibits the Malay princes from forming an alliance or maintaining correspondences with other foreign powers of potentate without the knowledge or consent of the

---

[196] The present copy of the 1824 treaty in the National Archives of Singapore (NAS) dates to September 1841, which was created at the request of the then Governor of the Straits Settlement Samuel George Bonham. See Kevin Khoo, "A Treaty Most Unfriendly," in *50 Records from History: Highlights of the National Archives of Singapore* (Singapore: National Archives of Singapore, 2019), 20–21. Two Malay copies were in fact created for the Sultan and the Temenggong to be invested in Singapore, but these do not seem to have survived.

[197] Thomas Braddell, "Notices of Singapore," *The Journal of the Indian Archipelago and Eastern Asia* VII, 350–354; Charles Buckley, *An Anecdotal History of Old Times in Singapore, etc.*, vol. 1 (Singapore: Fraser and Neave, 1902), 158–159, 172–173. Crawfurd himself candidly noted that "much pains have been taken with the Malayan version of the Treaty".

EIC, van Angelbeek furnished an extra line to say that, having left Singapore, the Malay princes would be again at liberty to deal with whomever they deemed fit. This uncanny addition would undoubtedly have been a clarification on Crawfurd's part. These are just some of the more obvious transgressions, which we can all too well freely nitpick. Nevertheless, we can excuse this transcript, since it remains an impressive specimen of language and memory, being largely accurate in interpretation and capturing surprisingly well the spirit of the 1824 treaty.

The Commentaries

Van Angelbeek's transcript of and commentaries about the 1824 treaty gives us a unique insight into what the Malay princes were unhappy about. This is because their own dissatisfaction with the treaty was liberally provided by John Crawfurd to van Angelbeek in conversation, which the young translator had the foresight to pencil in as commentary to the articles in the margins of the text. Therefore, through a close reading of van Angelbeek's points on the 1824 treaty and triangulating them with the available sources that have come down to us, we can not only get a more imaginative sense of what Sultan Hussein Shah and Temenggong Abdul Rahman were quibbling about with Crawfurd but also understand their perceptions of the circumstances in early Singapore. Let us look at them carefully.

There are only six comments in the margin, and they vary in length. The first is rather unimportant and concerns the conversion of currencies of the sum the EIC was paying to the Malay princes for the Governor-General's edification. Even though van Angelbeek made no further explanation about this sum, what is important on the part of the Malay princes is that they were insistent that 'the pension had to be hereditary and perpetual', likely because not only had they grown in prestige, wealth, and entourage in the meantime and they needed it to maintain 'their expenses and establishments', but also as safeguards for their heirs and successors.[198] It was a lucrative land-for-cash deal for the Malay princes that ascribed little value to land. Yet, by Crawfurd's admission, the British were conscious of the lack of contractual precedence and greatly resisted acceding to it. The success of the negotiation hinged on this sum and the payable pension and formed a sticking point between the parties. Considering how tied this treaty is to money, it would perhaps be more accurate, as others have remarked, to refer to this treaty as a 'buyout' of Singapore from Malay sovereignty.[199]

The second comment in the margin, which relates to Article 6 and 7 of the treaty (condensed by van Angelbeek into one point), confirms what we have known all along about Crawfurd's intention: It was an inducement to oust the Malay princes from Singapore's territory and, given their debt, 'to disencumber ourselves of them at such a price'. van Angelbeek here confirms that the clause is as Crawfurd states—to compensate them for their losses that they would eventuate as they had accumulated much property and land in Singapore, even though 'the dispositions evinced by them in the progress of negotiation show clearly that they little wish to relinquish'. So, as much as the British wanted nothing more to do with the Malay princes, the Malay princes, Sultan Hussein Shah and the Temenggong Abdul Rahman, were well loathed to leave the comfort and security they enjoyed on the island.

The third comment relates to Article 10 of the treaty (Point 6) and is more informative on the part of the Malay princes. As Crawfurd informs van Angelbeek, the purpose of these articles is to disentangle the British from native politics and to prevent

---

[198] Regarding the British colonial government compensation to the heirs of the sultan, which were made until the twentieth century, see Kwa Chong Guan, "Origins of Ordinances no. XII of 1904 to Make Provision for the Family of the Late Sultan Hussein," in *Beyond Bicentennial: Perspectives on Malays*, ed. Zainul Abidin Rasheed, Wan Hussin Zoohri, and Norshahril Saat (Singapore: World Scientific, 2020), 197–213.

[199] Mark Frost and Yu-Mei Balasingamchow, *Singapore: A Biography* (Singapore: Didier Millet, 2009), 74.

them from being embroiled in new Malay disputes. But the Malay princes were extremely unhappy with this, for which they ended up prolonging the signing of the Crawfurd Treaty for three months. If van Angelbeek's recollection is correct, this would then put the formulation of the treaty three months earlier to sometime in May 1824, long before the Malay princes arrived at a final decision.[200] As Crawfurd told Calcutta, the two royals had envisaged and had demonstrated 'evident desire throughout' to be engaged in a close alliance with the EIC, which would be an 'offensive party as we as defensive in their quarrels'. An earlier attempt to get the British involved in their claims on Johor against those of Riau had already been thwarted in late 1823, in which British abstention was felt by the Malay princes to be 'most repugnant to their wishes, and to certain ambitious views which they have been led to entertain'.[201] Considering that they had broken from the court at Riau to form this condominium of power, leaving the EIC as their only backers in their rebellion, the British extricating themselves from such a compact left them on a tenuous footing and without evident support. This was fatal to the Malay princes seeking to maintain their *negeri* (polity or state).

The fourth marginal note deals with the essence of Article 9, which stipulates that the Sultan and Temenggong, should they meet distress after being removed from Singapore, be afforded asylum at Penang and Singapore. Crawfurd explained that this article, which seemed like a gesture of generosity, was in fact to protect the British from being embroiled in a conflict with a foreign power. Van Angelbeek was informed that this referred

---

[200] This interpretation contradicts Mary Turnbull's claim, which seems unsubstantiated, that the delay and haggling was over the hereditary nature of their pension rights. C.M. Turnbull, *A History of Modern Singapore, 1819–2005* (Singapore: NUS Press, 2009), 47. A draft version of the Treaty had already been forwarded to Calcutta ceding the island of Singapore on 5 March 1824, putting its formulation sometime earlier in the year.

[201] Thomas Braddell, "Notices of Singapore," *The Journal of the Indian Archipelago and Eastern Asia* VII, 349; Charles Buckley, *An Anecdotal History of Old Times in Singapore, etc.*, vol. 1 (Singapore: Fraser and Neave, 1902), 158.

Marginal Notes to a Treaty: The Quibble of the Malay Princes   117

primarily to the Dutch. This little quote reveals that Crawfurd, unaware of the decisions in Europe, foresaw that the Malay princes, if left to their fragile devices, would eventually find themselves in trouble with the Dutch who were in the midst of concluding a circle of alliances from Borneo to Siak.[202] This proviso was thus intended to rein them in to British stations to prevent further trouble with the Dutch. However, it is here that van Angelbeek was able to relate that this provision had been entirely superseded by the Anglo-Dutch Treaty, which transformed the relationship that the Dutch and the British had with the entire Malay Peninsula. Crawfurd was thus rid of one source of worry.

Van Angelbeek's fifth comment returns to the proviso of the slave trade. The point here is complicated by Crawfurd's own politics, since he also deliberately used the term 'slave' to describe the Sultan and the Temenggong's followers.[203] According to van Angelbeek, both the Sultan and the Temenggong still had thousands of such followers or 'slaves' in 1825, all of whom maintained some sort of hierarchical relationship or dependence on their leaders. Several of their retainers, convinced of their unlawful status had appealed to Crawfurd and received thus their freedom.[204] The point here confirms Munshi Abdullah's account, which records that Crawfurd had, a month after the signing of the 1824 treaty, set twenty-seven young women of the Sultan's free, which inevitably led to an angry confrontation between the

---

[202] See NAB 1668: Foreign Pol Dept. 12 Mar 1824 No. 7 - Letter from J. Crawfurd, Resident at Singapore, to G. Swinton, Secretary to Government, reporting the result of the Dutch expedition into the interior of Borneo and their proposal to form an alliance with the Rajah of Siak, a 'Malayan State on Sumatra opposite the Town of Malacca'.

[203] Gareth Knapman, "Settler Colonialism and Usurping Malay Sovereignty in Singapore," *Journal of Southeast Asian Studies* 52, no. 3 (2021): 426.

[204] 2.21.007.57, Stukken betreffende Riouw en Malakka [Documents Concerning Riau and Melaka] (Oude inv., no. 24 Be.) 1818–1825, Nationaal Archief, The Hague, 143–144.

one-time ruler of Singapore and the Resident.[205] Therefore, one of the controversial points of the 1824 treaty, and from van Angelbeek's own musings, can be understood as the deliberate obscurity regarding what constituted 'slavery' and the issue of competing authorities in Singapore. For the Malay princes, Crawfurd was interfering with their *kerajaan's* (kingdom) economics;[206] in a world of migratory flows and shifting alliances, it was the size of the entourage of followers that reflected the stability of his reign, the measure of their wealth, and the greatness of their *nama* (name or renown), especially in competition with the alternative negeri across in Riau. Crawfurd, on the other hand, wanted to keep track and regulate the people who formed the Malay princes' following because he feared that a lack of jurisdiction might lead the residences of the Malay princes to become 'a sanctuary of criminals of any order or description'. If remained unchecked, Crawfurd envisaged 'the practice of introducing slaves' becoming common and jeopardizing the proper execution of law and order in the settlement.[207] Crawfurd admitted to Calcutta that the 'native princes were extremely urgent and importunate' with this clause in the 1824 treaty and van Angelbeek's reference in 1825 showed that this continued to be a source of tension; the Malay princes were still building their entourage in the traditional way, despite signing the treaty.

For his final comment, van Angelbeek offers us Crawfurd's understanding of the 1824 treaty in relation to Article 14. Evidently, Crawfurd was quite proud of driving it to its conclusion

---

[205] Abdullah bin Abdul Kadir, *The Hikayat Abdullah*, tr. A.H. Hill (Kuala Lumpur: Oxford University Press, 1970), 221–222.

[206] Anthony Milner, *The Malays* (Chichester: Wiley-Blackwell, 2008), 71–73.

[207] Crawfurd's draft treaty of 5 March 1824 had in fact four articles dealing with the Sultan's followers. See NAB 1673: Foreign Secret Cons 5 Mar 1824 No. 8 - Draft of a treaty with His Highness Sultan Mahomed Shah Sultan of Johore ceding 'by this Instrument all his rights of property and sovereignty in this Island of Singapore and the adjacent islets on its coast to the Honble East India Company'.

and related to his Dutch visitor that 'Sir Stamford Raffles in his usual carelessness never thought about concluding such a proper Treaty with the Sultan and the Temenggong.' From this, we can infer what Crawfurd thought about Raffles and the treaty that had earlier been signed.

The Conclusion

Almost 200 years after the 1824 treaty was signed, what can we draw from the margins of this treaty recorded by this Dutch emissary in Singapore, especially in the context of the existing sources, and how do they change our view of its conclusion? Furthermore, what new directions does this revisitation and close reading of this contract signal for Singapore's history? I present here four short takeaways in order of importance.

First, we can read and reconstruct, if somewhat liberally, Malay voices in the treaty negotiations of 1824, which have been hitherto ignored. As John Bastin has perceptively observed, one of the key problems of history in the modern period is how to come to an internal orientation of Malay personalities, especially since they have left us little native record of their thoughts and processes.[208] This intervention highlights how this can be done—through the discovery of new sources in the Dutch archives that have been neglected not only due to our Anglocentric preoccupations but also in reading between the lines of the codes and assumptions that lay behind the articles of the 1824 treaty. Since treatymaking set in motion elaborate processes of social division, initiated a redistribution of economic resources, and inaugurated new forms of doing politics in the Straits region, often to the exclusion of the local elites, it is important that we reread the agency of Malays and their own resistance to the power

---

[208] John Bastin, "Problems of Personality and the Reinterpretations of Modern Malaysian History," in *Malayan and Indonesian Studies: Essays Presented to Sir Richard Winstedt on His Eighty-Fifth Birthday*, ed. J.S. Bastin and R. Roolvink (Oxford: Clarendon Press, 1964), 151.

imbalance.[209] We can go slightly further here: that Crawfurd required the decision of Sultan Hussein Shah and Temenggong Abdul Rahman to marginalize them from decision-making in the first place reverses our understanding of the power dynamics between them. In view of the ad hoc nature of treatymaking with the EIC (and also earlier with the Dutch East India Company or VOC) in the years prior, we can also cast doubt on whether both Malay princes considered this latest iteration to be immutable and the cession of Singapore as final.

Second, the fundamental quibble of the Malay princes was not over pecuniary considerations,[210] which had already been a long-running squabble with the EIC.[211] Rather, it was over the continuation of security and alliances. Instead of looking at the 1824 treaty as the securing of the island for the EIC, we must also understand it from the local point of view—that it was concluded within the context of the native struggle for power in Johor-Riau that was playing out in the Straits. As van Angelbeek's margins to the 1824 treaty show, the Malay prince's resistance to the treaty, which caused a three-month delay, was primarily about whether Britain would remain a military and economic ally, not over the cession of Singapore. They were concerned, foremost, with maintaining their independence from the court at Riau but also with whether the British would sustain them as an alternative locus of power in the Straits. This pattern of shifting alliances is consistent with the traditional Malay political system that formed part of the eighteenth-century Malay world; it can also be surmised that the Malay princes saw that abrogation of this relationship represented a danger to their ascendancy and

---

[209] Stefan Eklöf Amirell, "International Treaties: The Foundations of Colonial Rule in Southeast Asia," The Newsletter 95 Summer, International Institute of Asian Studies, 2023, https://www.iias.asia/the-newsletter/article/international-treaties-foundations-colonial-rule-southeast-asia

[210] Abdullah bin Abdul Kadir, *The Hikayat Abdullah*, tr. A.H. Hill (Kuala Lumpur: Oxford University Press, 1970), 218–219.

[211] Ibid.

survival.²¹² Indeed, Sultan Hussein Shah's own complaint to the British Councillor much later in 1827 harped not about the loss of Singapore but about his own rights in the Karimun Island and his own status in Riau vis-à-vis the Bugis Raja Muda and the Dutch actions. This shows how alliances continued to loom in their conception of politics.²¹³ Furthermore, the concession not mentioned in the actual treaty is that the Malay princes were free to conclude arrangements should they leave Singapore, showing how Crawfurd preyed on the Malay princes' need for alliances rather than money. Incidentally, it was the precondition that the Malay princes vacate Singapore, which paved the road for the creation of modern Johor. Rereading this document is thus an invitation to consider historical moments in Singapore within their regional contexts, especially in relationship with Riau, Lingga, and Batavia along with the Malay Peninsula and Sumatra.

Third, the Treaty contained traces of the contest between two modes of government that were playing out in Singapore and came to centre the issue of the management of people. On one hand, you had the revivalist aspirations or the traditional vision of the Malay entrepôt, which was familiar to the Malay princes who had matured at Riau under the shadow of the VOC. The Europeans brought long- and short-distance trade to its shores while the Sultan and the Temenggong collected rent and taxes, monopolized the sale of goods, dispensed largesse to win loyalty, and built up a large following that enhanced their nama. Their actions flowed from a Malay past and contributed to the course of political life in their own world.²¹⁴ Crawfurd, on the other hand, conceived of a different type of polity organized upon different

---

[212] See, for example, Benjamin J.Q. Khoo, "The Changing Fortunes of the Raja Negara and the Orang Laut of Singapore," *Temasek Working Paper Series* 7 (2024).

[213] Sultan Hussein's letter can be found in Thomas Braddell, "Notices of Singapore," *The Journal of the Indian Archipelago and Eastern Asia* IX (1855): 477–482.

[214] C.H. Wake, "Raffles and the Rajas: The Founding of Singapore in Malayan and British Colonial History," *Journal of the Malaysian Branch of the Royal Asiatic Society* 48, no. 1 (1975): 71.

principles and foundations, one in which the Malay princes played no part, where European law was supreme, and in which land, people, and commodity flows could be closely controlled.[215] Here was a clash in state-building, the old traditional kerajaan against the emerging colonial state, and the battleground was the Sultan's followers. The 1824 treaty was one such attempt to end a grating aspect of the Anglo-Malay split of control in 1819—which for all intents and purposes proved an unsuccessful experiment.

Finally, it is highly likely that there were significant differences in the treaties, mostly in language and also of understanding, since there seemed to be unspoken agreements which both parties were well aware the text alluded to. A comparison with the Jawi version of the treaty would be most illuminating in this respect, but through van Angelbeek's comments on the treaty and Crawfurd's explication, it is evident that this was far from the clear and unequivocal document that Crawfurd himself proclaimed. The vague clauses on followers/slavery and the unmentioned potential agreement with other powers (should the Sultan and the Temenggong leave Singapore) are indicative of this. Despite ratification by Parliament, its validity hung very much on the Dutch East Indies government, which proposed little to no objection to it considering the more important Anglo-Dutch Treaty. Further, an oft-neglected third-party perspective can be located just across the Straits. Here, van Angelbeek was also aware that the 1824 treaty, though presenting little issue on the European front, was of limited applicability if the Riau court did not accept it; Riau considered Singapore to be part of their inalienable domain and not Sultan Hussein Shah and Temenggong's to give.

To conclude this with a larger question: Why, despite their objections and the evident disadvantages, did the Malay princes, Sultan Hussein, and the Temenggong, still put their seals to such an unfavourable treaty? Crawfurd seems to have admitted that their stubborn resistance was broken by letters that the

---

[215] Crawfurd's draft treaty of 5 March 1824 had explicitly prevented the native princes from any monopolies of imports or exports. See above.

Governor-General of Calcutta William Amherst sent to the Sultan and the Temenggong, which affected 'a marked and very favourable change [...] in their conduct'.[216] Crawfurd also remarked that the Temenggong was the more influential of the two, and his support helped ensure the success of the treaty.[217] What was contained in this letter and what lay behind the Temenggong's motivation? A clue to the latter can be found in another letter, dated 16 August 1824, where Crawfurd proposed to 'present a sum of money to a group of individuals to have contributed towards the progress of the treaty signed with the native chiefs'.[218] These turned out to be the sons of the royals as well as their close political advisors. These sources seem to suggest that while Sultan Hussein and Crawfurd have often been the focus of attention, we must perhaps look to Calcutta, the Temenggong Abdul Rahman, and his entourage for answers about the ceding of Singapore to the EIC. Exploring these lines of inquiry would lead to more novel interpretations of Singapore's early founding.

---

[216] Charles Buckley, *An Anecdotal History of Old Times in Singapore, etc.*, vol. 1 (Singapore: Fraser and Neave, 1902), 172–173.

[217] Crawfurd had initially conceived that two separate treaties were required, one with the Sultan and one with the Temenggong. The Temenggong's intervention into this treaty discussion in the five months preceding raises the question whether the Temenggong and his faction might have influenced Sultan Hussein into agreeing to sign away Singapore.

[218] NAB 1673: Foreign Secret Cons. 4 Mar 1825 No. 11 - Letter from J. Crawfurd, Resident at Singapore, to G. Swinton, Secretary to Government at Fort William, proposing to present a sum of money to a group of individuals whom Crawfurd feels have contributed towards the progress of the treaty signed with the native chiefs. The individuals in question were the Tengku Besar, the eldest son of Sultan Hussein Shah, the Daeng (likely Tun Haji Abdullah), Tengku Niat, the Temenggong's principal advisor, and Penghulu Hisang, another close advisor of the Temenggong, as well as other people attached to the native princes, a sum of which came up to 3,500 Spanish dollars. This sum approved by Calcutta, however, only came up to 2,000 Spanish dollars, see NAB 1673: Foreign Secret Cons. 4 Mar 1825 No. 13 - Letter from the British Government at Fort William to J. Crawfurd, Resident at Singapore, giving approval and ratification of the Treaty of 1824, and making mention of on the 10th Article (regarding the area coming under British control), etc.

Part III

The Theoretical: Orientalism, Eurocentrism, and Raffles

Preface to Part III

The Theoretical: Orientalism, Eurocentrism, and Raffles

It is challenging to talk about Singapore's history without mentioning the name Thomas Stamford Raffles. Depending on who you ask, he could be a hero or a villain; as Chris Hale has shown, there was also a period in the nineteenth century when he was completely forgotten. It is now a well-established fact that there was even a 500-year-long period before he arrived on Singapore's shores. However, many contemporary debates over how Singaporean history should be taught and understood inevitably touch on Raffles and his legacy.

As was previously argued, the founding of Singapore was much more than a 'discovery' in 1819; it involved complex legal and political processes in which Raffles played little to no part. A major intellectual impetus behind the shift to a newer 700-year Singaporean history has been moving away from both 1819 and a 'great man' approach that reduces Singapore's success to the deeds of one man. This is to say that changes in Singaporean history have been about shifting perspectives as much as about discovering novel material and information.

Much of the intellectual weight behind these perspective shifts came from outside the field of history, from a tradition of critical theory called 'post-colonialism'. The general idea here is that colonialism and its conditions ('coloniality') was a reality-defining paradigm—it was a way of experiencing the world that permeated everything from our sexual desires to self-perceptions of our identities.

In Edward Said's book *Orientalism*, arguably the most famous post-colonial study, he suggests that colonialism was not only about physical control but about using information and knowledge to codify the world. Recall the overused maxim: 'Knowledge is power.' In other words, colonialism was about getting people to adopt, accept, and internalize certain Eurocentric frames of reference. The example he gives is how information about 'the Orient' were defined more by the stereotypes that Western intellectuals imposed on Asia. However, when these stereotypes were repeated enough times, they went on to become indisputable 'facts', despite having little to no basis in reality. He called this a 'discourse'. Because of this, post-colonial theory argues that even after the dissolution of empires, vestiges of colonial knowledge and epistemology continue to impact the way that we understand the world.

History is no exception. As this volume has discussed over and over again, the 'history' that we read is a narrative constructed from a series of interpretations, and thus heavily influenced by biases, perspectives, and the conventions of the present. Much in the same way that myths can parade themselves as facts, historical narratives with minimal relation to the underlying events can also be taken for granted as an objective account of what happened. Post-colonial theory implores us to adopt a more critical lens when studying the histories that have been heavily shaped by colonialism. As Chris Hale explained, there was a close relationship between the writing of history and the British imperial project. Syed Farid Alatas and Tim Hannigan provide additional examples of how post-colonial theory can enrich the study of Singapore's history.

Alatas' essay will use Raffles as a case study for assessing the continued influence of Eurocentrism on Singapore's history. He applies the historical philosophy of the fourteenth-century Muslim intellectual Ibn Khaldun, who argued that there are two versions of history: the stories that are told about it on the one hand and the underlying facts on the other. In Raffles' case, the facts are his complicated retinue of deeds, ranging from the benevolent to the violent. Despite this, stories of Raffles, until recently, have portrayed him in an overwhelmingly heroic manner. Alatas implores us to consider a more balanced and critical perspective along the lines of the late Syed Hussein Alatas' seminal work *Thomas Stamford Raffles: Schemer or Reformer*, one of the first books to apply post-colonial theory to Singaporean history.

Hannigan makes a complementary argument but applies Edward Said's *Orientalism* and his theory of 'discourses' to the study of Raffles. He suggests that the 'Raffles' we learn of today is a literary construction more than a historical figure. There is a rich scholarship on Raffles dating to the late nineteenth century that was pioneered by his wife, Sophia Raffles, and has perpetuated a particular impression of the man—much in the same way that Said's discourses perpetuate Western stereotypes about Asia. To study Raffles is to accept that there are two versions of him: Raffles the man and Raffles the archetype. In the same way that the facts and narratives of history do not always align, so too do stories of Raffles deviate from his actual life.

That any discussion of colonialism takes us back to Raffles is telling. As a historian and scholar of Southeast Asia, he embodied the knowledge–power nexus of the colonial state; as a conqueror, he embodied its violence; as the heroic founder of Singapore's history, he embodied the 'great man' trope of history writing and gave the story an uncomplicated protagonist. However, again, one of the premises of Singapore's 700-year history is a decentering of Raffles and his singlehanded impact on Singapore's future. In reality, he was but one among many other actors and institutions, both colonial and local, that played a role in charting Singapore's future. To emphasize Hannigan's poignant conclusion, the good-versus-evil debate over Raffles' legacy is, therefore, frivolous. Rather, we should move on completely from Raffles by accepting that he is but one piece in a much larger, more complex, and certainly more interesting story.

Chapter 5

Raffles and the Coloniality of History

Syed Farid Alatas

Introduction

I have one objective in this chapter. I would like to use the case of history writing, particularly the historiography on Thomas Stamford Raffles, to illustrate a larger problem in the discipline of history, which is Eurocentrism.[219]

About 600 years ago, there was an Arab historian and philosopher of history, Abd al-Rahman Ibn Khaldun (1332–1406), who, in his *Muqaddimah* or *Prolegomenon*, distinguished between the surface (*zahir*) and inner meaning (*batin*) of history:

> At the level of the surface, history is no more than information about political events, dynasties, and occurrences of the remote past, elegantly presented and spiced with proverbs. The inner meaning of history, on the other hand, refers to subtle explanations of the causes and origins of existing things, and deep knowledge of the how and why of events

---

[219] I would like to thank Matthew Christian Oey for the invitation to speak at the conference Reimagining Southeast Asian History, which took place on 26 August 2023 at the Asian Civilisations Museum, Singapore. This chapter is a slightly revised version of the conference presentation.

and is arrived at through speculation and an attempt to get at the truth.[220]

Ibn Khaldun's zahir–batin dichotomy is particularly pertinent to the case of Singapore's history. For many decades, Singapore's '1819 paradigm', centred around Raffles as a great man of history, was presented as consisting of objective and immutable facts about the past. Upon a more critical reading, however, it becomes clear that this was merely the surface (zahir), a specific construction of history with certain causes and origins. Determined by specific interests, these refer to the inner meanings, the batin of history. In this case, it is the Eurocentric perspective that has historically dominated writings about Singapore's history to the exclusion of other narratives.

The Problem of Eurocentrism

The portrayal of Thomas Stamford Raffles in history writing in Singapore is part of a larger problem of the Eurocentric manner in which we understand history. In the specific case of Raffles, there is generally the failure to evaluate his misdeeds in the context of the overall worldview of colonial capitalism and the ideology of imperialism. Therefore, you have a kind of silencing. The larger context within which this kind of silencing takes place is a Eurocentric reading of history. It is sometimes difficult to understand that the 'facts' reported to us about what happened in the past are not always factual. They are, rather, interpretations based on specific interests, biases, and prejudices.

Let me give you a couple of examples from history. Everybody knows about the 'discovery' of America by Christopher Columbus. The whole world takes it as an empirical, historical fact that America was discovered in 1492. What a lot of people don't

---

[220] Ibn Khaldun, *Ibn Khaldûn: The Muqadimmah - An Introduction of History*, 3 vols., tr. Franz Rosenthal (London: Routledge & Kegan Paul, 1967), vol. 1, 6.

think about is that this was not humanity's discovery of America. Although often presented this way, it would be more accurate to say that this was the Europeans' discovery, not humanity's discovery in general. This is because people were already living in America who obviously knew about it. It is also likely that others, such as the Africans, already knew about America before Columbus 'discovered' it. It would be more accurate to refer to this as the European discovery of America. Therefore, what we mean by Eurocentrism here is the European generalization of their own experiences as universal truths.[221]

Professor Kwa Chong Guan, in his presentation at the 2023 Reimagining Southeast Asian history conference, on which this anthology is based, mentioned the Orang Laut—the so-called sea nomads. They created aquatic, nomadic economic systems or modes of production, in many ways similar to desert political economy systems of land nomads. However, in the historical study of the Malay world's political economic systems, even in the pre-colonial period, we are influenced by Eurocentric ideas that tend to be 'terracentric' or 'land-centric'. By this, I mean a bias towards land where sea and water are seen merely as a means of communication and transportation. We tend not to try and understand the sea as a political and economic system unto itself. At sea, you have nomads who live on the sea, not just people who traverse its waters on boats. That, of course, constitutes a very different kind of political economic system, one that had very intimate relations with the sea. But we tend not to look at history that way because historical studies that originated from European minds had a more terracentric way of viewing history based on their own experiences.

Let me provide another example. In the social sciences of Singapore, Malaysia, and Indonesia, unlike the European social sciences, we tend not to do class analysis. We tend not to study

---

[221] Syed Farid Alatas, "Knowledge Hegemonies and Autonomous Knowledge," *Third World Quarterly* (2022): 1–18. https://doi.org/10.1080/01436597.2022.2124155

societies in terms of power differences that are characteristic of hierarchical societies. We study them in terms of religious or ethnic differences. This is not because class does not exist. The problem has more to do with the legacy of colonialism and Eurocentric scholarship. When the British and Dutch began to study this part of the world during the colonial period, they stressed the ethnic, as opposed to the classist, nature of our societies. The seminal work in this respect is that of J.S. Furnivall, who studied what he called the plural society, one characterized by ethnic and religious differences. There was no attention given to class.[222] In his analysis, the societies of the Malay world were simply divided along ethnic lines, separate but coexisting. And while they lived separately, they would come together in the marketplace. This is what he called the plural society. There is no doubt that this element of pluralism existed in this part of the world, but this is not to say that people were not stratified or divided along class lines as well as along the lines of occupation and access to resources. We cannot deny that power differentials were not based on class differences. But this Europe-centred perspective insisted that so-called Eastern societies were thoroughly different from European societies in that ethnicity, not class, was the main dividing line—a perspective that has affected us until today. So much so that we still think in mainly ethnic rather than class terms.

This problem of Eurocentrism in history was recognized by the European scholars, particularly beginning with the Dutch scholars in the late 1940s, followed by the English-British scholars. But the discussion was for decades misled, misguided, and confusing. When Dutch and British scholars spoke about Eurocentrism and criticized the problem of Eurocentric writing of Malay and Indonesian histories, they tended to equate Eurocentric history with a European perspective. This is very problematic. We need to understand that the problem is not a European perspective. The problem is the *Eurocentric* perspective.

---

[222] J.S. Furnivall, *Colonial Policy and Practice: A Comparative Study of Burma and Netherlands India* (New York: New York University Press, 1956).

When we speak about a Eurocentric perspective, we are referring to bias, distortions, silencing, and false universalisms. But the historical account by Europeans about certain events based on their interests and their concerns is perfectly legitimate. Every community, every group, provides a historical account based on their interests and their concerns, which is legitimate. In the writing of history, it is perfectly legitimate to have different vantage points from which accounts of particular events of the past are presented.

In the historian John Bastin, we find an extreme position. Bastin was at the University of Malaya in the 1950s. He suggested that since everybody has been colonized and studies the Western discipline of history, it is impossible to have any understanding of history apart from a Eurocentric one.[223] Now this would suggest that there cannot be a critical study of Raffles. There can only be the one presented by the British, the one that silences Raffles' misdeeds, his criminality, and so on. This is clearly a very difficult position to accept. We may wonder why Bastin thought in such a manner when alternative, more critical approaches to colonial history were available to him. He may have known of the works of Jose Rizal, the Filipino anti-colonial scholar who reconstructed Filipino history away from a colonial perspective. Bastin would also have known of the work of the Dutch colonial officer and writer, Eduard Douwes Dekker (1820–1887), known by his pen name, Multatuli. He is celebrated for his novel, *Max Havelaar; or, The Coffee Auctions of the Dutch Trading Company*, an 1860 novel in which the protagonist, Max Havelaar, wages a battle against a corrupt Dutch colonial government on Java in

---

[223] John Bastin, "The Study of Modern Southeast Asian History: An Inaugural Lecture delivered in the University of Malaya in Kuala Lumpur on 14 December 1959, Kuala Lumpur," (University of Malaya, 1959). A shorter version of this was published as "The Western Element in Modern Southeast Asian History," *Papers on Southeast Asian Subjects*, no. 2 (Kuala Lumpur: Department of History, University of Malaya, 1960). For a response to Bastin, see Syed Hussein Alatas, "Theoretical Aspects of Southeast Asian History: John Bastin and the Study of Southeast Asian History," *Asian Studies* 2, no. 2 (1964): 247–260.

the Netherlands East Indies, with a focus on the coffee trade.[224] Critical perspectives with regard to colonialism were available.

On the other hand, the historian John Smail, in critiquing Bastin, suggests that we ought to be critical of Eurocentric history and move to an Asian-centric history. But, he is not at all clear about what is meant by Eurocentric and Asian-centric histories. He seems to equate Eurocentric with a European perspective and Asian-centric with an Asian perspective. What is meant by perspective is not discussed.[225] Does the European perspective simply mean a perspective from the vantage point or standpoint of a European or does it refer to something more than that—the distortion, silencing, and false universalism? We have not worked out these historiographical problems. In this sense, the history writing of Southeast Asia has not progressed in comparison to the historical scholarship on West Asia, India, and Latin America.

The Case of Raffles

I now want to focus on Eurocentrism in the particular case of the study of Raffles. The first critical assessment of Raffles in the English language was the sociologist Syed Hussein Alatas' 1971 study *Thomas Stamford Raffles: Schemer or Reformer*. Here, Alatas presented a critique of the philosophy of Raffles well ahead of its time—when there was hardly any critical assessment of the man in Singapore scholarship. His intervention in the literature was a balanced, rather than Eurocentric or Anglocentric, account of the thoughts and deeds of Raffles.

His book's specific objective was to review Raffles' political philosophy and conduct in light of new findings and less-known events. Alatas felt that the silence among scholars about Raffles'

---

[224] Multatuli [Eduard Douwes Dekker], *Max Havelaar: or The Coffee Auctions of a Dutch Trading Company* (London: Penguin Books, 1987).

[225] John R.W. Smail, "On the Possibility of an Autonomous History of Modern Southeast Asia," *Journal of Southeast Asian History* 2, no. 2 (1961): 72–102.

questionable political philosophy and disturbing conduct was strange in that even by colonial standards he fell short of the humanitarianism that was attributed to him.[226]

Alatas had noted the ethnic bias of British historians and biographers in their treatment of Raffles. In their bid to present Raffles as a progressive statesman and humanitarian reformer, there is a virtual absence of a critical treatment of Raffles' ethnically prejudiced views of the different Asian communities, his involvement in the Palembang Massacre, the corruption case known as the Banjarmasin Affair, and other questionable acts, all of which should be put in the proper context of British imperialism and the ideology of colonial capitalism. Behind the so-called 'facts' is this silencing.

With respect to the Palembang Massacre, Alatas leans towards the view that Raffles was complicit in the events that led up to the murders of twenty-four Europeans and sixty-three Javanese from the Dutch fort in Palembang, comprising both soldiers and civilians.[227] According to some, such as Ahmat Adam, Raffles is held to have instigated the massacre.[228]

On the Banjarmasin Affair or Banjarmasin Enormity, Alatas suggested that Raffles engaged in a suspicious acquisition of a territory along the Borneo coast with his friend, Alexander Hare, which involved nepotism and corruption.[229] Raffles had appointed Hare as commissioner and resident of Banjarmasin. The provision

---

[226] Syed Hussein Alatas, *Thomas Stamford Raffles: Schemer or Reformer* (Sydney: Angus & Robertson, 1971), 50–51. For the re-edition, see Syed Hussein Alatas, *Thomas Stamford Raffles: Schemer or Reformer* (Singapore: NUS Press, 2020). All references to this work in this chapter are to the 1971 edition.

[227] Syed Hussein Alatas, *Thomas Stamford Raffles: Schemer or Reformer?* (Singapore: NUS Press, 2020), 18.

[228] Ahmat Adam, *Letters of Sincerity: The Raffles Collection of Malay Letters (1780–1824). A Descriptive Account with Notes and Translation* (Kuala Lumpur: Malaysian Branch of the Royal Asiatic Society, 2009).

[229] Syed Hussein Alatas, *Thomas Stamford Raffles: Schemer or Reformer?*, 34–35.

of labour supply to Hare included the transportation of forced labour from Java,[230] which in today's terms would amount to kidnapping, enslavement, and human trafficking.[231]

During his lieutenant-governorship in Java as well as his time in Singapore, it is true that Raffles attempted to limit slavery by placing some restrictions on the local slave trade, keeping in line with British policy. Nevertheless, his biographer, Emily Hahn, claimed that Raffles himself kept a large retinue of slaves at his official residences in Java.[232] In other cases, Raffles had advocated for the replacement of slavery with contract labour and debt bondage.[233]

Raffles was appointed lieutenant governor of Java during its brief period of British rule (1811–1816). During this tenure, he was directly involved in the terrible events of 21 June 1812, known as the rape of Yogyakarta, the cultural capital of Java at the time, which ended in looting, sacking, and the killing of hundreds.[234] The barbaric nature of the attack on Yogyakarta was conveniently left out by Raffles in his *The History of Java*.[235] Said to have been the first time an indigenous court was taken in this manner by

---

[230] Ibid. 36-37.

[231] Leon Moosavi, "Decolonising Criminology: Syed Hussein Alatas on Crimes of the Powerful," *Critical Criminology* (2018). https://doi.org/10.1007/s10612-018-9396-9.

[232] Emily Hahn, *Raffles of Singapore: A Biography* (Kuala Lumpur: University of Malaya Press, 1968), 290.

[233] Syed Hussein Alatas, *Thomas Stamford Raffles: Schemer or Reformer?*, 41, 47.

[234] Peter Carey, "The End of the Beginning: The Last Months of the Franco-Dutch Government and the British Rape of Yogyakarta, 1811-1812," in *The Power of Prophecy: Prince Dipanagara and the End of an Old Order in Java, 1785-1855* (Leiden: Brill, 2007), 261–343.

[235] Thomas Stamford Raffles, *The History of Java*, 2 vols. (London: Black, Parbury, and Allen, 1817). Of relevance to this discussion is Farish Noor, "Don't Mention the Corpses: The Erasure of Violence in Colonial Writings on Southeast Asia," *Biblioasia* 15, no. 2 (2019). http://www.nlb.gov.sg/biblioasia/2019/08/30/dont-mention-the-corpses-the-erasure-of violence-in-colonial-writings-on-southeast-asia/.

a European army, the Yogyakarta *kraton* was stormed, damaged, and looted by the British, with much of the contents of its archive stolen by Raffles.[236]

Raffles also supported the opium trade and was concerned about how licensing would affect the EIC's revenues. Viewing Singapore's function as an outlet for the distribution of opium throughout the region, he made every effort to ensure that the EIC's opium trade would be 'protected and offered every facility'.[237] Eventually, opium licenses were introduced, that is, 'a certain number of houses may be licensed for the sale of *madat* or prepared opium'.[238] Raffles' instructions to William Farquhar were that these licenses were to be auctioned and re-auctioned 'every three months until further orders'.[239] In addition to that, Raffles took for himself a 5 per cent commission on the sale of each opium licence.[240] With regards to the trade, Raffles said:

---

[236] M.C. Ricklefs, *A History of Modern Indonesia since c. 1200*, 4th ed. (Houndmills: Palgrave Macmillan, 2008), 137–138.

[237] Raffles to Mackenzie, 20 December 1819, enclosed in Raffles to Dart, 28 December 1819, vol. 50, Sumatra Factory Records, East India Company, National University of Singapore; India Office Library and Records. London: Recordak Microfilm Service. 1960. Monash University. Cited in Nadia Wright, "Farquhar and Raffles: The Untold Story," *Biblioasia* 14, 4 (2019). https://biblioasia.nlb.gov.sg/vol-14/issue-4/jan-mar-2019/fnr-untold-story/.

[238] Raffles to Travers, 20 March 1820, vol. 50, Sumatra Factory Records, East India Company, National University of Singapore; India Office Library and Records. London: Recordak Microfilm Service. 1960. Monash University. Cited in Nadia Wright, "Farquhar and Raffles: The Untold Story," *Biblioasia* 14, 4 (2019). https://biblioasia.nlb.gov.sg/vol-14/issue-4/jan-mar-2019/fnr-untold-story/.

[239] Jennings to Farquhar, 15 August 1820, L. 4, SSR; Accountant General's office, 8 March 1826, vol. 71, Java Factory Records, East India Company, London: Recordak Microfilm Services, 1956. Microfilm, Monash University. Nadia Wright, "Farquhar and Raffles: The Untold Story," *Biblioasia* 14, 4 (2019). https://biblioasia.nlb.gov.sg/vol-14/issue-4/jan-mar-2019/fnr-untold-story/.

[240] Ibid.

> Opium is one of the most profitable articles of eastern commerce: as such it is considered by our merchants [...] it is impossible to oppose trading in the same. In this situation of affairs, therefore, we would rather advise that general leave be given to import opium at Malacca, and to allow the expectation from thence to Borneo and all the eastern parts not in the possession of the state.[241]

The British opium trade out of Singapore, sanctioned by Raffles, was its single largest source of revenue from 1824 until 1910.[242] Opium was also a major source of revenue during Raffle's governorship of Java.[243] The hypocrisy was lost on Abdullah bin Abdul Kadir Munshi, the Malay writer who was also for a time Raffles' scribe and copyist. While Abdullah counselled the Malays against the evils of opium smoking and praised the reputable Europeans for avoiding it, he seemed blind to the reality that while the Europeans did not consume opium, they traded in it, and even offered it, as Raffles did, to Malay emissaries.[244]

Raffles' supporters and admirers, as noted by Alatas, have generally remained silent about his questionable views and activities. The purpose of Alatas' *Thomas Stamford Raffles* is to call for a balanced approach. This involves, on the one hand, recognizing his role in the founding of Singapore as a trading settlement. But, on the other hand, it also requires an accurate

---

[241] Thomas Stamford Raffles, *The History of Java*, 2 vols. (London: Black, Parbury, and Allen, 1817), 104.

[242] C. Trocki, *Singapore: Wealth, Power and the Culture of Control* (London: Routledge, 2006), 20.

[243] Hans Derks, *History of the Opium Problem: The Assault on the East, Ca. 1600 – 1950* (Leiden: Brill, 2012), Appendix 4.

[244] A. H. Hill, "The Hikayat Abdullah," *Journal of the Malayan Branch of the Royal Asiatic Society* 28, pt. 3 (1955): 80. Cited in Syed Hussein Alatas, *The Myth of the Lazy Native: A Study of the Image of the Malays, Filipinos and Javanese from the 16th to the 20th Century and its Function in the Ideology of Colonial Capitalism* (London: Frank Cass, 1977), 138–139.

assessment of his political philosophy and conduct in Java and Singapore without shying away from exposing his faults and hypocrisy as well as his possible involvement in the crimes of the powerful.[245]

In fact, Alatas' work on Raffles can be viewed as a discussion of criminology in the decolonial mode.[246] To the extent that criminology as a field is Eurocentric, its research agenda is such that many topics and themes of great relevance to the Global South are omitted. Once such theme is colonization.

Mainstream criminology, for example, does not take into account the role of colonialism in the interplay between past and contemporary globalization, global inequality, and insecurity.[247] There is a silencing that goes on in Northern theory for which the colonial and coloniality are often deemed irrelevant. Missing or omitted is empire and the role of European capitalism in state formation, and the development of ideas and institutions, often accompanied not only by violence and criminal behaviour of the colonial state but also the ideological criminalization of anti-colonial resistance.[248] According to Moosavi, another tendency of mainstream criminology is to focus on low level crime, street crime, everyday crime, or crimes of the powerless, at the expense of ignoring the crimes of the powerful.[249] The study

---

[245] On colonial hypocrisy see Aimé Césaire, *Discourse on Colonialism* (New York & London: Monthly Review, 1972), 11.

[246] See Moosavi's important contribution to this idea in Leon Moosavi, "Decolonising Criminology: Syed Hussein Alatas on Crimes of the Powerful," *Critical Criminology* (2018). https://doi.org/10.1007/s10612-018-9396-9.

[247] Katja Franko Aas, "Visions of Global Control: Cosmopolitan Aspirations in a World of Friction," in *What is Criminology?*, eds. M. Bosworth and C. Hoyle (Oxford: Oxford University Press, 2011); Katja Franko Aas, "The Earth is One but the World is Not: Criminological Theory and its Geopolitical Divisions," *Theoretical Criminology* 16, no. 1 (2012): 5–20, 13–14.

[248] K. Carrington, Russell Hogg and Maximo Sozzo, "Southern Criminology," *British Journal of Criminology* 56 (2016): 1–20.

[249] Leon Moosavi, "Decolonising Criminology: Syed Hussein Alatas on Crimes of the Powerful," *Critical Criminology* (2018). https://doi.org/10.1007/s10612-018-9396-9.

of Raffles is at once a study of the crimes of the powerful as well as the criminality of the colonial state.

Conclusion

In most countries, the idea of nominating an imperialist as the founder of a newly independent state would have been considered 'outrageous and most definitely reactionary'.[250] But, when Alatas' *Thomas Stamford Raffles* appeared in 1971, the dominant view in Singapore was that it was inadvisable to search for a 'golden past' in the pre-colonial era. History prior to 1819 was considered one of 'ancestral ghosts' that should be forgotten.[251] K.G. Tregonning (1923–2015), formerly Raffles professor of History at the University of Singapore, had this to say: 'Modern Singapore began in 1819. Nothing that occurred on the island prior to this has particular relevance to an understanding of the contemporary scene; it is of antiquarian interest only.'[252] Thus, 'history' began after 1819 and Raffles, as the prime mover, was elevated to a 'great man' of history—not only by colonial historians but also officially by the post-colonial state.[253] The coloniality of such a perspective is all the more glaring when we take into consideration the growing critical literature on colonialism in the form of post-colonial theory and decolonial thought.

---

[250] S. Rajaratnam, "Raja Tells Why We Still Honour Raffles' Name," *The Straits Times*, 25 May 1983.

[251] S. Rajaratnam, "Untitled Speech," in *The Prophetic and the Political: Selected Speeches and Writings of S. Rajaratnam*, ed. Chan Heng Chee and Obaid Ul Haq (Singapore: Graham Brash, 1987), 140; S. Rajaratnam, "S'pore's Future Depends on Shared Memories, Collective Amnesia," *The Straits Times*, 20 June 1990.

[252] K.G. Tregonning, "The Historical Background," in *Modern Singapore*, ed. Ooi Jin-Bee and Chiang Hai Ding (Singapore: Singapore University Press, 1969), 14.

[253] Kwa Chong Guan, "Introduction," in *Studying Singapore Before 1800*, ed. Kwa Chong Guan and Peter Borschberg (Singapore: NUS Press, 2018), 1–26, 3–4, 201.

Nevertheless, scholarship on Singapore's history has progressed. No longer is Singapore's history said to have begun in 1819. It is now known that it began 500 years before that in 1299 as the seaport of Temasek.[254] The authors of *Singapore: A 700-Year History* state that their book differs from other works on the history of Singapore by providing a long-sighted view of the past, dating the start of Singapore's history to the arrival of Seri Tri Buana from Palembang, about 500 years before Raffles arrived here.[255]

What has not changed, however, is Raffles' position as a 'great man' of history. In post-colonial Singapore, Raffles is to this day a canonized figure. How is it that a British colonial administrator has eventually attained a glorified, heroic status as a humanitarian reformer of sorts? While it is quite understandable that this is the case with his British biographers, it is surprising that the post-colonial state of Singapore adopted a very positive image of the man. The decision to keep the Raffles statue at Boat Quay was based on the Dutch Economic Adviser to Singapore Albert Winsemius' advice to Lee Kuan Yew. Winsemius' point was keeping the statue was a friendly gesture to foreigners and signified that their capital would be safe in Singapore.[256] In fact, Raffles was presented by the independent state of Singapore as a hero of sorts, one of the rare instances in history of a colonial administrator serving as a national icon, in a world where most post-colonial nations adopted an extremely critical approach towards colonialism and the colonial figures who ruled over them.

---

[254] "About the Singapore Bicentennial," *SG Bicentennial*, accessed 9 April 2025, https://www.sg/sgbicentennial/about/.

[255] Kwa Chong Guan, Tan Tai Yong, and Derek Heng, *Singapore: A 700-Year History - From Early Emporium to World City* (Singapore: National Archives, 2009). See also the important edited book: Kwa Chong Guan and Peter Borschberg, eds., *Studying Singapore Before 1800* (Singapore: National University of Singapore Press, 2018).

[256] Lee Kuan Yew, *From Third World to First: The Singapore Story, 1965-2000* (New York: HarperCollins, 2000), 50.

Kwa notes perceptively that the idea of 1819 as the beginning of Singapore's history presents three categories of historiographical problems. One is attributing to Raffles the foreknowledge of recognizing the strategic importance of Singapore, resulting in his elevation to a 'great man' of history and the subsequent focus on generations of 'great men'. History is explained through the impact of great men. The second category of problems is that it possibly aggravated Singapore's post-1965 identity crisis by depriving it of its origins as a fourteenth century Malay state. The third category of problems is that it distorts our perspective on the role of the Malay sultans and their courts in Singapore, suggesting that they were not active subjects in their own history.[257] To this I suggest adding a fourth category of problems: Our attitude towards colonialism. To deal with such historiographical problems means to advance an anti-colonial, post-colonial, or decolonial mode of history writing.

The critical anti-colonial spirit is not completely absent in Singapore. An alternative account in literary form of the 'founding' of Singapore can be found in the work of the Singaporean writer, Isa Kamari.[258] The anti-colonial sentiment can also be seen in the Singaporean poet, Suratman Markasan's poem, 'Balada: Seorang Lelaki di Depan Patung Raffles' ('The Ballad of a Man Before the Statue of Raffles').[259] I reproduce

---

[257] Kwa Chong Guan, "From Temasek to Singapore: Locating a Global City-State in the Cycles of Melaka Straits History," *Studying Singapore Before 1800*, ed. Kwa Chong Guan and Peter Borschberg (Singapore: National University of Singapore Press, 2018), 201–203.

[258] Isa Kamari, *Duka Tuan Bertakhta (Sadly You Rule)* (Kuala Lumpur: Al-Ameen Serve Holdings, 2011). For the English translation see Isa Kamari, *1819*, tr. R. Krishnan (Kuala Lumpur: Silverfish, 2013). See also Harry Aveling, "1819: Isa Kamari on the Foundation of Singapore," *Asiatic* 8, 2 (2014): 88–108.

[259] Suratman Markasan, "Balada Seorang Lelaki di Depan Patung Raffles - The Ballad of a Man Before the Statue of Raffles," in *Suratman Markasan: Puisi-puisi Pilihan - Selected Poems of Suratman Markasan* (Singapore: NLB, 2014), 18–29.

a few lines here below, in both Malay, the national language of Singapore, and the English translation:

> *Raffles tersenyum kaku*
> *Lelaki hilang kepala menggerutu*
> *Telah kukatakan seribu kali*
> *kau menipu datuk-nenekku hidup mati*
> *kau rampas hartanya pupus-rakus*
> *kau bagikan kepada kawan-lawan*
> *kau dengar Raffles? Kau dengar?*
> *Seharusnya kau kubawa ke muka pengadilan di PBB kota New York*
> *tapi sayang hakim tak punya gigi*

> Raffles smiles rigidly
> the man who has lost his mind grumbles
> I've said it a thousand times you deceived my grandparents totally
> you seized their properties until they're gone, greedily
> you gave them away to your friends, enemies
> do you hear, Raffles? Do you hear?
> I should have brought you to face justice at the UN office in New York
> but unfortunately the judge has no clout

To note that Raffles was a product of his time and was informed by the dominant ideology of his age, that is, imperialism, is to state the obvious. In our assessment of him today, though, that recognition cannot be an excuse to allow the embarrassing facts of the colonial adventure to disappear.

Chapter 6

The Myth and the Man: Bringing Singapore's History Out of Stamford Raffles' Shadow

Tim Hannigan

Some years ago, I wrote a book called *Raffles and the British Invasion of Java*. It was originally conceived as a narrative account of the five-year period from 1811 to 1816, during which Britain usurped Holland as the colonial power in Java and other parts of what is now Indonesia. But the book also, almost by accident, served as a revisionist biography of Thomas Stamford Raffles, who headed the British interregnum in Java. There had been many previous biographies of Raffles, all of which portrayed him as heroic, honourable, visionary, and morally impeccable—though, possibly, rather boring. The more recent of these books tended to present him as that rare thing: a notable figure from British imperial history still deserving of straightforward admiration in a postcolonial era, the 'last colonialist it's okay to like'. The apparent popular veneration of Raffles in Singapore—where his name remains commemorated in various institutions and urban spaces and where not one but *two* commemorative statues remain prominent near the riverfront—surely made this presentation easier.

But researching the British period in Java, reading Raffles' own official and private correspondence, and other archival materials from the time, generated, for me, an impression impossible to square with the image of the biographies. My own book, then, became a reactive text, an attempt, as I then saw it, to set straight a record that had somehow gone badly awry in the course of the previous two centuries.

The book was launched at the 2012 Singapore Writers' Festival—quite by chance at exactly the same time as another new biography, *Raffles and the Golden Opportunity*, by the senior and very well-established British writer Victoria Glendinning. Her book took the traditional positive line on Raffles, and she was, I suspect, a little perturbed by the serendipitous appearance of my rival account. With an eye for manufactured controversy, the festival organizers decided to stick us together for what they billed as an 'exclusive face-off' in the National Museum of Singapore, moderated by Timothy Barnard and titled 'Raffles: Saint, Scoundrel or . . .'

Glendinning elected to speak first, reading a prepared paper (I had come expecting to debate rather than present, so I didn't have a written statement). Rather unexpectedly—for me, at least—she began not with Raffles himself but with a dismissal of the contemporary relevance of Edward Said. When she was at university, she said, lots of people were very excited by 'a new book by Edward Said called *Orientalism*'. It was very good, according to Glendinning, but *very much of its time*. 'We are now in the twenty-first century,' she said, 'and *things have moved on*.' This did generate a certain frisson in the audience, which contained a good few humanities students and professors from Singapore's universities. In the question-and-answer session that followed, Glendinning was challenged by an audience member on the alleged irrelevance of Said—and she did row back a little. I chipped in to say that he absolutely was still relevant and that even if he wasn't, when it came to literature and colonial history, it really wasn't for the likes of Glendinning and me—both white Britons, albeit from very different backgrounds and generations—to say so.

She was absolutely right, though, in having latched onto Said in response to reading my account of Raffles. It is a narrative history book of the very poppiest sort—all purple prose and dramatic reconstructions, intended to be a 'good read' first and foremost, rather than a serious scholarly treatise. It certainly doesn't contain any direct references to post-colonial theory. But if Glendinning suspected that Said's ideas were floating around in there somewhere, particularly when I discussed Raffles' intellectual project in Java—the cataloguing of temples, the accumulation of manuscripts, the gathering of ethnographic notes—which ran alongside his military and political endeavours, she was spot on.

As for many others over the decades, Edward Said provided my introduction as an undergraduate to post-colonial theory and really to critical thought more generally. Two decades after the original 1978 publication of *Orientalism*, it was still an invigorating first encounter with the critique of ideas, the analysis of discourse, the argument that texts—all texts—are both political and interconnected, the sense that whenever a writer says something, it's worth asking *why* and *where* did that something come from. I am heartened to see, another two decades on and now more than forty years since *Orientalism* appeared, that it so often still has the same effect on new generations of students all over the world. Still relevant, then. And still a touchstone for my own work, both critical and creative, even when it appears to have nothing to do with colonial or post-colonial history.

This chapter approaches Raffles from a Saidian perspective. I begin by tracing his career as a British official in Southeast Asia in the early nineteenth century. I argue that he can reasonably be seen as an individual personification of Said's entire concept of Orientalism, combining an aggressively acquisitive militarism; a sustained effort to politically, economically, and socially restructure the territories he governed; and a concerted intellectual project to construct academic knowledge of—and therefore have power over—the regions he was to administer. The chapter, then, moves on to consider the biographical discourse that has, over the course of two centuries, firmly established the heroic portrayal of Raffles, which Glendinning sought to reiterate at the Writers' Festival in 2012. I turn, again, to Said to help make sense of this, arguing that just as Orientalist writers 'fell back on texts', deferring to the antecedent authority of the books they had read thus reinscribing the tropes contained therein in their own work, Raffles' biographers have repeatedly been controlled by the heroic discourse of their own predecessors, even where it runs contrary to archival evidence. To illustrate this point, I pay particular attention to one of the many controversial episodes of Raffles' career—the Palembang Affair, in which he deviously incited a local ruler to action, which he then used as a pretext to unseat him and annex the most valuable parts of his sultanate—and the way it has been underplayed or erased in biographical accounts. Finally, I consider how we might escape the valorizing biographical feedback loop, and how we might move beyond crudely binary debates that ultimately serve to maintain Raffles' prominence in the discussion of Singapore's past.

Who is 'Raffles'?: An Orientalist Career and a Biographical Feedback Loop

Raffles today is most closely associated with Singapore; but the establishment of the British settlement there in 1819 was really a coda at the end of a long and often controversial career in Southeast Asia. Having served initially as a junior clerk in the EIC London headquarters, he arrived in Penang in 1805 as assistant secretary to the British governor there. This was the era of the global Napoleonic conflict, and after the French annexation of Holland, the British made plans to seize Dutch colonial territories in Asia. In 1810, Raffles was appointed by Lord Minto, the EIC's governor-general in India, as an agent tasked with gathering intelligence and making local political provisions for a mooted British invasion of Java—then the key Dutch possession in the region. That invasion was successfully launched in 1811, with Raffles appointed by Lord Minto to administer Java and other former Dutch territories in what is now Indonesia as lieutenant governor. This was in direct defiance of the London headquarters' instructions for Lord Minto himself. He was to merely oust the Dutch from Java and return the island to the rule of its own local courts. Raffles' five-year tenure in Java was wildly ambitious but politically chaotic, financially ruinous, and frequently violent. The episode irrevocably tainted his reputation in official colonial circles; but after a partial rehabilitation—effected in significant part by his publication of the two-volume *The History of Java* in 1817, for which he gained a knighthood—he took up a post as lieutenant governor at the minor British outpost at Bengkulu on the west coast of Sumatra in 1818. This remained his official seat in Southeast Asia until the end of his career in 1824, though it was his key role in the founding and early development of British Singapore that gained him enduring posthumous fame.

Beyond the bare narrative of his career, I would argue that what makes the historical Raffles most significant today from a critical post-colonial perspective is that he is an almost perfect embodiment of Orientalism, especially in Java, even though he was actually operating well before the Victorian high-water-mark of Orientalism in the Saidian conception. His career epitomizes what Farish Noor, following Said, has called the 'militarised commercial-academic enterprise'[260] of nineteenth-century European colonialism. It was violent and involved aggressive military assaults on local polities, characterized as 'chastisements'—punishments for native 'insolence'. This was violence with a deliberately performative quality, designed, as Raffles himself put it of his attack on Yogyakarta in Java, to teach the local rulers 'a lesson which may impress upon them the Character and power of our Government'[261]—to show them who was boss. His career also had extractive commercial impetus—Raffles' 'reforms' were

---

[260] Farish A. Noor, *The Discursive Construction of Southeast Asia in 19th Century Colonial-Capitalist Discourse* (Amsterdam: AUP, 2016), 75.

[261] This quote is drawn from correspondence in Mss Eur F148/31, part of the Raffles-Minto Collection held in the British Library, London. Research in this collection formed the original basis for *Raffles and the British Invasion of Java*.

almost always intended to generate revenue and, ultimately, channel wealth from Southeast Asia towards the colonial metropolis. And perhaps most significantly of all, his so-called scholarship was always part of the colonial knowledge project, less a strictly objective accounting of an existing situation than a textual *construction* of a new actuality—as Farish Noor and others have amply demonstrated. 'Knowledge is power,' Raffles once wrote, 'and in the intercourse between the enlightened and ignorant nations the former must and will be the rulers.'[262]

As mentioned above, I wrote *Raffles and the British Invasion of Java* as a piece of narrative non-fiction that I principally hoped would entertain a general audience, rather than as a formal academic work to be cited by future scholars. Despite that, it was firmly rooted in original archival research. I rather naively failed to anticipate that such a radically revisionist portrayal might have an impact on public discourse about Raffles, and even on future historiography. Had I done so, I might have presented the text rather differently and paid more attention to academic conventions—though I certainly wouldn't have altered the substance. I have attempted to make up for this past naivety over the subsequent years by returning to Raffles from time to time in a number of papers, journal articles, and contributions to edited collections—reiterating the arguments from *Raffles and the British Invasion of Java* in a far more robustly academic mode.

However, I am always at pains to point out that I am *not* a historian by training. My own academic background is in literary studies, and my enduring scholarly interest in Raffles is less about the historical figure himself than about another textual construction—the 'Raffles' of popular imagination, the product of a biographical discourse, a 200-year process of valorization and reiteration. This Raffles, and not the actual man, I would argue, is the one represented by the two statues that stand close to the Singapore River—one dating from the colonial 1880s

---

[262] Sophia Raffles, *Memoir of the Life and Public Services of Sir Thomas Stamford Raffles* (London: John Murray, 1830), 478.

and another from the notionally post-colonial 1970s, but both significantly identical in form, if not colour and material.

At the time of his death in 1826, Raffles' reputation, particularly within official colonial circles, was not particularly positive. He'd left Java in 1816 in semi-disgrace, and though he went on to receive acclaim for his scholarship and his association with Singapore, suggestions of overreach, incompetence, and corruption still lingered. Obviously, that all changed by the time the first statue was erected in 1887, and this was largely down to the efforts of his widow, Sophia. In 1830, just four years after his death, she produced the *Memoir of the Life and Services of Sir Thomas Stamford Raffles*. This 800-page volume, in-line with biographical convention at the time, was largely made up of Raffles' own letters and their replies, arranged to form a coherent narrative, and was embedded with explicatory introductions and footnotes. Sophia Raffles was working with an explicit motive of reputational rehabilitation, 'a desire to do justice to her husband's memory', as she put it.[263] And she was, obviously, very selective about what she included.

Since Sophia Raffles' *Memoir*, there have been around a dozen further Raffles biographies, beginning with Charles Demetrius Boulger's *Life of Sir Stamford Raffles* in 1897,[264] followed by several others in the 1900s and 1920s, then Emily Hahn's *Raffles of Singapore* in 1946,[265] the voluminous *Raffles of the Eastern Isles* by C. E. Wurtzburg in 1952,[266] and a run of shorter biographies in the 1950s and 1960s. There was then a bit of a gap before Nigel Barley's 1991 biography-cum-travelogue *The Duke of Puddle*

---

[263] Ibid. viii.

[264] Demetrius Charles Boulger, *Life of Sir Stamford Raffles* (London: Horace Marshall & Son, 1897).

[265] Emily Hahn, *Raffles of Singapore* (New York: Doubleday, 1946).

[266] C.E. Wurtzburg, *Raffles of the Eastern Isles* (London: Hodder and Stoughton, 1954).

Dock: Travels in the Footsteps of Stamford Raffles,[267] and then Victoria Glendinning's *Raffles and the Golden Opportunity* in 2012.[268] There have also been myriad shorter biographical texts, from children's picture books to entries in travel guidebooks. And as mentioned earlier, virtually all of them present Raffles in exactly the same positive light—just as Sophia Raffles might have hoped, despite contrary archival evidence and the more critical take on colonialism one might have expected of the later twentieth- and twenty-first-century biographers. How did this happen?

There's another Saidian resonance here. Said wrote in *Orientalism* of the 'textual attitude' that people adopt in certain situations:

> One is when a human being confronts at close quarters something relatively unknown and threatening and previously distant. In such a case one has recourse not only to what in one's previous experience the novelty resembles but also what one has read about it.[269]

Said was talking specifically here about travel and travel writing. Newly arrived and confronted by all those unknown complexities, a traveller is likely to 'fall back on a text', Said says, because a place 'can always be described by a book, so much so that the book (or text) acquires a greater authority, and use, even than the actuality it describes'.[270] And this is absolutely central to Orientalism as Said conceives it. Even if 'the Orient' has ever actually existed as a discrete, readily demarcated unit of territory and block of human geography (a highly debatable proposition in itself), in all its vastness it must remain entirely beyond summation. But a

---

[267] Nigel Barley, *The Duke of Puddle Dock: Travels in the Footsteps of Stamford Raffles* (London: Henry Holt & Company, 1991).

[268] Victoria Glendinning, *Raffles and the Golden Opportunity* (London: Profile, 2012).

[269] Edward W. Said, *Orientalism*, 3rd ed. (London: Penguin, 2003), 93.

[270] Ibid.

textually constructed Orient—textually constructed on specifically European terms—*could* very readily be contained in a book. So, the book wins over the actuality; and the statements made in the earliest Orientalist texts about a particular aspect of 'the Orient' are likely to be found repeated over and over and over in subsequent texts. This is not to say that Orientalist writers actively fabricated their narratives. And it is not to say that they didn't honestly believe they were basing their judgements on authentic empirical data or direct observational experience.

A classic and apt example of the process involved was identified by the Malaysian scholar, Syed Hussein Alatas, who is often named alongside Edward Said as a significant figure in the first major wave of post-colonial scholarship. In fact, some of his most influential work predates *Orientalism*, and he might reasonably be placed with Frantz Fanon among the original progenitors of the critical approaches that Said later popularized. Alatas' seminal 1977 book, *The Myth of the Lazy Native*,[271] provides a compelling example of what we now think of (thanks to Said) as Orientalism in action. A colonial traveller arriving in Southeast Asia would probably already have read that the natives were incurably 'indolent' (a trope that Alatas himself convincingly traces to early local resistance to the exploitative labour demands of the colonial economy). And so, when the traveller would spot a local man snoozing under a tree in the middle of the afternoon, they'd see therein clear evidence of that indolence, confirmed by their own eyes. The fact that the man in question might have been up since before dawn digging a ditch and was sensibly taking a break during the hottest part of the day doesn't enter into it; the traveller was still in bed at the time, so they didn't notice the work going on, and even if they did, it was less likely to make an impression because it didn't resonate with the texts they'd read. The book wins.

---

[271] Syed Hussein Alatas, *The Myth of the Lazy Native* (London: Frank Cass and Company, 1977).

Something very similar has happened in the biographical discourse around Raffles. Because Sophia Raffles' *Memoir* has some of the characteristics of an archive—a collection of correspondence written by, to, or about Raffles during his own lifetime—that is how later biographers have often used it, despite the fact that it is a highly partial, and indeed partisan, archive. Thus, the 'Raffles' that most of the early biographers first encountered is Raffles precisely as Sophia wished him to be seen—heroic, visionary, selfless, moral (even in this century, Glendinning has said that her interest in Raffles began when her husband brought her a copy of Sophia's *Memoir* home to Britain from a business trip to Southeast Asia).[272] So, once these biographers enter the *unedited* archive, where they may well find irrefutable evidence of Raffles behaving with cruelty, avarice, and dishonesty, they are predisposed to take more notice of the equivalent of the man snoozing under the tree—the bits that make Raffles look good. This may not even happen consciously. But it happens.

The Palembang Affair and the Biographical Feedback Loop

At this point, I want to step aside from the biographical discourse to look at a specific episode from Raffles' career in Southeast Asia before returning to the biographies to look at how that episode has been presented—or *not* presented—there.

Several controversial aspects of Raffles' career have become much better known in recent years—in particular the sacking and looting of Yogyakarta and the so-called Banjarmasin Outrage. The first of these episodes took place on 20 June 1812, less than a year into Raffles' tenure as lieutenant governor of Java. At the time, the Yogyakarta Sultanate was the most substantial of the various royal courts in Java—all of which had treaty arrangements with

---

[272] Lee Randall, "Interview: Victoria Glendinning, author of *Raffles and the Golden Opportunity*," *The Scotsman*, 3 November 2012.

the Dutch but some of which retained a high level of de facto independence. Raffles quickly identified Yogyakarta as the greatest challenge to the absolute and uncontested authority he wished for himself in Java. He was particularly distressed by a suspicion that the court authorities there viewed the British as a weaker power than the Dutch-Napoleonic colonial government that had preceded them: 'It becomes absolutely necessary for the tranquillity of the Country that he should be taught to think otherwise,' he wrote to Lord Minto.[273] Under the flimsiest of pretexts, Raffles thus ordered a major military assault on Yogyakarta. This direct attack on a major court was unprecedented in the previous two centuries of Dutch engagement in Java. The court itself was badly damaged during the assault, large numbers of the defenders were killed, the Sultan himself was arrested and removed from the throne, and all the contents of the court archive and most of its portable treasures were looted by the British forces—Raffles himself claimed a large personal booty. The Yogyakarta Sultanate is still lobbying to have some of these looted materials returned from British institutions today.

The Banjarmasin Outrage, meanwhile, was the result of Raffles' friendship with the adventurer Alexander Hare, a man who had a reputation for unethical behaviour even within his own lifetime. Raffles appointed Hare resident at Banjarmasin in southern Borneo, where he set about attempting to develop a personal fiefdom, reputedly typified by egregious abuses and sexual excesses. In support of this project (which violated EIC rules for official British residencies), Raffles shipped from Java an unknown number of people (certainly hundreds) as de facto slaves for Hare—again, in violation of regulations that Raffles was supposed to uphold.[274]

---

[273] Mss Eur F148/31, British Library, London.

[274] Syed Hussein Alatas, *Thomas Stamford Raffles, 1781–1826: Schemer or Reformer?* (Sydney: Angus & Robertson, 1971), 34–38; J.C. Baud, "De Bandjermasinsche Afschuwelijkheid," *Bijdragen tot de Taal-, Land- en Volkenkunde* 3 (1860): 1–25;

The large-scale violence of the Yogyakarta episode, and its resonance with wider debates about the continued presence of cultural materials obtained through colonial violence in London and other former imperial metropolises, and the salacious details of the Banjarmasin Outrage, have encouraged recent attention. But for me, a more significantly revealing controversy in Raffles' career is the still relatively little-known Palembang Affair of 1810–1811. This was actually my own first detailed encounter with the Raffles of the archive. By pure chance, the first box I called up and dove into in the British Library when starting my own research—Mss Eur F148/6—contained the correspondence surrounding that episode.

In late 1810—before Java and long before Singapore—Raffles was based in Melaka as agent of the governor general to the Malay states, laying the groundwork and conducting advance research for the mooted British invasion of Dutch territories in Indonesia. Part of that groundwork involved initiating correspondence with sultans and rajas across the archipelago, some of them notional Dutch vassals, others wholly sovereign. These included Sultan Mahmud Badaruddin II of Palembang, a state in southern Sumatra that controlled two large islands in the Straits of Melaka, Bangka, and Belitung, home to a long-established tin-mining economy, which Raffles knew all about. For nearly a century, the sultanate had a treaty with the Dutch authorities in the colonial headquarters at Batavia (modern-day Jakarta), and the Dutch maintained a trading post at the Palembang capital on the Musi River, home to about 100 Dutch citizens in 1810. The treaty meant that the Sultan, in theory, acknowledged Dutch suzerainty; but, in practice, Palembang continued to function autonomously.

In late December 1810, Raffles had a messenger carry his first letter to Sultan Badaruddin II in which he wrote thus:

Andrew F. Smith, "Borneo's First 'White Rajah': New Light on Alexander Hare, His Family and Associates," *Borneo Research Bulletin* 44 (2013): 93–131.

I lose no time in dispatching this letter to put Your Majesty on your guard against the evil machinations of the Dutch, a Nation that is desirous of enriching itself from the property of your Majesty as it has done with that of every Prince of the East with which it has had connection [. . .]

I would recommend your Majesty to drive them out from your country at once, but if your Majesty has reasons for not doing so, and is desirous of the friendship and assistance of the English [. . .] I have power over many ships of war and if I think proper to do it, I can drive the Dutch out even were they 10,000 in number.[275]

He kept up the same theme in subsequent letters, telling the Sultan that the Dutch were 'a bad Nation' and a people with a 'sinister disposition, want of faith, and rapacious spirit of aggrandisement', repeatedly urging him to break his treaty arrangements and evict the occupants of the Dutch trading post. He even sent an unsolicited draft treaty stating, 'His Majesty the Sultan hereby engages to dismiss from his Territories the present Dutch Resident, and all Persons acting under the authority of the Dutch Government.'[276] Raffles explained that the sultan needed to do this because Britain was probably going to invade Java, and if Palembang wanted to be truly independent, it needed to break with the Dutch before that happened. If not, it would be automatically transferred to Britain, and there would be nothing Raffles could do about it. All of this advice, as he presented it, was for Palembang's own good. Raffles even sent the Sultan a shipment of guns to assist the eviction process.

Badaruddin himself had no particular complaints about his long-standing arrangement with the Dutch, so he ignored the treaty and politely fobbed Raffles off, insisting that 'while Batavia

---

[275] Mss Eur F148/6, British Library, London. Subsequent quotes from Raffles' correspondence with Palembang are drawn from this same manuscript file, part of the Raffles–Minto Collection.

[276] Mss Eur F148/15, British Library, London.

is not yet taken, as this might occasion some distress to his Majesty, the Hollanders shall continue to occupy [their compound in Palembang.'[277] But eventually, after many months of back and forth, he got news that the British really had invaded Java and that Raffles had been appointed as the lieutenant governor there. At this point, quite logically, Badaruddin decided he'd better do what Raffles had asked—and possibly try and make it look like he'd done it some time ago. Exactly what happened is unclear, but the net result was that all the Dutch citizens in Palembang were killed, probably on 14 September 1811, just three days after Raffles' appointment as lieutenant governor and actually before the final Dutch surrender of Java. But when Raffles himself found out what had happened, he didn't send a thank you-note to Badaruddin for his compliance. He fulminated instead about the Sultan's 'abhorrent deeds' and despatched a punitive force, which chased Badaruddin out of his court, placed his brother on the throne as a British vassal, and directly annexed the tin-rich islands of Bangka and Belitung, which British correspondence from the time suggests was the plan right from the start. Long before he found out about the massacre of the Dutch, Raffles' immediate superior, Lord Minto, had written, 'Palembang is to be occupied as soon as possible [. . .] With regard to Banca and the tin, the Lieutenant Governor [Raffles] knows my sentiments.'[278] He and Raffles had wanted the islands, ideally, to be seized from a sovereign Asian state rather than a Dutch signatory because that would provide a legal argument for them to be retained as British possessions, even if Britain and Holland eventually made peace and other former Dutch territories were handed back (as did indeed happen in 1816).

This is all a matter of fact, plainly evidenced by archival sources. It is also, I think, very revealing of Raffles' modus operandi. Palembang was the first significant local court that he dealt with

---

[277] Ibid.
[278] Ibid.

closely—and those dealings were strikingly Machiavellian. He tried to forcefully incite the Sultan to a course of action, and then when the Sultan did precisely what he had asked, he used that very action as an excuse to unleash military violence, remove the Sultan from his throne, and annex the most valuable chunk of his territory. And Raffles was entirely cavalier about the likelihood of people losing their lives in the process. This was a pattern that repeated in the years that follow. It was how Raffles dealt with Yogyakarta in 1812, of course; there were similar interactions with local courts throughout his term as lieutenant governor. In late 1812, he ordered an assault on Sambas in Borneo as part of a policy of 'chastisement and destructions',[279] supposedly to discourage 'piracy'.[280] In 1814, Raffles ordered a military incursion against the Balinese kingdom of Karangasem in response to the 'insolence' of the Raja. That same year, Raffles decided that the 'insulting' conduct of the Raja of Bone in southwest Sulawesi 'demanded an example'. He despatched a naval force, which burned the Raja's palace and all its contents to the ground. This, Raffles reported to his superiors in India, had made a 'deep and lasting impression [. . .] on the inhabitants of the more Eastern Isles'.[281]

Archipelago courts were well networked, and we can reasonably assume that by 1819, Raffles' reputation was well known throughout the region—with a general understanding that it was probably bad news if you started getting letters from Thomas Stamford Raffles, that it might well end up with British and Indian sepoy soldiers destroying your palace. And so, that iconic moment traditionally presented as the 'founding of Singapore', when Raffles and Farquhar stepped ashore and met the Temenggong Abdul Rahman on 29 January 1819—and then still more so, the moment a week later, 6 February, when they signed their treaty

---

[279] C.E. Wurtzburg, *Raffles of the Eastern Isles*, 268.

[280] Farish Noor has convincingly argued that the very concept of 'piracy' in the region was often itself a constructed pretext for colonial violence. See Farish A. Noor, *The Discursive Construction of Southeast Asia*, 121–156.

[281] C.E. Wurtzburg, *Raffles of the Eastern Isles*, 353.

with Sultan Hussein Shah of Johor—should be understood as an act of latent violence—a latent violence that, I would suggest, everyone present at the time recognized. But neither will you find that discussed in any of the biographies nor, typically, will you find any proper discussion of the Palembang Affair.

In Sophia Raffles' *Memoir*, we do find an account of the British advance on Palembang but no mention of Raffles' motives there nor excerpts of his correspondence with the Sultan. And that sets the tone. When we get to the next biographer, Boulger, we are told simply that Badaruddin had acted '[f]or some reason that cannot be confidently explained' and that Raffles had despatched a fleet to 'bring the Sultan to a proper sense of his position'.[282] Many subsequent biographers do not mention Palembang at all, and only Wurtzburg makes brief reference to Raffles' correspondence with Badaruddin from Melaka—a correspondence that, we are told, 'was to have unexpected repercussions', though without any summary of its contents or of Raffles own purpose (annexing the tin islands) in starting the correspondence in the first place.[283] In Maurice Collis' 1966 biography the whole episode is covered in a single line about an unnamed sultan in Sumatra 'who had massacred the Dutch residents'.[284] And so it continues right down to Glendinning who simply says without explanation that Badaruddin ordered the 'massacre of the Dutch garrison', and that Raffles was 'outraged' when he found out.[285]

Some of these biographers will surely have looked into that same box file that I first examined in the British Library and been exposed to the same evidence. But, operating within a discourse, falling back on the earlier biographic image of Raffles to which they had been exposed and which they themselves were in the process of reiterating, they did not think it was significant, decided not to tell people about it, or simply could not process it.

---

[282] Demetrius Charles Boulger, *Life of Sir Stamford Raffles*, 140.

[283] C.E. Wurtzburg, *Raffles of the Eastern Isles*, 118.

[284] Maurice Collis, *Raffles* (London: Faber & Faber, 1966), 68.

[285] Victoria Glendinning, *Raffles and the Golden Opportunity* (London: Profile, 2012), 99.

Every so often I happen upon another biographical text about Raffles that I've previously missed and feel that old sense of outraged bafflement: *How did this happen?* And then, of course, Edward Said helps me to understand. These texts are often what we might call 'minor biographies', briefer accounts of Raffles within larger texts, or self-contained in shorter forms. Several years ago, I came across a 2002 graphic novel, illustrated by Zhou Yimin: *Stamford Raffles: Founder of Modern Singapore*. This book, produced by a Singaporean publisher, is essentially hagiographic and unwavering in its adherence to the narrative originated by Sophia Raffles in her memoir. Raffles was 'from a poor family'; he 'learnt to speak Malay at a time when few other English officials could speak the language'[286]—things that are plainly false. And there's certainly no mention of the violence he unleashed in places like Palembang and Yogyakarta.

More recently, browsing in a second-hand bookshop, I encountered *The Lost Temple of Java* by Phil Grabsky, produced in 1999 to accompany an episode of the BBC history series *Timewatch* about Borobudur, the eighth- and ninth-century Buddhist temple in Central Java that Raffles is often miscredited with 'discovering'. The book is effectively a brief biography of Raffles as well as an account of Borobudur. We are told, among other things, that Raffles was always motivated by 'the general good. His desire to improve living conditions [in Java] motivated him to press on with introducing vaccinations, reducing the flow of opium, and improving health care. He also prohibited, from the beginning of 1813, the importation of slaves into Java.'[287] The part about opium is really not true at all, and the part about slavery is just spin. Raffles was simply—and belatedly—putting into practice what was already since 1807 supposed to be a universal British interdiction on the trade in slaves, and under his supervision, it was a very patchy prohibition. Raffles exempted children from the ruling, allowing those under the age of fourteen still to be

---

[286] Zhou Yimin (illustrator), *Stamford Raffles: Founder of Modern Singapore* (Singapore: Asiapac Books, 2002).

[287] Phil Grabsky, *The Lost Temple of Java* (London: Orion, 1999), 45.

imported as slaves to Java.²⁸⁸ The buying and selling of slaves between Europeans in Batavia continued unabated; even the official British government newspaper there carried adverts for domestics slaves.²⁸⁹ Raffles himself was served by a large retinue of government slaves at his official residences²⁹⁰—and then there's the Banjarmasin Outrage.

Unsurprisingly, neither the Asiapac comic nor the BBC book make any mention of Palembang. It's important to realize exactly why that is if we are to recognize how pernicious a discourse like the one around Raffles can be. It is unlikely that the authors of either of these books did any original archival research. They drew their own account of Raffles entirely from secondary sources, mostly previous biographies. They, therefore, had no direct contact with the matter of history, the traces left by the actual Thomas Stamford Raffles for our analysis. They *only* had contact with the very textual construction to which they, in turn, contributed: a perfectly tuned feedback loop. They did not mention Palembang, not because they were trying to cover it up but because they knew nothing about it. Within the constructed reality of the feedback loop, it simply never happened.

Moving Beyond Binaries: Minimizing Raffles?

I want to end by asking if we can ever move on from this situation. While working on an early draft of this chapter, I spotted in the BBC radio listings that Raffles was to be discussed on a show called *Great Lives*. My heart sank. Surely not, still, in the third

---

²⁸⁸ Mss Eur F148/8, British Library, London

²⁸⁹ For example, the final edition of the paper, *The Java Government Gazette*, on 10 August 1816, carries a front-page advert for 'valuable MEN and WOMEN SLAVES' with interested parties directed to make enquires at the newspaper office itself.

²⁹⁰ Emily Hahn, *Raffles of Singapore*, 290.

decade of the twenty-first century! Luckily, production and research seem to have become more nuanced since the *Timewatch* documentary in 1999. In the recent show, the man who proposed Raffles as a 'great life', Matthew Gould, CEO of the Zoological Society of London (which Raffles co-founded after his time in Asia), was offset by a thoroughly critical voice: Stephen Murphy, now of the School of Oriental and African Studies (SOAS) in London, but formerly of the Asian Civilisations Museum, who was heavily involved in some of the bicentennial activities around Raffles in 2019. Murphy did an excellent job of intervening whenever uncritical hagiography threatened, questioning Raffles' alleged anti-slavery credentials, critiquing his scholarship, and even mentioning the Banjarmasin Outrage. But listening to the show did confirm for me an emerging frustration—and a wish, perhaps, for my own obsolescence in this field.

To be clear and fair, there have been critical voices speaking against the dominant discourse on Raffles for a very long time. He had critics—including critics on moral grounds—among his own British contemporaries. There was also a strong anti-Raffles line among Dutch historians of the later nineteenth century. But perhaps most significant for us is Syed Hussein Alatas' scholarly account published in 1971, *Thomas Stamford Raffles: Schemer or Reformer?* During my own original research on Raffles, it was a great relief to encounter this book, to feel that I was not alone. Alatas outlined details of the Palembang Affair, the Banjarmasin Outrage, and other episodes long ignored by Raffles' conventional biographers. He wrote:

> It is hoped that the portrayal of Raffles' thoughts and actions in this book will be considered as an attempt to correct the persistent historical canonization of Raffles as a loveable and gentle personality surrounded by jealous competitors, as an heroic reformer who wanted to bring peace and progress to the people of the area in which he operated [. . .] There is great need to review the entire historical writing in this

region with a view to accomplish a deeper, more meaningful and objective portrayal of history.[291]

Alatas' own answer to the titular question was clearly 'schemer'—and that would be my answer too. But half a century has now passed since Alatas' book, thirteen years since mine, and sometimes I fear we are still trapped in a simple binary, a never-ending debate. 'Schemer or reformer?' asked Alatas; 'Saint or scoundrel?' asked my debate with Glendinning; 'Pirate or hero?' asked the media at the time of the bicentennial.[292] And great life or not great life, asked the recent BBC radio show. To be clear, the fact that there are still people out there who would, fairly uncritically in the first instance, consider him a 'great life' worthy of straightforward admiration does mean that continuing to research and draw attention to, for example, the Palembang Affair, is a worthwhile endeavour. But I would like, eventually or sometime soon, for that to no longer be the case.

In the last decade or so, parts of the ongoing conversation about Raffles that I have found most invigorating are less the continuing scholarly work than some of the creative explorations emerging from within Singapore. Alfian Sa'at's and Neo Hai Bin's 2019 play *Merdeka*—staged in bicentennial year—was both a creative performance and a direct critical engagement with the historiography around Raffles, to powerful effect.[293] Jimmy Ong's artwork has very much foregrounded what we might call 'the nasty bits' of the Raffles story but in subtle, and subtly subversive, ways. There's much more too. One of my favourites is a poem called 'Effigies' by Ng Yi-Sheng (who has, it should be

---

[291] Syed Hussein Alatas, *Thomas Stamford Raffles*, 51.

[292] Tom Benner, "Pirate or Hero? Raffles Bicentennial Fuels Singapore Debate," *AlJazeera*, 29 January 2019, https://www.aljazeera.com/news/2019/1/28/pirate-or-hero-raffles-bicentennial-fuels-singapore-debate.

[293] Alfian Sa'at, Faris Joraimi, and Sai Siew Min, eds., *Raffles Renounced: Towards a Merdeka History* (Singapore: Ethos Books, 2021) reproduces some of the material from the play, alongside various original essays and commentaries.

noted, also produced other more serious and sustained creative responses to Raffles, as well as critical commentaries). Posted on Facebook for Singapore Poetry Writing Month in 2018, it was inspired by a bizarre children's picture book by Janet Appleyard called *Raffles Finds A Friend*, published in 1992, in which the two riverside statues come to life and go on jolly japes around the nocturnal city (also providing yet another a standard hagiographic biography of the man in the process).[294] In Ng Yi-Sheng's version, things take a very X-rated turn, and the statues end up in bed together—at the Raffles Hotel, of course. The poem ends with bronze and poly-marble in a state of postcoital bliss while: 'Elsewhere / in moonlight stand their pedestals, / blissfully empty.'[295] This final line is arguably much more suggestive and provocative than the hilariously explicit content that precedes it. I find Ng Yi-Sheng's poem appealing not only because it is consciously intertextual, a direct reaction to *Raffles Finds a Friend*, but also because it is directed specifically at the statues, which are, in turn, as I've already argued, a representation of the textually constructed image of Raffles rather than the historical man. This begs the question of what should really be done about the statues.

In 2020, when protestors toppled a statue of the slave trader Edward Colston into a dock in Bristol in the UK, various jokes were made about how uneasy the Raffles statues must be feeling given how close they are to the Singapore River. And there have been voices arguing that Raffles, too, must fall. But if we push him into the river of infamy, someone will, surely, immediately start arguing for his restoration to the pedestal of heroism—thus prolonging the binary debate. I think it might ultimately be better for us to reach a point where we simply stop talking about him, for the statue to not be toppled but to be made figuratively smaller through focusing scholarship elsewhere, through creative work that both diminishes Raffles' traditional stature and embiggens

---

[294] Janet Appleyard, *Raffles Finds a Friend* (Singapore: EPB, 1992).

[295] Ng Yi-Sheng, "Effigies," Facebook, 10 April 2018, https://www.facebook.com/groups/singpowrimo/posts/1664082880373623/.

other things; make the statues so small that we might walk right past without ever noticing them. Again, I am talking figuratively here in the first instance, but if someone successfully proposes doing it *actually* too then why not? A tiny Raffles, dwarfed by his own pedestal on the Singapore waterfront, seems a symbolically apt monument, and perhaps one worth retaining. And if that reduction of Raffles comes to pass, then when it is time for the 250-year acknowledgement of the establishment of a British presence in Singapore, surely no one will feel the need to organize a debate or to deliver a conference paper on the question of whether Raffles was a schemer or a reformer. Things will then *really* have moved on.

Part IV

The Possibilities: Revisiting Malay Perspectives in Modern Singaporean History

Preface to Part IV

The Possibilities: Revisiting Malay Perspectives in Modern Singaporean History

Another major critique of the 1819 paradigm is the treatment of the role and agency of Malaysia and the Malay world in Singapore's history. It is impossible to talk about Singapore without Malaysia, whether in history or the contemporary age. In the fourteenth century, the port city of Temasek was part of the Malay-speaking world. When Raffles arrived in 1819, Singapore was a fiefdom of the Johor Sultanate, and it was the Malay princes who sold Singapore to the British in 1824. Thereafter, Singapore would serve as the capital of the colonial administrative region known as British-Malaya. Even after Malaysia gained independence in 1957, Singapore remained part of it until it was ousted and became a separate entity in 1965.

Despite the historical intertwining of Singapore and Malaysia, traditional narratives on Singapore's past devote little attention to its Malay roots, the agency of the sultans, and its connections to the Malay world. There were expedient reasons for this. When Singapore split from Malaysia in 1965, it had to carve out a national identity that distinguished itself from that of Malaysia. As a tool of politics, history played a role in defining the nation and, therefore, was forced to adopt a narrative that centered around the modern Singaporean state. The year 1819 was significant for this project because Raffles' arrival set Singapore on a path away from Johor's sphere of influence—providing a convenient start date for the nascent country's national history when it split from Malaysia in 1965.

Pushing back Singapore's start date to the fourteenth century has invited a closer appreciation of its historical connection to the Malay world between the time of Temasek and British colonialism. However, even after 1819, the Malay world and its rulers continued to play an important role in Singapore's modern development. One such example was given by Benjamin Khoo, who reconstructed the Malay perspective on the 1824 Treaty of Friendship and Alliance where the Johor Sultanate sold Singapore to the British. Wilbert Wong and Mohamed Effendy Abdul Hamid give two more examples of how Malay perspectives can be revisited to enrich our understanding of modern Singaporean history.

Effendy visits another crucial nineteenth-century treaty between the Malay sultans and the British. Often overshadowed by its 1819 and 1824 predecessors, the 1855 Treaty of Johor was a turning point in the joint history of Singapore and Malaysia. Here, Sultan Ali—the eldest son of Sultan Hussein Shah, who signed the 1819 treaty with Raffles—signed away Johor to Temenggong Daing Ibrahim for a lump sum and stipend. The treaty was facilitated by the British colonial administration, which had the most to gain from sidelining the Johor Sultanate, thereby consolidating their control over British Malaya. Although the failure of Sultan Ali's reign has often been caricatured as simply resulting from shortsightedness or incompetence, Effendy argues that he was a capable ruler who faced insurmountable challenges. Histories of Singapore's treaties in the nineteenth century tend to focus solely on the colonial perspectives to the exclusion or stereotyping of local voices. In revisiting Sultan Ali's reign, Effendy provides a model for filling our knowledge gap on Malay rulers and their impact on modern Singaporean history.

Wong's essay breaks down the impact of Richard Olaf Winsted's contributions to Malay studies, particularly its impact on

Malaysia's national narratives. Winsted was a prominent colonial scholar and administrator whose work *Kitab Tawarikh Melayu* (*Book on Malay History*) is one of the most influential studies in Malaysian history. In contrast to Singapore's 1819 paradigm and its exclusive focus on post-Raffles Singapore, Winsted's *Kitab Tawarikh Melayu* traces the entire region of British Malaya, including Singapore—back in time to the legacies of the Melaka-Johor Sultanate and the ancient Srivijaya Empire of Sumatra. As such, Singapore was included in a wider regional history that went beyond the confines of a nation-state approach. His work has thus often been used to criticize Singapore's national narrative by demonstrating the deep historical ties that conjoin Singapore and Malaysia.

Rewriting the Malay perspective into Singaporean history brings together a number of themes in this volume. Before 1819, as Borschberg has stressed, Singapore was never a singular entity as we understand it today but always part of a larger regional body or international trade network. Those largely centered around its key position within Nusantara or the Malay Archipelago. As Singapore progresses into a more globalized and international twenty-first century, it thus makes perfect sense to recognize its pre-British roots as part of a highly diverse and interconnected Malay-speaking world, one that has sat right at the tradewinds of global merchant empires. The 1819 paradigm in carving out Singapore's distinct national identity was, no doubt, useful at a particular point in history. But now that it has served its purpose, it is finally time to recognize the shared histories that bind Singapore to Malaysia, the region, and the world.

Chapter 7

Sultan Ali's Reign and the Impact of the 1855 Treaty: A Reassessment

Mohamed Effendy

Introduction

The role of Sultan Ali, son of Sultan Hussein, has not been extensively explored in the writing of Singapore history. The British recognized him as the Sultan of Johor only in 1855, twenty years after his father had died. Sultan Ali failed to designate his royal-born son, Tengku Alam, as his successor on his death in 1877, and the title of Sultan of Johor lapsed until 1886, when Maharaja Abu Bakar, son of Temenggong Daeng Ibrahim, was recognized as Sultan of Johor by the British. This chapter attempts to fill a major lacuna about Sultan Ali in the history of Singapore and explains how filling in the lacuna can be useful in furthering out understanding of Singapore's past. The British decision to not recognize Tengku Alam as Sultan Ali's successor, recognizing Maharaja Abu Bakar instead, effectively sidelined the descendants of Sultan Hussein and ended any political role of his lineage in Singapore's future. This allowed the British to further cement their control over Singapore, challenging the traditional narrative of British rule in Singapore as a purely benevolent and progressive force.

This essay moves our understanding of Sultan Ali beyond simplistic explanations that attribute his failure to indebtedness and incompetence. He was shortchanged in the 1855 Treaty he signed with the British to be recognized as Sultan and forego his claim to rule Johor except for the Muar-Kesang area. This chapter argues that Sultan Ali failed not because he was accorded rule over the resource-poor area of Muar-Kesang, but that he actually received a resource-rich area which could have strengthened his financial and political position. The essay shows that Sultan Ali had the opportunity to become a successful ruler. His failure ultimately stemmed from an inability to solve the major challenges to effectively govern and capitalize on the region's potential. The essay analyses the cultural and historical context of Malay kingship and examines the complexities that confronted Sultan Ali and shaped his actions and decisions.

By reassessing Sultan Ali's reign, the chapter addresses a poignant gap in knowledge about the local rulers of Singapore that has been neglected. Though not much can be found in terms of local sources about Sultan Ali, it is still possible to gain some insights about Sultan Ali and the area that he ruled when nineteenth-century colonial sources about the Muar-Kesang area are examined further. They show that Sultan Ali had the opportunity to become a successful ruler. This has never been discussed before in the production of knowledge about Sultan Ali and his reign.

The chapter aims to gain a more nuanced understanding of Sultan Ali's failure by moving beyond simplistic explanations, such as the long-held notions solely attributing everything to his indebtedness and even shortsightedness. Instead of relying on colonially derived racial stereotypes, this analysis considers the cultural and historical context of Malay kingship and examines the complexities that Sultan Ali faced, taking into account his actions and decisions, the British, and other relevant actors.

Collaboration as a Fundamental

The Portuguese conquest of Melaka in the sixteenth century heralded major processes of change for many kingdoms in Southeast Asia. The Iberians took on numerically superior forces at Melaka and emerged victorious. The establishment of a permanent fort at Melaka enabled them to hold on to their conquest, where they defended themselves against repeated attacks from Acehnese and Malay forces throughout the sixteenth and seventeenth centuries. However, a crucial factor for the Portuguese in their rule of Melaka was their reliance on local collaborators.[296] Collaboration with local rulers and their forces enabled the Dutch and their Johor-Malay allies to defeat the Portuguese in the sixteenth century.[297] Establishing local alliances and entreating with Malay rulers was thus a key impetus behind Dutch success in the region during the seventeenth century; for example, in Sulawesi, the alliance with Arung Palakka, a Bugis prince of the Kingdom of Bone, helped the Dutch defeat the Makassar kingdom.[298]

However, the nineteenth century witnessed a dramatic shift in European engagement with local rulers, sometimes resulting in the massacre of local elites. An often-used example is the massacre of Balinese elites at Klungkung, known as the *puputan* event, where a Balinese ruler marched his royal entourage into Dutch guns.[299] Another example was the destruction of the Riau court, which the Dutch crushed in 1911, leading to its members seeking refuge in Singapore.[300] The British were also reliant on force. Their

---

[296] Paulo Jorge de Sousa Pinto, *The Portuguese and the Straits of Melaka, 1575-1619: Power, trade and Diplomacy* (Singapore, Kuala Lumpur: NUS Press, Malaysian Branch of the Royal Asiatic Society, 2012), 179.

[297] Peter Borschberg, "The Seizure of the Sta. Catarina Revisited: The Portuguese Empire in Asia, VOC Politics and the Origins of the Dutch-Johor Alliance (1602-c.1616)," *Journal of Southeast Asian Studies* 33, no. 1 (2002): 31–62, http://www.jstor.org.proxy.lib.sg/stable/20072387.

[298] Leonard Andaya, "The heritage of Arung Palakka: A history of South Sulawesi (Celebes) in the seventeenth century," *Verhandelingen van het Koninklijk Instituut voor Taal-. Land- en Volkenkunde* 91 (Leiden: Springer, 1981), 73–100.

[299] Margaret J. Wiener, *Visible and Invisible Realms: Power, Magic, and Colonial Conquest in Bali* (Chicago: University of Chicago Press, 1995).

[300] Virginia Matheson, "Strategies of Survival: The Malay Royal Line of Lingga-Riau," *Journal of Southeast Asian Studies* 17, no. 1 (1986): 5–38. https://doi.org/10.1017/S002246340000518X.

battles with the rulers of Burma not only led to the extermination of the Burmese monarchy but also caused traumatic changes for the population of Burma, who were left kingless with the capture and exile of King Thibaw in the nineteenth century.[301] Despite employing military force, the British also relied heavily on treaties to gradually subordinate the Malay rulers of Singapore. The establishment of a British outpost in 1819 initiated a process that progressively stripped both the descendants of Sultan Hussein and Temenggong Abu Bakar of political and economic power. However, the Temenggong's descendants—especially Daing Ibrahim and Maharaja Abu Bakar, who adapted to British-induced political and socio-economic change—enabled them to thrive in comparison to Sultan Hussein's descendants.[302]

The 1855 Treaty in Retrospect

The signing of the Treaty of Johor in 1855 was curious. The event was reported in detail by *The Straits Times* on 13 February 1855.[303] The ceremony took place at noon in a large room, presumably within the government offices of Singapore. Despite limited preparation time, local authorities strived to create an impressive atmosphere. The reception chamber was filled with decorations that included various national flags. A raised platform covered in scarlet dominated the room, with three chairs for Governor Butterworth, Sultan Ali, and the Temenggong of Johor Daing Ibrahim. The report also described that above the chairs hung the British Union Jack and the EIC's ensign, and behind the Governor's chair stood a marble bust of Raffles erected on a

---

[301] Michael Aung-Thwin, "The British 'Pacification' of Burma: Order without Meaning," *Journal of Southeast Asian Studies* 16, no. 2 (1985): 245–261. http://www.jstor.org/stable/20070866.

[302] C.A. Trocki, *Prince of Pirates: The Temenggongs and the Development of Johor and Singapore, 1784-1885* (NUS Press, 2007).

[303] "Recognition of the Sultan of Johore," *The Straits Times*, February 13, 1855, https://eresources.nlb.gov.sg/newspapers/digitised/article/straitstimes18550213-1.2.18.

pedestal. On both flanks of the platform, a set of tables held the state sword, inkstand, state seals, and three copies of the treaty. Seating arrangements included the sons of Sultan Ali and the Temenggong, Resident Councillor Mr Dunman, Commander Blane of the HMS Rapid, and even ladies. British military personnel formed a significant portion of the audience, making the ceremony replete with armed presence.

The report went into greater detail on the proceedings: The ceremony began when Sultan Ali, son of Sultan Hussein of Singapore, entered with an escort and received a guard of honour. Governor Butterworth greeted Sultan Ali with a handshake and formally recognized him as the Sultan of Johor in a firm voice followed by an eleven-gun salute. The Temenggong Daing Ibrahim then arrived and paid his respects to Sultan Ali before taking his designated seat. Mr Thomas Church, the resident councillor of Singapore, then read the Treaty of Johor, outlining the transfer of the territory of Johor from Sultan Ali to Temenggong Daing Ibrahim, with the exception of Kesang.[304] Also read were financial arrangements: a lump sum of 5,000 Spanish dollars and a monthly allowance of 500 Spanish dollars were to be allocated to Sultan Ali. The treaty was then signed and Governor Butterworth gave an address. He mentioned that he was happy with elevating the 'almost powerless and nearly penniless' princes to a state of affluence and prosperity.[305] He then presented the state sword to Sultan Ali, who received it and acknowledged the British government's support.

Despite receiving a substantial sum of money in the 1855 treaty, Sultan Ali appeared to struggle with a great amount of debt. He borrowed sums of 53,600 Spanish dollars in 1860 and 15,000 Spanish dollars in 1862 from a Chettier named Kavana

---

[304] "Government Notification," *Singapore Chronicle and Commercial Register*, 18 March, 1837, https://eresources.nlb.gov.sg/newspapers/digitised/article/singchronicle18370318-1.2.2. Mr Thomas Church was appointed Resident Councillor of Singapore in 1837.

[305] Ibid.

Chana Shellapah.[306] Though there is little information as to why such amounts were borrowed, the reasons for this could be varied: the expenses of maintaining a court, a taste for a lavish lifestyle, or potential mismanagement. Evidence of prodigal expenditure echoed in a 1938 report, based on the account of a witness who attended Sultan Ali's funeral in 1874, offers a glimpse into the aftermath of his reign as well as echoes of lavish expenditure.[307] The report, citing a seventy-four-year-old man named Jani bin Jaafar from Umbai, Melaka, describes the unforgettable scene he witnessed during Sultan Ali's funeral. Several members of the royal household gathered in Umbai to follow the coffin from the Sultan's palace in Bukit Dara to the mosque, a distance of roughly 2 miles (3.2 kilometres). The mourners threw thousands of gold leaves into the air—valuable tokens neatly wrapped in paper and rice—for the Sultan's subjects to collect as keepsakes. Some Malays even used inverted umbrellas like bowls to catch the falling leaves.

Previous Writings on the Failure of Sultan Ali

Colonial reports offer intriguing insights into the reasons behind the decline of Sultan Ali's power. Frank Swettenham attributed part of the failure to the EIC's mistreatment of him. He also highlighted the growing tension between Sultan Ali and Temenggong Ibrahim, exacerbated by the British refusal to recognize Ali as sultan after his father died in 1835. Swettenham suggested that the British installed Ali as sultan to weaken his claim to Johor and arrogate control under the more compliant Temenggong Ibrahim, who would pay tribute. This strategic move

---

[306] "Enclosure 1: Precis History of the History of Sultan Ali," in *Accounts and Papers*, Volume 12, ed. House of Lords (Oxford: Oxford University, 1879), 5–6.

[307] 'Inverted Umbrellas to Catch Gold Leaves at Funeral," *The Straits Times*, November 20, 1938, https://eresources.nlb.gov.sg/newspapers/digitised/article/straitstimes19381120-1.2.97.

to quell internal conflict and protect British interests ultimately undermined Sultan Ali's authority, contributing to his downfall.[308]

William Henry Read, a European advisor to Sultan Ali, offered a more critical perspective on Sultan Ali's management. Read characterized Sultan Ali as incapable of managing his affairs, even describing himself as the Sultan's custodian. This assessment suggests that Sultan Ali was financially imprudent and required oversight. Read expressed doubts about the Sultan's mental acumen, noting 'The Sultan was a man of very poor mental capacity, in fact, one might say, of weak mind.'[309] Underscoring this distrust, Read retained custody of the Sultan's seal from 1852 onwards. This was due to Sultan Ali's habit of issuing unauthorized orders and documents under his seal, often to his detriment.[310]

Fawzi and Hasrom's 1978 study, based on correspondence between British officials and Sultan Ali, reveals a complex power struggle. They argue that Sultan Ali's ambitions were met with persistent resistance, ultimately leading to the downfall of his reign. Initially denied the title of Sultan of Johor in 1846, he eventually secured it in 1855 through British mediation. However, this came at a heavy price: the surrender of Johor and the acquisition of a largely unproductive territory. Subsequently, conflicts erupted over resources and the legitimacy of the treaty, particularly with Temenggong Ismail of Muar, whose territory overlapped with Kesang. Sultan Ali's attempts to assert authority, including the use of Bugis mercenaries to subdue Ismail, proved futile. Faced with dwindling resources and a deteriorating

---

[308] Frank Swettenham, *British Malaya: An account of the origin and progress of British influence in Malaya* (London: Routledge 2018 reprint of 1948 edition), 78–104 on "The Straits from 1825–67–The arrangement made to settle the claims of the Sultan and Temenggung in regard to Johore."

[309] W.H.M. Read, *Play and Politics, Recollections of Malaya by an Old Resident* (London: W. Gardner, 1901), 14.

[310] Ibid. 15.

situation, Sultan Ali was ultimately forced to relocate to Umbai, Melaka in 1862.[311]

Haji Buyong Adil, in his book *Sejarah Johor*, sheds another light on the power struggle faced by Sultan Ali. He alludes that British duplicity led to Sultan Ali's failure as a ruler. He details the circumstances surrounding the British denial of the Johor kingship to Tengku Ali (later Sultan Ali). Relying on colonial sources, Buyong Adil suggests that the British selected the area between the Muar and Kessang rivers due to its significance as a burial ground for Sultan Ali's ancestors.[312] However, Buyong Adil's account of events in 1856, a year after the treaty, suggests some British dishonesty. According to him, Sultan Ali faced resistance from the Temenggong of Muar, who refused to pay taxes. This was a significant problem for the Sultan because, unknown to both Sultan Ali and Governor Butterworth of Singapore, the previous sultan, Hussein, had already appointed the Temenggong of Muar as the leader of the region. This oversight about the position of the Temenggong of Muar's position was not addressed in the 1855 treaty, indicating a lack of transparency.[313] However, the claim that the British (Buyong Adil mentioned that Governor Butterworth claimed that he did not know of the existence of the Temenggong of Muar when asked by Sultan Ali) did not know of the Temenggong Muar and Sultan Hussein's role in selecting Muar's rulers was false. The British did know about this relationship, which can be seen in T.J. Newbold's meeting with Temenggong Datu Syed in Gresik, Muar, who was made the Temenggong of Muar by Sultan Hussein of Singapore in 1830.[314]

---

[311] M.A. Fawzi Basri, Haron Hasrom, and Malaysia Muzium Negara, *Sejarah Johor Moden 1855-1940: Satu Perbicangan Dari Pelbagai Aspek*, Monograf siri pustaka tinta emas (Kuala Lumpur: Muzium Negara, 1978), 1–11.

[312] Buyong Adil, *Sejarah Johor* (Kuala Lumpur: Dewan Bahasa dan Pustaka, 1980), 228.

[313] Ibid. 238.

[314] J. H. Moor, *Notices of the Indian archipelago & adjacent countries: Being a collection of papers relating to Borneo, Celebes, Bali, Sumatra, Nian, and the Philippines islands* (London: Frank Cass, 1968 reprint of 1837 edition), 75.

Abdullah Zakaria Gazali's 1997 work further adds to our understanding of Sultan Ali's weakness and failure as a ruler. One major factor that weakened him was that the area of Muar-Kesang was not very productive and Sultan Ali did not invest much into developing it. This was made worse with the Temenggong Daeng Ibrahim's control of revenue collection in Kesang and throughout Muar.[315] Sultan Ali's difficulties in ruling were stymied by the defiance of Temenggong Ismail of Muar who did not accept Sultan Ali's power and authority. This led Sultan Ali to adopt harsh measures to exert his authority over the Temenggong, which caused a breakdown in his rulership.[316]

Contemporary historian C.M. Turnbull's 2009 work identifies Sultan Ali's financial difficulties as the key failure of his rule. She goes further by exposing the manipulative actions of British individuals like William Read, who exploited Sultan Ali's vulnerabilities, particularly his perceived lack of intelligence. Furthermore, Turnbull argues that the 1855 treaty, while granting Sultan Ali his coveted title and allowance, effectively recognized Daeng Ibrahim as Johor's true ruler. This departure from Malay customary law, bypassing both Sultan Mahmud of Lingga and Bendahara Ali (Daeng Ibrahim's previous patron), generated considerable resentment and further weakened Sultan Ali.[317]

More recent historians such as Hadijah Rahmat in a 2020 work reemphasize the same themes that have been identified as weakening Sultan Ali's rule: rivalry with Temenggong Ibrahim and debt that led him to sign the Treaty of Johore on 10 March 1855.[318] However, Kwa Chong Guan goes further. In 2020, he wrote that the 1855 treaty was a continuation of the 2 August 1824 treaty, which further weakened the financial and political position

---

[315] Ghazali Abdullah Zakaria, *Istana dan politik Johor, 1835-1885* (Kuala Lumpur: Yayasan Penataran Ilmu, 1997), 35.

[316] Ibid. 35.

[317] C.M. Turnbull, *A History of Modern Singapore, 1819-2005* (Singapore: NUS Press, 2009), 69–70.

[318] Hadijah Rahmat, *Abdullah Bin Abdul Kadir Munshi: His voyages, legacies and colonial history*, 2 vols. (Singapore: World Scientific, 2021), 411.

of Sultan Hussein and his son, Tengku Mohamed Ali (Tengku Ali), who proved less capable of managing their affairs. By 1855, Tengku Ali faced dire financial straits and was forced to accept a British-brokered bailout. In exchange for British recognition as sultan and a lump sum of 5,000 Spanish dollars, along with an annual payment of 500 Spanish dollars from the Temenggong's family, he ceded Johor, with the exception of the small territory of Muar-Kesang on the Melaka border.[319]

In 2023, Soon-Tzu Speechly, architectural historian and author of the work *Malayan Classicism: From the Architecture of Empire to Asian Vernacular*, pointed out that the treaty of 10 March 1855 significantly bolstered Temenggong Daeng Ibrahim's power and territorial claims. Following the treaty, he actively encouraged Chinese planters to settle in the area, promoting the cultivation of pepper and gambier. Additionally, the treaty granted him greater access to Gutta Percha, a highly valuable resin or sap-like substance gathered from trees in Southeast Asia that proved invaluable as insulation for underwater cables in the nineteenth century.[320] Although the treaty seemingly increased Temenggong Daeng Ibrahim's wealth and influence, on introspection, it reduced Sultan Ali's wealth sources and allowed Temenggong Daeng Ibrahim to establish a monopoly over such resources, contributing to Sultan Ali's impoverishment.[321]

Muar-Kesang Area: A Strategic Domain

These perspectives on Sultan Ali's impoverishment, however, require further qualification. Sultan Ali actually ruled a resource-rich

---

[319] Z.A.Rasheed, W.H. Zoohri, and N. Saat, eds., *Beyond Bicentennial: Perspectives on Malays* (Singapore: World Scientific, 2020), 200.

[320] John Tully, "A Victorian Ecological Disaster: Imperialism, the Telegraph, and Gutta-Percha," *Journal of World History* 20, no. 4 (2009): 565, http://www.jstor.org.libproxy1.nus.edu.sg/stable/40542850.

[321] S. T. Speechley, *Malayan Classicism: From the Architecture of Empire to Asian Vernacular* (London: Bloomsbury Publishing, 2023), 36–37.

area. This chapter will show that the Muar-Kesang territory of the nineteenth century was not only full of resources but also located in a strategic area that was suitable for a ruler to establish his power base—if successfully developed. An 1877 *Straits Times* report offers a succinct description of Sultan Ali's lands.[322] His domain was 89 kilometres from the north-east and stretches 37 kilometres in breadth in the east-west direction. It has a sea frontage of 5 kilometres and is situated in close proximity to Melaka, long regarded to be a centre of not only Malay civilization but also of economic wealth. It is located between the Kessang River, which forms the Southern boundary of Melaka, and the Moar (Muar) River, which forms the northern boundary of the principality of Johore, giving it access to the Melaka Straits, an important and ancient maritime trade route. At the centre of Sultan Ali's domain stands a mountain named Gunung Ledang or Mount Ophir, long regarded to be the abode of powerful spirits.[323] The Muar-Kesang area was also noted as significant in the early seventeenth century by Emanuel Godinho de Eredia (1563–1623 CE), who did an illustration of the area in a 1601 CE map.[324]

Eredia's seventeenth-century map clearly delineates the Kessang and Muar rivers, positioned in close proximity to Melaka, which were then under Portuguese control. J. Kathirithamby-Wells highlights the critical role these waterways played in the economic and political success of Malay rulers.[325] In the middle is the Muar River, considered one of the largest in Johor and among the oldest. Apart from the Muar, the Kessang River is also significant.

---

[322] "Moar State," *The Straits Times*, August 18, 1877, https://eresources.nlb.gov.sg/newspapers/digitised/article/straitstimes18770818-1.2.5.

[323] J.V. Mills, "Eredia's Description of Malaca, Meridional India, and Cathay," *Journal of the Malayan Branch of the Royal Asiatic Society* 8, no. 1 (109) (1930): 40–41, http://www.jstor.org.proxy.lib.sg/stable/41560454.

[324] "New Geographic Map of the Interior of Malaca," *Library of Congress*, 1602, https://www.loc.gov/resource/gdcwdl.wdl_00972/?st=image&r=0.264,0.198,0.959,0.373,0

[325] J. Kathirithamby-Wells, "Hulu-hilir unity and conflict: Malay statecraft in East Sumatra before the mid-nineteenth century," *Archipel* 45 (1993), 77–96.

Though much smaller than the Muar, it splits into two smaller rivers. One is the Tangkak River, which originates from the foot of Gunung Ledang.[326] A ruler who can maintain a harmonious relationship between *hulu* (inland) and *hilir* (coastal) areas will be able to establish a successful *kerajaan* (kingdom). The hulu regions provided valuable resources like jungle products that could be traded for profit. Meanwhile, the hilir regions provided access to trade routes across the strategically important Melaka Straits, a hub of maritime commerce. The proximity to a mythical mountain could hold significant meaning, as mountains have historically been revered as sacred places, particularly for rulers.

Leonard Andaya highlights that mountains hold spiritual importance not just for land-dwelling communities but also for seafaring ones like the Orang Laut.[327] The importance of mountains for kingship is reinforced by historian Kenneth R. Hall, who emphasizes the role of rivers in connecting the symbolic power of mountains and the sea. Throughout Southeast Asian history, river basins have served as the cradles of early kingdoms.[328] Therefore, it is likely that Sultan Ali viewed the area near the mythical mountain as favourable, aligning with traditional Malay and Southeast Asian beliefs about suitable locations for establishing a Malay kingdom. It was no surprise that Sultan Ali decided to establish his residence at the *kwala* (*kuala* or mouth) of Muar as he could be at the junction of two symbolically powerful areas—the mountain and the sea—the ideal location for a Malay kingdom.[329]

---

[326] Dato' Haji Abdul Shukor Ismail, *Sejarah Ringkas Muar* (Muar: Penerbitan Toko Buku Manaf, 1984), 1.

[327] Leonard Y. Andaya, *Leaves of the Same Tree: Trade and Ethnicity in the Straits of Melaka* (Honolulu: University of Hawai'i Press, 2008), 180–181.

[328] K.R. Hall, *A History of Early Southeast Asia: Maritime Trade and Societal Development, 100–1500* (Lanham: Rowman & Littlefield, 2011), 110.

[329] Martin Lister, "Malay Law in Negri Sembilan," *Journal of the Straits Branch of the Royal Asiatic Society* (Malaysian Branch of the Royal Asiatic Society) nos. 20–22 (1889): 301.

Access to Gold and Tin

Beyond the previously mentioned advantages of being located at the hulu–hilir or between the mountain and rivers that connect the area to the sea, Sultan Ali's selection of Muar-Kesang was also strategic because of the area's well-known deposits of gold and tin. According to J.R. Logan, the area was full of gold and tin resources as well as communities that could be useful for the kerajaan.[330] Pierre Étienne Lazare Favre's 1846 report on a survey trip to Johor highlights the area's abundance. Favre (1812–1887) was a French Roman Catholic missionary who joined the Missions Etrangères de Paris in 1842 and served as a priest in Malaysia, initially teaching at the College General of Penang before establishing a mission in Malacca. He describes the land between the Muar and Kessang rivers not only as rich in tin and gold but also as home to major communities of Jakun and Malay inhabitants. According to Favre:

> It is probable that the country is rich in gold and tin [. . .] There are tin mines on the banks of the Johore River. Several new ones were lately discovered in the piece of ground which lies between the two rivers of Muar and Cassang [Kesang]; and everyone is aware of the considerable quantity of gold which is extracted every year from the mines of mount Ophir, though worked without proper means, and by a few persons only[331]

Hence, Favre's observations of the Muar-Kesang area show that the Muar-Kesang area had abundant resources for mining. More

---

[330] P. E. L. Favre, "A journey in Johore," *The Journal of the Indian Archipelago and Eastern Asia*, ed. J. R. Logan, Series I, vol. 3 (1849), 60–65.

[331] P. E. L. Favre, *An account of the wild tribes inhabiting the Malayan peninsula, Sumatra and a few neighbouring islands, with a journey in Johore and a journey in the Menangkabaw states of the Malayan peninsula* (Paris: Imperial Printing Office), 148–149.

information on the area's richness in gold and tin is provided by J.B. Westerhout, the assistant resident at Melaka, further reinforcing the availability of the wealth from the gold and tin mines of Sultan Ali's domain.

Westerhout reported on the gold and tin mining activities near Kesang. He focused on the gold mines of Mount Ophir (Gunung Ledang), which lay within Sultan Ali's Muar-Kesang territory and had been worked on since 1817 and earlier by Malay, Chinese, and Indian miners from Coromandel. The gold mines are located at the foot of Mount Ophir. However, these mines, according to Westerhout, were under the control of the Temenggong of Muar as well as various Penghulu. The amount of gold excavated from the area was 24–40 *katis* (14.4–24 kilograms) of gold annually.[332] Westerhout also mentioned that the principal tin mine was located at Kesang, and 2,200 Chinese miners worked on it, excavating 300–350 *pikuls* (18,000–21,000 kilograms) monthly.[333] In 1852, Balfour even marvelled at the productivity of the tin mines of Kesang, located north of Ayer Panas near Melaka. He mentioned that since 1844, Chinese tin miners had worked on them and increased production from 146 pikuls to 12,000 pikuls (8,760–720,000 kilograms) in 1852.[334] Hence, Sultan Ali's domain contained precious metals that could have been extracted and shows that he did really rule a resource-rich area.

Access to Jakun Communities

Sultan Ali also had access to Jakun communities in the area as a ruler of Muar-Kesang. Favre's report sheds light on how the

---

[332] J.B. Westerhout Esq, Assistant Resident at Malacca, "Notes on Malacca," in *The Journal of the Indian Archipelago and Eastern Asia*, vol. 2, ed. J.R. Logan (Singapore: Mission Press, 1848), 171–172.

[333] Ibid. 172.

[334] E. Balfour, *The cyclopaedia of India and of Eastern and Southern Asia, Commercial, Industrial, and scientific: Products of the mineral, vegetable, and animal kingdoms, useful arts and the manufactures* (London: Bernard Quaritch, 1885), 891.

Jakun population was a potentially valuable asset for Sultan Ali. He describes a Jakun leader (an eighty-year-old Batin), appointed by both the Sultan of Johor and the Temenggong of Singapore to rule 200–300 Jakun, which suggests that these indigenous communities were seen as strategically important. Favre further described that he had been appointed fifteen years ago (approximately in 1831) by both of them and received two written documents both with the seals of the Sultan and Temenggong and spears adorned with gold and silver as a mark of his Batinship or authority.[335]

This information suggests that Sultan Ali recognized the strategic value of the Jakun people. They represented a potential source of manpower for his growing kingdom. Gifts could have served as a way to secure their loyalty and cooperation, crucial for various activities. The Jakun's deep knowledge of the land would have been invaluable for tasks like resource collection and, potentially, military service. Significantly, even after Sultan Ali's death in 1877, Jakun involvement in camphor collection continued. In an 1882 report, Dudley Francis Amelius Hervey (1849–1911), a British colonial administrator in Malaya who explored the Endau region of Johor, wrote about the Jakun community's participation in collecting camphor, a valuable commodity traded with the Malays and highly prized by the Chinese.[336] Further evidence comes from an 1894 description of camphor collection by the Jakun of Johor by Harry Lake, a miner and surveyor, and H.J. Kelsall, who was a lieutenant with the Royal Engineers in Singapore. They highlight the profitability and complexity involved. The search for camphor could take months, requiring the Pantang Kapur language—a specialized skill set—to identify camphor in older trees. The collected camphor fetched a high price, selling to Chinese

---

[335] P.E.L. Favre, *An account of the wild tribes*, 121.

[336] D.F.A Hervey, "Endau and Its Tributaries," in *Journal of the Straits Branch of the Royal Asiatic Society* 8 (1881): 101, https://books.google.com.sg/books?id=y3icdojOauwC.

traders.[337] It was highly lucrative and strategically located, which further suggests that Sultan Ali's decision to establish his residence near the mouth of the Muar River was not merely coincidental.

By positioning himself at this key intersection of resources, trade routes, and potentially loyal allies like the Jakun, Sultan Ali could have significantly bolstered his kingdom's growth and prosperity. These reports illustrate the potential value the Jakun communities held for Sultan Ali. Their expertise in resource collection, particularly of a valuable commodity like camphor, could have significantly benefited his kerajaan's economy.

Access to Fertile Soil

Sultan Ali's domain actually had very fertile soil and this attracted planters to the area in search of land grants. Among these planters was Adolf Gottwald Studer, a member of the United States consul in Singapore. He was appointed to the position in 1871 and heard about the 'extreme fertility and richness of the then almost unoccupied lands in Kassang [Kesang] or Muar'.[338] On 3 February 1877, Studer went to Muar and chose a tract of land on the western bank of the Muar River, after which Sultan Ali wrote a formal concession that enabled Studer to acquire the land. Studer not only acquired a large tract of land 45 square miles in size but found that it was a very fertile land rich in minerals. It also had great soil, which was suitable for tobacco growing. The area was also full of rare and valuable woods. The Muar River was quite navigable and accessible. Studer, together with another planter, made plans to further develop the area and even invested in a

---

[337] H. Lake and H.J. Kelsall, "The Camphor Tree and Camphor Language of Johore," in *Journal of the Straits Branch of the Royal Asiatic Society* 26 (1894): 40, https://books.google.com.sg/books?id=RZnwqKpCQvcC.

[338] "Appendix to the Memorial: In the Matter of the claim of Adolf Gottwald Studer against Abu Baker, Sultan of Johore and ruler of Muar," in *American and British Claims Arbitration* (Washington D.C.: U.S. Government Printing Office, 1913), 280.

small steamship.[339] Hence, Sultan Ali's strategic location near a fertile agricultural area offered several advantages. It likely ensured a consistent food supply for his growing population, reducing dependence on external sources and potential vulnerability. Additionally, these fertile lands could have generated surpluses beyond what his subjects needed. These surpluses could have been used to trade with other regions, potentially bringing in important resources and strengthening the kingdom's economy.

Therefore, Sultan Ali's decision to establish Muar-Kesang as the centre of his kerajaan after 1855 stands out as a well-calculated move. The proximity to Melaka, a major port city, provided access to established trade routes and markets. The Kesang and Muar rivers offered a dual advantage: facilitating both maritime trade and access to inland resources through crucial waterways. This geographical advantage positioned Muar-Kesang at the heart of a well-trodden trade route, bolstering the potential for economic prosperity. Beyond its geographical advantages, Muar-Kesang was rich in natural resources. Gold and tin could have been mined and traded, significantly increasing Sultan Ali's wealth and contributing to his kingdom's economic success. The presence of Jakun communities in the area presented another strategic advantage. Their knowledge of the land and their expertise in resource collection, as evinced by the reports on camphor gathering, made them a valuable human asset. Even the land in Muar-Kesang was fertile and suitable for large-scale cash crop enterprises such as tobacco. Therefore, Sultan Ali's domain was actually a suitable centre for the development of a wealthy and potentially powerful kingdom.

Limitations to Development

However, Sultan Ali's vision for success might not have been fully realized. Developing and managing mines and plantations requires significant investment in manpower, expertise, and

---

[339] Ibid. 281–282.

infrastructure. One of the greatest impediments to Sultan Ali's rule was his crippling debt, which limited his ability to fully exploit the area's potential. He was in debt even before the signing of the Treaty of Johor in 1855. A report entitled 'Precis History of Sultan Ali', published in 1879, mentioned that in 1860 Sultan Ali borrowed 53,600 Spanish dollars from a chitty (Chettiar) in Singapore named Kavana Chana Shellapah. As security for the payment of the debt, Sultan Ali agreed to give the Chettiar 500 Spanish dollars, which was the monthly payment allotted to him for signing the 1855 treaty. Sultan Ali also 'assigned to the chitty the monthly pension of 170 dollars which he received from the British government' and mortgaged five acres of his land in Singapore. In 1862, another 15,000 Spanish dollars were borrowed from Kavana Chana Shellapah along with a sum of 20,000 Spanish dollars as security, which Sultan Ali was to claim from the British government. However, these sums were never repaid by Sultan Ali, who secretly fled Singapore in November 1862.[340]

He also owed substantial sums of money for the services of the Bugis mercenary that he hired shortly after he was made ruler in 1855. The mercenary Suliwatang Kalek Aji and his men were hired to forcibly collect taxes from the population of Muar-Kesang and to enforce his rule over the area. However, the Bugis mercenary encountered great resistance from the men of the Temenggong of Muar, and some of his men were even killed. The resistance was so great that the mercenary was forced to take up defensive positions by building a fort in Dok. The Bugis mercenary wanted Sultan Ali to pay for his losses, which amounted to several hundred thousand dollars, but this was, of course, never done. Tensions between Sultan Ali and the Suliwatang escalated, ultimately leading to Suliwatang's decline in influence and reputation. Suliwatang lost men and money working for Sultan Ali from 1856 to 1857. Apart from losing his

---

[340] "Correspondence with Regard to the Muar Territory, Enclosure 1: Precis History of Sultan Ali," in *Accounts and Papers*, Vol. 12, ed. House of Lords (Oxford: Oxford University, 1879), 6.

men, the greatest loss sustained by the Suliwatang was the loss of 8,000 *gantangs* of rice as well as money at Muar, where they were attacked by the various *penghulu* (headmen) of the area.[341]

Recent works on the nature of the Sultan's debt attempt to highlight the consequences of his many defaults. According to D. Graeber, debts, unlike other obligations, are emotionless transactions focused solely on the bottom line, which can have significant consequences for human relationships and individual well-being. Furthermore, histories of debt show that there are long-standing moral virtues associated with the repaying of borrowed money.[342] In other words, a person who defaults on his debt compromises his morality. Furthermore, Sultan Ali reigned during a time when there was a growing anti-aristocratic sentiment in nineteenth-century Britain. Historian Antony Taylor analyses in the work *Lords of Misrule* how negative sentiment towards British aristocracy developed throughout the nineteenth century among Britain's population, who increasingly viewed the debt and debauchery of aristocrats as the ultimate detriments to British society and politics.[343] These negative perceptions could thus have framed nineteen-century British observations in Malaya who viewed Sultan Ali's indebtedness and may have equated it with weak rulership. As a result, he would have been unlikely to gain support from the British community in Malaya.

While financial constraints posed a significant challenge to Sultan Ali's rule in Muar-Kesang, an even greater obstacle was his inability to cultivate a loyal and powerful following to support his authority. Unfortunately, information about the nature of Sultan Ali's rule and of his followers remains scarce. However, based on his perceived role as heir to the Melaka Sultanate, we can

---

[341] "Tunku Silawatang Qualla Kessang to the Resident of Malacca," in *American and British Claims Arbitration* (Washington D.C.: U.S. Government Printing Office, 1913), 96–97.

[342] D. Graeber, *Debt: The First 5,000 Years, Updated and Expanded* (New York: Melville House, 2014), 21–27.

[343] A. Taylor, *Lords of Misrule: Hostility to Aristocracy in Late Nineteenth and Early Twentieth Century Britain* (Basingstoke: Palgrave Macmillan UK, 2004), 14.

infer certain aspects of his government. If he indeed sought to follow the Melaka model, his *kerajaan* likely included traditional Malay elites holding positions like *bendahara* (chief minister), *bendahari* (treasurer), temenggong (military leader), and *laksamana* (admiral). This structure aligns with the traditional Malay system of governance with lesser nobles such as the *orang kaya* (literally meaning a wealthy man) and penghulu (village heads), with pendekar and *hulubalang* (warriors) complementing the structure. Furthermore, we can assume that Sultan Ali adhered to prevalent Malay concepts of a good ruler, which often emphasized leadership qualities like justice, piety, and concern for the well-being of his subjects.

This quality of a good Malay ruler has been the subject of discussion among many scholars. Noor Aisha observes that Islam serves as a check on a ruler's despotic powers and describes the famous agreement in the *Malay Annals* between Demang Lebar Daun and Sang Sapurba (Sri Tri Buana) where Malay subjects pledged their loyalty and subservience to rulers as long as the ruler does not mistreat or punish them arbitrarily.[344]

Anthony Milner goes further to describe the centrality of a good ruler in a traditional context, and he maintains that the 'Kerajaan System' was a social order based on public reputation and hierarchy. The sultan was the centre of this system, and rank was determined by one's relationship to him. The sultan needed a large population to bolster his own status, so he focused on keeping his subjects happy. This meant adhering to proper *adat,* or customs and ceremonies, emphasizing the importance of public perception. Following these rules ensured one's place in society and protected one's reputation. The system placed a high value on rank and following proper etiquette. Transgressions were seen as a threat to social order and could lead to harsh punishments.[345]

---

[344] Noor Aisha Abdul Rahman, *Colonial Image of Malay Adat Laws: A Critical Appraisal of Studies on Adat Laws in the Malay Peninsula during the Colonial Era and Some Continuities* (Leiden: Brill, 2006), 125.

[345] A. Taylor, *Lords of Misrule: Hostility to Aristocracy in late nineteenth and early twentieth century Britain* (London: Palgrave-Macmillan, 2004), 14.

Sultan Ali's position as ruler in Muar-Kesang directly challenged the existing power structure. As observed by T.J. Newbold in 1839, the area already possessed a well-established network of traditional elites, which included various figures like the temenggong of Muar, orang kaya, and penghulu, each governing specific territory. Notably, the temenggong of Muar, who controlled a vast region from Melaka to Parit Siput, wielded significant authority. Further south, the penghulu of Batu Pahat oversaw a prosperous territory exporting ebony, rattan, and aloe wood. Additionally, penghulu controlled various regions like Banut and Pontian. According to T.J. Newbold, these chiefs, similar to the Temenggong of Singapore, were originally vassals of the Sultan of Johor.[346]

Therefore, Sultan Ali's arrival disrupted this established system of governance, inevitably leading to conflict with the existing power holders, particularly Temenggong Ismail Paduka Tuan. This clash made it nearly impossible for Sultan Ali to adhere to traditional Malay principles of governance, which often emphasized cooperation and established hierarchies.

Dato Haji Abdul Shukor Ismail's 1984 work provides a more detailed description of the various temenggongs of Muar from the eighteenth century. Beginning with Dato Seri Maharaja Di Raja (also named Dato Semada Raja), who was appointed temenggong of Muar by Sultan Abdul Jalil Syed Kota Tinggi in 1707 CE. Dato Semada Raja passed in 1732 CE and his son, Paduka Tuan anak Semada Raja, was made temenggong of Muar. Temenggung Engku Buruk reigned from 1762 and Temenggong Dato Kamil (also named Temenggong Sonet and Temenggong Konik) reigned in 1801. In 1834, Temenggung Engku Said was appointed temenggong of Muar by Sultan Hussein Shah of Singapore. In 1847, Temenggong Ungku Ismail (Paduka Tuan) became the temenggong of Muar. He was also said to have moved to Kuala Segamat to distance himself from Johor's control. In 1879, Temenggong Wan Mohamad Salleh became temenggong

---

[346] T.J. Newbold, *Political and Statistical Account of the British Settlements in the Straits of Malacca, Viz: Pinang, Malacca, and Singapore* (London: John Murray, 1839), 41–43.

of Muar and finally, in 1910, Temenggong Wan Abdul Rahman bin Wan Mohamed Salleh was appointed temenggong of Muar.[347]

Dato Haji Abdul Shukor Ismail diligently collected vital information from local residents who were knowledgeable about the various temenggongs of Muar, then at Lubuk Batu Segamat. Among his informants was Wan Ambak binti Temenggong Wan Abdul Rahman, daughter of a former temenggong. Following Muar's incorporation into Johor, Temenggong Ismail persisted in collecting taxes and other revenues from his domain. Appointed to this territory in 1847, his reluctance to join Sultan Ali's kingdom after 1855 is understandable, as it would likely have entailed relinquishing control over his prosperous fiefdom.[348]

The defiance of the Temenggong of Muar significantly exacerbated Sultan Ali's already precarious financial situation. This defiance had a two-fold impact. Firstly, Sultan Ali's reliance on expensive Bugis mercenaries further drained the treasury. Secondly, their presence fuelled a negative perception of his rule. The mercenaries' actions likely alienated both the British and his Malay subjects, shattering any attempts to project himself as a just and benevolent leader. A report in 1858 by the *Singapore Free Press and Mercantile advertiser* showed that the Bugis sent by Sultan Ali to Muar to assert his rights there had been defeated by the Temenggong of Muar. They had taken up defensive positions on Kesang and raided villages in Melaka. This caused much disturbance to the villagers and the police even captured some of them.[349] However, the damage to the population of Muar and Kesang was greater. The use of Bugis mercenaries to collect taxes from the population further impoverished the area and this likely led Sultan Ali to abandon Muar-Kesang, moving instead to Umbai, Melaka where he finally died in 1877.

---

[347] Dato' Haji Abdul Shukor Ismail, *Sejarah Ringkas Muar* (Muar: Penerbitan Toko Buku Manaf, 1984), 163–164.

[348] Ibid. 165–168.

[349] "Muar," *The Singapore Free Press and Mercantile Advertiser,* July 31, 1858, https://eresources.nlb.gov.sg/newspapers/digitised/article/singfreepressa18580731-1.2.4 .

Conclusion

Reports of instability in Muar-Kesang were rife. In 1857, a report by Chinese miners rioting in Kesang made tin mining operations difficult.[350] Violence in the area only seemed to increase in 1859, leading to many police constables being deployed in the area from 1857–1858.[351] Despite Muar-Kesang's strategic location and resources, Sultan Ali's reign was ultimately defined by struggle. Internal unrest—including discontent, rebellions, and financial pressures—consumed his limited resources and eroded his authority. These internal challenges were further worsened by external forces, particularly the rising influence of the British and the Temenggong of Johor. These challenges restricted Sultan Ali's autonomy and the economic development in Muar-Kesang. Faced with these overwhelming challenges, Sultan Ali was unable to fully capitalize on his territory's potential. The Treaty of Johor, though initially presented as a solution, ushered in the decline of his rule. Sultan Ali's legacy thus became one of a ruler who was ultimately overwhelmed by many obstacles.

The reign of Sultan Ali of Johor was a crucial turning point in Singapore's history, as his failure allowed the British to sideline Sultan Hussein's descendants and consolidate their power further. The chapter also shows that Sultan Ali's failure cannot be attributed solely to factors like indebtedness or shortsightedness. Instead, we must consider the cultural and historical context of Malay kingship and the complexities of the situation, including the actions of Sultan Ali, the British, and other key actors. By doing so, we can get a more nuanced understanding of Sultan Ali's reign especially the challenges of ruling a resource-rich Muar-Kesang region.

---

[350] "The Free Press," *The Singapore Free Press and Mercantile Advertiser*, March 26, 1857, https://eresources.nlb.gov.sg/newspapers/digitised/article/singfreepressa18570326-1.2.4

[351] "Singapore: Saturday, 25th June, 1859," *The Straits Times*, June 25, 1859, https://eresources.nlb.gov.sg/newspapers/digitised/article/straitstimes18590625-1.2.4.

More can be done to fill the significant gap in our knowledge about the role of Malay rulers in Singapore's history. By re-reading nineteenth-century colonial sources, this chapter offers fresh insights into further possibilities for challenging conventional narratives and providing a more comprehensive understanding of Singapore's Malay rulers and their role in history.

Chapter 8

Colonialism, the Historical Construction of 'Tanah Melayu', and its Significance to Malaysia's and Singapore's National Narratives

Wilbert W. W. Wong

Introduction

The prominent colonial scholar administrator Richard Olaf Winstedt (1878–1966) is widely recognized for his contributions to Malay studies, especially his studies on Malay literature, language, culture, and history. His pioneering influence in Malay(si)a's nation-state historiography, however, is more significant than is often appreciated and has largely gone unnoticed. Notwithstanding that, his publications are still widely referenced today in both Malay and non-Malay historical works. Using a microhistory approach to uncover broader historical developments by analysing a single event or subject, this chapter will analyse the historical construction of 'Tanah Melayu' (which literally translates as 'Malay Land' and is generally used today in Malaysia to refer to Peninsular Malaysia) by examining Richard Winstedt's writing of *Kitab Tawarikh Melayu* (*Book on Malay*

History), which was first published in 1918 and used as a history textbook in Malaya.

Winstedt's writing of this history, as will be demonstrated, is significant for several key reasons. It was the first work in the Malay language to construct a Malay history that is centred on the portions of the Malay Peninsula that came under British political control or protection. He placed historical emphasis on the British side of Tanah Melayu, with the Melaka Sultanate or *kerajaan* accorded a central and founding role in the region's history. The legacies of Winstedt's historical construction of Tanah Melayu can be seen in Malaysia's post-colonial national narrative, which continues to emphasize the central role of the Melaka Sultanate in its historiography. Although there have been competing narratives that challenge this approach, such as the Malay world-oriented histories that place their attention more broadly on the Malays across the Malay Archipelago and other polities in the region rather than just Melaka, the Melaka-centric discourse remains significant. Given the continued influence of this Melaka-centric narrative in Malaysia's historical discourse, analysing the ways in which Winstedt constructed the history of Tanah Melayu in *Kitab Tawarikh Melayu* can help uncover the ideological and historical roots of Malaysia's nation-state narrative. Within the broader context of the legacies of imperialism, this chapter also seeks to uncover the colonial roots of Malaysia's national narrative as well as the colonial impact on the historical discourse and consciousness of post-colonial societies, such as Malaysia.

With its historical emphasis on the Melaka Sultanate, a polity located squarely within the boundaries of 'British Malaya', which the post-colonial state of Malay(si)a inherited, Winstedt's narrative provides a unifying founding point for the nation's national narrative. His *Kitab Tawarikh Melayu* also presents a Tanah Melayu that is founded on the tradition of Malay culture and history, which were built on the legacies of the Melaka–Johor Sultanate. This complements Malaysia's nation-building narrative by providing the historical endorsement to the nation that its Malay nationalist post-colonial nation builders have wanted to create. Winstedt's historical construction of Tanah

Melayu also has a crucial place in Singapore's national narrative. While his history endorses the state narrative in Malaysia, the opposite, however, is true for Singapore. Winstedt's monoethnic Malay-centric histories, such as *Kitab Tawarikh Melayu*, can challenge Singapore's state narrative, and they have been criticized for downplaying the historical presence and agency of the Malays in the building of a multicultural or pluralistic state. *Kitab Tawarikh Melayu* is a reminder that an alternative history that emphasizes Singapore's Malay identity by positioning the island as a crucial part of the Malay sultanates in Tanah Melayu is possible. Indeed, Winstedt's histories, as will be discussed, have been featured in the recent debates in Singapore's historiography. His Malay-centric approach to the region's history has been, furthermore, used to give greater recognition to Singapore's Malay past. The legacy of his historical construction of the region can also be observed in Singapore's attempt to give some acknowledgment that it was part of a Malay polity when covering the region's history before British colonialism in 1819.

Richard Winstedt's Works in Malaysia's and Singapore's Historiographies

Winstedt's key contributions to Malay(si)a's and Singapore's historiographies came from his key historical works on the Malays, Malaya, and its individual states that were published between 1918 and 1948.[352] Many of his works, such as his

---

[352] Richard O. Winstedt and Abdul Hamid bin Tengku Muhammad Salleh Daing, *Kitab Tawarikh Melayu*, First edition (Singapore: Education Department, S.S. and F.M.S, 1918); Richard O. Winstedt, "Malaya: The Straits Settlements and the Federated and Unfederated Malay States," *Journal of the Malaysian Branch of the Royal Asiatic Society (JMBRAS)* 1, no. 2 (88) (1923): 388–389; Richard O. Winstedt, "A History of Kedah," *JSBRAS* 81 (1920): 29–35; Richard O. Winstedt, "A History of Johore (1365-1895 A.D.)," *JMBRAS* 10, no. 3 (1932): 1–167; Richard O. Winstedt, "A History of Johore (1673–ca. 1800 A.D.)," *JMBRAS* 10, no. 1 (1932): 164–201; Richard O. Winstedt, "Negeri Sembilan: The History, Polity and Beliefs of the Nine States," *JMBRAS* 12, no. 3 (1934):

state histories of Perak and Johore, have been regarded as pioneering, for example in a 1995 special issue on the history of the *Journal of the Malaysian Branch of the Royal Asiatic Society*. This was because they were the first full-scale histories on the region that were produced using the modern 'scientific' approach of evidence-based historical writing.[353] Winstedt's general histories of Malaya were the first full-scale works of their kind to cover all the states within the boundaries of present-day Peninsular Malaysia from antiquity up to the twentieth century. His later historical works, such as his 1948 *Malaya and Its History*, cover the period up to the immediate post-World War II years.[354] As will be discussed below, his Malay-centric histories place the most emphasis on the Malay monarchies, or kerajaan, especially the Melaka-Johor Sultanate, which he accorded a founding and central role in the region's history.

Winstedt's Malay-centric histories are also of relevance to Singapore's history today. This can be observed in the way his works have been featured in a recent criticism of Singapore's national narrative by the historian Michael Barr. Joining the chorus of scholars and leading historians of Singapore, such as Peter Borschberg and Kwa Chong Gwan, in their re-evaluation of the nation's historiography, Barr criticizes Singapore's disregard

---

37–111; Richard O. Winstedt and R.J. Wilkinson, "A History of Perak," *JMBRAS* 12, no. 3 (1934): 1–34, 112–114; Richard O. Winstedt, "A History of Selangor," *JMBRAS* 12, no. 3 (1934): 1–34; Richard O. Winstedt, "A History of Malaya," *JMBRAS* 13, no. 1 (1935): 1–270; Richard O. Winstedt, *The Malays: A Cultural History* (Singapore: Kelly & Walsh, 1947); Richard O. Winstedt, *Malaya and its History* (London: Hutchinson, 1948).

[353] Choy Chee Meh (née Lum) et al., "History of the Malaysian Branch of the Royal Asiatic Society," *JMBRAS* 68, no. 2 (1995): 97.

[354] My analysis of Winstedt's general histories here is based on my study of Padma Daniel's 1941 catalogue of books relating to Malaysia that are held in the Raffles Museum and Library in Singapore: Padma Daniel, "A Descriptive Catalogue of the Books Relating to Malaysia in the Raffles Museum & Library Singapore," *JMBRAS* 19, no. 3 (1941): 1–125.

of the Malay presence and role in its mainstream history.[355] He does this in one of his works by referencing some of Winstedt's Malay-centric histories of the region, such as his 1932 *A History of Johor*, among other works, to undermine and deconstruct Singapore's national narrative. He demonstrates that the Malays have a deep historical connection to and greater agency in the region's past than is often portrayed in Singapore's historical discourse.[356] Barr's use of Winstedt's histories to support his point demonstrates the crucial position of Winstedt's works in the nation-state historiographies of Singapore and Malaysia. In the context of Singapore, it shows that Winstedt's narratives can provide a historical alternative to its modern national narrative.

According to critics of the official state narrative, Singapore has overemphasized the British colonial period, particularly the role of Stamford Raffles in its founding in 1819 and the subsequent achievements of his successors in developing the city as a major port with its predominantly Chinese inhabitants.[357]

---

[355] See for example: Hong Lysa and Huang Jianli, *The Scripting of National History: Singapore and Its Pasts* (Singapore: NUS Press, 2008); Kwa Chong Guan, "From Temasek to Singapore: Locating a Global City-State in the Cycles of Melaka Straits History," in *Studying Singapore Before 1800*, ed. Kwa Chong Guan and Peter Borschberg (Singapore: NUS Press, 2018), 179–205; Kwa Chong Guan et al. eds., *Seven Hundred Years: A History of Singapore* (Singapore: Marshall Cavendish International (Asia), 2020); Afian Sa'at, Faris Joraimi, and Siew Min Sai, eds., *Raffles Renounced: Towards a Merdeka History* (Singapore: Ethos Books, 2021); Benjamin Khoo and Peter Borschberg, *Knowing Singapore: The Evolution of Published Information in Europe, c.1500-1819* (Kuala Lumpur: Malaysian Branch of the Royal Asiatic Society, 2023). See also: Terence Chong, "The Bicentennial Commemoration: Imagining and Re-Imagining Singaporeâs History," in *Southeast Asian Affairs 2020*, ed. Malcolm Cook and Daljit Singh (Singapore: ISEAS–Yusof Ishak Institute, 2020): 323–34.

[356] Michael D. Barr, "Background Figures in a British Portrait: The Johor Royal Family in Nineteenth-Century Singapore," *History Australia* 18, no. 2 (2021): 287–289.

[357] Michael D. Barr, "Singapore Comes to Terms with Its Malay Past: The Politics of Crafting a National History," *Asian Studies Review* 46, no. 2 (16

This narrative suits the nation-building purpose of fostering a multicultural Singapore that is grounded on the spirit of innovation and meritocracy.[358] On closer examination, this interpretation of Singapore's state history can be traced back to the colonial period in Lennox A. Mills' 1925 *British Malaya: 1824–1867*.[359] Despite its title, his history is focused on the Straits Settlements (namely Singapore, Penang, and Melaka) while the Malay states are only mentioned to add historical context to them.[360] Without being dismissive of the Malays, his history comes across as multicultural, as he places significant attention on the role of the non-Malay settlers, especially the Chinese and Europeans, in the historical development of Singapore and the other parts of the Straits Settlements.[361] Mills gives the impression that the region's development was, in his words, '[T]he main product of British initiative and Chinese labour.'[362] Constance Mary Turnbull, who provided an annotated bibliography and wrote the preface to the 1960 reprint of Mills' work calling it a 'standard work in the field', would later herself write *A History of Modern Singapore*, which

---

September 2021): 351, 357; Hong Lysa and Huang Jianli, *The Scripting of National History: Singapore and Its Pasts* (Singapore: NUS Press, 2008), 3–7.

[358] Michael D. Barr, "Singapore Comes to Terms with Its Malay Past," 352; Terence Chong, "The Bicentennial Commemoration: Imagining and Re-Imagining Singapore's History": 325. On Singapore's post-colonial state goal of building a nation grounded on the image of multiculturalism, see: Kevin Blackburn and ZongLun Wu, *Decolonizing the History Curriculum in Malaysia and Singapore* (Abingdon: Routledge, 2019), 138–139; Hong Lysa and Huang Jianli, *The Scripting of National History: Singapore and Its Pasts* (Singapore: NUS Press, 2008), 92. It should be noted, however, that Singapore's national narrative in recent years is heading towards giving greater recognition to its pre-1819 history. Time will tell how the Malays will be positioned in its future state narrative, as the region's histories are rewritten and reimagined. See Michael D. Barr, "Background Figures in a British Portrait": 300–301.

[359] L.A. Mills, "British Malaya: 1824-1867," *JMBRAS* 3, no. 2 (1925): 1–339.

[360] Ibid. 36–42, 56–59.

[361] Ibid. 43, 210.

[362] Ibid. 199.

became, and remains, the standard reference on Singapore's state history since its first publication in 1977.[363] Her widely acclaimed history, however, seems to have followed some of the key aspects of Mills' work in emphasizing the achievements of the British and Chinese in Singapore's history. It has been criticized for downplaying Singapore's precolonial history (by starting in 1819) and the historical importance of the Malays.[364]

In summary, the discussion above has shown that Winstedt's histories can help, and have been used to, deconstruct and reposition (or reconnect) Singapore as part of the history of the Malay world. Contrary to the state's histories that follow the line of Mills and Turnbull, Winstedt's histories place the historical attention on the Malays by positioning the island as part (site) of the history of the Malay kerajaan of Tanah Melayu. It is not surprising that Singapore's history textbook, at least the recent edition, has adopted aspects of Winstedt's Melaka- and Johor-centric approach to Singapore's history in what appears to be its attempt to be more inclusive of Singapore's pre-colonial Malay past. Across the Singapore Strait, however, Winstedt's histories present a different issue for Malaysia's historiography in the sense that their Malay-centric focus disregards the non-Malay historical presence in the region, including of its indigenous Orang Asli inhabitants, who are only mentioned in passing. These features are present in his *Kitab Tawarikh Melayu*, which will be analysed below.

---

[363] Constance Mary Turnbull's preface to L.A. Mills, "British Malaya: 1824-1867," *JMBRAS* 33, no. 3 (1960): 1–424; Constance Mary Turnbull, *A History of Modern Singapore: 1819-1975* (Kuala Lumpur: Oxford University Press, 1977).

[364] Michael D. Barr, *Singapore: A Modern History* (London: Bloomsbury, 2019), 4; Michael D. Barr, "Singapore Comes to Terms with Its Malay Past": 356–357; Terence Chong, "The Bicentennial Commemoration: Imagining and Re-Imagining Singapore's History": 325.

The Historical Significance of *Kitab Tawarikh Melayu* and the Creation of a Tanah Melayu History

One of Winstedt's important works on Malay(si)a's history is *Kitab Tawarikh Melayu* (*A Book of Malay History*), which he wrote with Daing Abdul Hamid bin Tengku Muhammad Salleh, a Bugis from Selangor. Although he was co-author, much of the book's contents were shaped by Winstedt and are consistent with his general views on the region's history. For example, its diffusionist interpretations of Malay culture and literature were shaped by copying (the word *tiru* was used) from other cultures, such as Hinduism.[365] The book was first published in 1918 and continued to be used as a history textbook in Malay colleges during the colonial period.[366] It was probably used as a guide for Malay teachers to prepare them for history teaching. According to the historian Naoki Soda, *Tawarikh Melayu* was still in use at the Sultan Idris Training College (SITC) in 1927 before being superseded by Abdul Hadi bin Haji Hassan's (1900–1937) *Sejarah Alam Melayu*.[367] About 2,000 copies of the first edition of *Tawarikh Melayu* were

---

[365] See for example: Richard O. Winstedt, *Kitab Tawarikh Melayu*, Third edition (Singapore: Kelly & Walsh, 1921), 6–14. The *Kitab Tawarikh Melayu* was first published in 1918, but I have used the 1921 version that is now held at the National Library of Singapore because I could not get access to the 1918 edition.

[366] Naoki Soda, "The Malay World in Textbooks: The Transmission of Colonial Knowledge in British Malaya," *Southeast Asian Studies* 39, no. 2 (2001): 200. According to Cheah Boon Kheng, it was also used in Malay primary schools, 'which went up to the sixth standard'. See: Cheah Boon Kheng, "Writing Indigenous History in Malaysia: A Survey on Approaches and Problems," *Crossroads: An Interdisciplinary Journal of Southeast Asian Studies* 10, no. 2 (1996): 44; Richard O. Winstedt, *Kitab Tawarikh Melayu*, 6.

[367] Naoki Soda, *Conceptualizing the Malay World* (Kyoto: Kyoto University Press, 2020), 31; Naoki Soda, "The Malay World in Textbooks: The Transmission of Colonial Knowledge in British Malaya": 196.

printed every year.³⁶⁸ It was revised in 1921 and 1925, each time after 10,000 copies had been printed.³⁶⁹

Winstedt's 1918 history, *Kitab Tawarikh Melayu*, holds a special place in Malaysia's historiography. It is arguably the first book written in the Malay language that carries a semblance of a national or state history in the way it constructs a history of Tanah Melayu by narrowing its geographical focus to just the British-controlled areas of the Malay Peninsula, which Malaysia initially inherited at independence. 'Tanah Melayu' is used today both in a political sense to refer to Peninsular Malaysia and as a geographical signifier for the Malay Peninsula. Even when used in a purely geographical context, emphasis is placed on the Malay sultanates and polities of the Malay Peninsula. The term is also used to refer to the Malaysian portion of the region, although the Malay Peninsula can also be seen as extending to the Isthmus of Kra in contemporary Thailand. This political framing of Tanah Melayu can be traced back to the colonial period, as an evaluation of Winstedt's *Kitatb Tawarikh Melayu* will demonstrate.

Before the twentieth century, 'Tanah Melayu' was a broad and vague term that did not carry the same political meaning as it does in post-colonial Malaysia. Tanah Melayu is not even mentioned in the Kedah-based text *Hikayat Merong Mahawangsa* or the Melaka-centred *Sejarah Melayu*.³⁷⁰ *Ujong tanah* (land's end) or the general term *negeri-negeri di bawah angin* (lands or states beneath the wind) were used to refer to the Malay Peninsula or more broadly the Malay Archipelago.³⁷¹ The nineteenth-century *Tuhfat*

---

³⁶⁸ Cheah Boon Kheng, "Writing Indigenous History in Malaysia": 44.

³⁶⁹ Ibid.

³⁷⁰ Syed Nasir bin Ismail, ed., *Hikayat Merong Mahawangsa* (Kuala Lumpur: Dewan Bahasa dan Pustaka, 1968); Richard O. Winstedt, "The Malay Annals of Sejarah Melayu," *JMBRAS* 16, no. 3 (1938): 1–226.

³⁷¹ See, for example, Raja Ali Haji, *Tuhfat Al-Nafis: Sejarah Melayu-Islam*, ed. Virginia Matheson Hooker (Kuala Lumpur: Dewan Bahasa dan Pustaka, 1991), 428; Richard O. Winstedt, "The Malay Annals of Sejarah Melayu": 49, 88, 93.

Al-Nafis mostly uses the term *sebelah barat* (the Western side) when pointing to the Malay Peninsula or its Malay inhabitants, and *di sebelah Johor* (the Johor side) in the case of Johor.[372] Tanah Melayu, however, is mentioned in the *Tuhfat Al-Nafis,* but it is a vague term that is used to point to any places that have a Malay settlement.[373] Tanah Melayu appears in the *Hikayat Hang Tuah* (at least in the century-old Dewan Bahasa dan Pustaka version of the text that this paper uses, which was obtained from Kelantan), in a way suggesting that the term was also used to refer to the Malay Peninsula in the nineteenth-century, if not earlier.[374] Its vagueness, however, suggests that the term was used in a regional rather than in a political sense. An example of the regional or geographical usage of Tanah Melayu in the *Hikayat Hang Tuah* can be observed in the way Tanah Melayu is positioned in the context of other regions. At one point in the *Hikayat Hang Tuah*, a reference is made by one of the characters, Sang Jaya Nantaka, to being a *raja* (or ruler) in Tanah Melayu, Benua Keling Keling (Kalinga continent), Tanah Jawa (Jawa), and Tanah Minangkabau (Minangkabau).[375] Tanah Melayu in *Hikayat Hang Tuah* also includes Bintan, which is today part of Indonesia's Riau Island province.[376] Nonetheless, when placed in the context of other Malay classical texts, it is possible that the *Hikayat Hang Tuah* used 'Tanah Melayu' to refer to other Malay polities beyond the Malay Peninsula.

In *Tawarikh Melayu,* Winstedt creates a distinct geopolitical entity in the way he sketches out Tanah Melayu. By narrowing the focus of 'Tanah Melayu'—a previously broad and vague term

---

[372] Raja Ali Haji, *Tuhfat Al-Nafis*, 259–260.

[373] Ibid. 539.

[374] On the age of the Dewan Bahasa dan Pustaka edition of the *Hikayat Hang Tuah*, see: Kassim Ahmad, "Introduction," in *Hikayat Hang Tuah*, ed. Hassan Ahmad, Second edition (Kuala Lumpur: Yayasan Karyanan dan Dewan Bahasa dan Pustaka, 2008), xv, xxiii. It will be interesting to see how Tanah Melayu is used in the other, earlier versions of the *Hikayat Hang Tuah*.

[375] Hassan Ahmad, ed., *Hikayat Hang Tuah*, 83. *Tanah Benua Keling* (literally translates to 'land of the Kalinga continent') is also used to refer to *Benua Keling*.

[376] Ibid. 35, 55, 61.

that had no political meaning—to 'British Malaya', Winstedt effectively transforms the term and historically gives it a new geopolitical significance. He turns it into a historical space or even something that is equivalent to a Malay nation—that is, rather conveniently, based on a collection of Malay polities and sultanates that eventually came under British political control or protection by the twentieth century. In other words, his Tanah Melayu is centred on the boundaries of British Malaya at its fullest extent. This Tanah Melayu is presented in Winstedt's history as if it was an entity that had always existed, as will be further discussed below. His historical construction of Tanah Melayu in *Tawarikh Melayu* and the way he frames the region is similar to how he constructs Malaya in his other general histories of the region that he wrote and published in English. In these histories, he equates Malaya to all the portions of the Malay Peninsula that had come under British political control by the early twentieth century.[377]

Like Tanah Melayu, Malaya was a general and vague term before the twentieth century that was used to refer to the entirety of the Malay Peninsula, including parts that are in Thailand today or other regions of the Malay Archipelago. An example of this broad usage of 'Malaya' can be observed in an 1882 article by A.M. Skinner on the 'Outline of the British Connection with Malaya'. He uses 'Malaya' to refer to a broad geographical area that includes the Malay Peninsula and the Indonesian Archipelago—chiefly Sumatra, Java, and Borneo.[378] The vague and broad usage of Tanah Melayu and Malaya, and the absence of a political definition of the terms make sense, given that the Malay Peninsula consisted of various political entities and sultanates that emerged and vanished over time. The region, even

---

[377] Richard O. Winstedt, ed., *Malaya: The Straits Settlements and the Federated and Unfederated Malay States* (London: Constable, 1923); Richard O. Winstedt, *Malaya and its History*; Richard O. Winstedt, "A History of Malaya," *JMBRAS* 13, no. 1 (1935): 1–270.

[378] A.M. Skinner, "Outline History of the British Connection with Malaya," *JSBRAS*, no. 10 (1882): 272.

in the areas that came under British control, was once part of polities or states that were based outside of the Malay Peninsula, such as the Javanese empire of Majapahit, the Sumatran-based Srivijaya, and Siamese-based kingdoms.[379]

Winstedt understood the vague and broad aspect of the term 'Malaya' well, as can be seen in his attempt to narrow down its definition to just the British-controlled portions of the Malay Peninsula in his 1923 book *Malaya: The Straits Settlements and the Federated and Unfederated Malay States*. In the opening to that book, he acknowledges the wide meaning of Malaya.[380] What follows next is an admission of his geopolitical framing of Malaya when he states that he is now using the term 'politically' to refer to 'that part of the Malay Peninsula under British rule or protection', hence transforming the definition of Malaya to British-controlled Malay Peninsula or British Malaya.[381] The title of his 1923 book provides a further indication of his attempt to geopolitically equate Malaya with British Malaya. He would even state later in his 1948 book, *Malaya and its History*, that he believed Malaya was a British invention that was used as a 'name for the whole of the Malay Peninsula'.[382] Earlier historical works on the region by his contemporaries such as Frank Swettenham (1850–1946) and Richard James Wilkinson (1867–1941) did not define Malaya in the way Winstedt had done in his histories. The geographical boundaries of Swettenham's 1906 book *British Malaya*, for instance, are vague and also cover those parts of the Malay Peninsula that were controlled by the Kingdom of Siam (and remain part of modern Thailand), such as Junk Ceylon

---

[379] Barbara Watson Andaya and Leonard Andaya, *A History of Malaysia*, Third edition (London: Palgrave Macmillan, 2017), 32, 36; Paul Wheatley, *The Golden Khersonese* (Kuala Lumpur: University of Malaya Press, 1961), 299, 301–302.

[380] Richard O. Winstedt, ed., *Malaya: The Straits Settlements and the Federated and Unfederated Malay States*, 2.

[381] Ibid.

[382] Richard O. Winstedt, *Malaya and its History*, 8.

(Phuket).[383] R.J. Wilkinson's *History of the Peninsular Malays*, which first appeared in 1908 as part of the 'Papers on Malay Subjects' series, excludes the northern Malay states of Perlis, Kelantan, and Terengganu, while its coverage does not go beyond the late nineteenth century.[384] Interestingly, it was not Winstedt's 1923 *Malaya* but his 1918 Malay-language *Kitab Tawarikh Melayu* that would be his first historical attempt to geopolitically narrow the focus of Tanah Melayu—the Malay equivalent of Malaya—to British Malaya.

The historical importance of *Tawarikh Melayu* does not lie only in its historical construct of Tanah Melayu, as if it was a political entity. It was also perhaps the first Malay history written taking the modern approach of factual history. *Tawarikh Melayu's* significance in Malay historiography is highlighted by the prominent Malay scholar and literary figure Zainal Abidin bin Ahmad (Za'ba) (1895–1973), who regarded it as the first scientific work ever produced in the Malay language on Malay history in Malaya.[385] Za'ba's appraisal is crucial. He was a Malay teacher during the colonial period and was, therefore, able to appreciate the historical significance of *Kitab Tawarikh Melayu* in Malay literature. Early Malay histories were mainly courtly narratives that focused on genealogies, proper conduct, and customs that were written under royal decrees.[386] Modern historians such as the late Khoo Kay Kim have noted that most Malay historical works until the beginning of World War II focused almost exclusively on the

---

[383] Frank Swettenham, *British Malaya* (London: Bodley Head, 1907), 313.

[384] R.J. Wilkinson, ed., "A History of the Peninsular Malays," Third edition (London: Oxford University Press, 1923), 15–151.

[385] Zainal Abidin bin Ahmad, "Modern Developments," an Additional Chapter to R.O. Winstedt, "A History of Malay Literature," *JMBRAS* 17, no. 3 (1939): 151.

[386] Khoo Kay Kim, "Local Historians and the Writing of Malaysian History in the Twentieth Century," in *Perceptions of the Past in Southeast Asia*, ed. Anthony Reid and David Marr (Singapore: Heinemann Educational Books (Asia) (1979), 300–302.

royal family.³⁸⁷ Many were not published at the time because they were not intended for public consumption.³⁸⁸

Tawarikh Melayu was also different because, as a colonial history of the region, it was written for a Malay audience rather than a European one. In it, Winstedt, probably with the help of Daing Abdul Hamid, pretends to be a Malay by writing Tanah Melayu history and speaking as if he was one of them, which he probably did to make his history more relatable to Malay readers. This attempt to appear Malay can also be seen in his closing statement in *Tawarikh Melayu*—where, after expressing his hope that Allah would enhance the peace and prosperity of the inhabitants of the Malay Peninsula that came under British tutelage, he exclaimed 'Amin! Amin! Ya rabu'il alamin.'³⁸⁹ Another example of Winstedt's attempts to sound like a local in his history can be seen in his statement that some of the Hindu elements in Malay culture are very sinful (*sangat berdosa*) in the view of Islam.³⁹⁰ Winstedt even refers to Tanah Melayu as 'Tanah Melayu *kita*' (our Tanah Melayu), which would have further cultivated a local, or perhaps even a nationalistic, sense of belonging to the land among his Malay readers.³⁹¹ According to Kevin Blackburn and Zonglun Woo, history was seen at the time by colonial administrators as a way of fostering a sense of imperial citizenship, of being part of a commonwealth of nations within the British Empire.³⁹² It is plausible that Winstedt was writing *Kitab Tawarikh Melayu* with this intention of creating a distinct sense of identity and nationhood among the Malays within the British Empire. After all, in 1918, when he published his history, Winstedt was a chief education

---

³⁸⁷ Ibid. 302–303.

³⁸⁸ Ibid.

³⁸⁹ Richard O. Winstedt, *Kitab Tawarikh Melayu*, Third edition (Singapore: Kelly & Walsh, 1921), 88–89.

³⁹⁰ Ibid. 8.

³⁹¹ Ibid. 1, 12.

³⁹² Kevin Blackburn and ZongLun Wu, *Decolonizing the History Curriculum in Malaysia and Singapore* (Abingdon: Routledge, 2019), 18–19, 39.

officer whose responsibility included overseeing the curriculum of the Malay schools in Malaya.[393]

Another crucial feature of *Tawarikh Melayu* that is worth noting is Winstedt's emphasis on 'Tanah Melayu *ini*' (this Tanah Melayu) to distinguish it from the other Malay provinces outside of the region, such as Sumatra, which he calls 'Daerah Melayu itu' (that Malay province).[394] What is interesting is that he also refers to Sumatra as Tanah 'Melayu' ('Malay' land), but there is a noticeable difference in the way he frames the term when he uses it in the context of Sumatra and the Malay Peninsula. Whenever he uses Tanah 'Melayu' to refer to Sumatra, Winstedt puts the word 'Melayu' or 'Malay' in quotation marks to distinguish it from his Tanah Melayu (Malay land) in the Malay Peninsula or, more specifically, British Malaya. This can be seen in the way he positions Sumatra in Tanah 'Melayu' when discussing the Javanese conquest of the Sumatran regions of Siak and Kampar.[395] Interestingly, he does not put 'Melayu' in quotation marks whenever he uses the term Tanah Melayu to cover historical events in Malaya, as can be observed in his discussion of the Dutch and their ships sailing '*ka*-Tanah Melayu *ini*' (to this Tanah Melayu) and engaging in diplomacy, war, and peace with the 'raja-raja Melayu di sini' (Malay kings here).[396] The way he puts 'Melayu' in quotation marks in Tanah 'Melayu' to differentiate Sumatra from the Tanah Melayu of Malaya is another indication of Winstedt's geopolitical attempt to historically construct a Malay nation in the Malay Peninsula

---

[393] Naoki Soda, "The Malay World in Textbooks: The Transmission of Colonial Knowledge in British Malaya," *Southeast Asian Studies* 39, no. 2 (2001), 195–196, 199; Kevin Blackburn and ZongLun Wu, *Decolonizing the History Curriculum in Malaysia and Singapore* (Abingdon: Routledge, 2019), 162.

[394] Richard O. Winstedt, *Kitab Tawarikh Melayu*, 27.

[395] Ibid. 24, 95. For example, on page 95: '*Tanah "Melayu" di-Pulau Percha itu, ia-lah Kampar dan Siak agak-nya di-datangi oleh tentera Jawa.*'

[396] Ibid. 68–69. For example: '*Maka mana-mana kapal Belanda yang lain ditegahkan berlayar ka-tanah Melayu ini sahaja; dan berkuasalah pula Kompeni itu berjanji dan berperang serta berdamai dengan raja-raja Melayu di sini.*'

that is drawn along the territorial lines of the British Empire. The way he distinguishes one Tanah Melayu from another in his history furthermore hints at his awareness that the term could be inclusive of other parts of the Malay World that were not under British control. When placed in the context of how he uses the terms Tanah Melayu and Tanah 'Melayu', his phrasing of 'Tanah Melayu *di sini*' could be more than just a literary convention to provide clarity in the discussion and may also have had a political intent. It was possibly done to emphasize and distinguish this Malay Land (Tanah Melayu *di sini*) from the other 'Malay' land(s) outside the borders of British Malaya, historically creating and carving out a political space in the Malay world in the process.

Za'ba also observed that *Tawarikh Melayu* was the book that opened the eyes of the Malays to the modern scientific meaning of history as a subject distinct from fiction.[397] It can be seen that his statement is not without basis when the contents of *Tawarikh Melayu* are analysed. In it, Winstedt outlines the strengths and weaknesses of some of his sources (Portuguese, Malay, English, Chinese, and Javanese) and encourages his readers to decide the facts for themselves, therefore promoting critical reading of historical sources along the lines of Western historiographical practices.[398] Through his treatment of Malay sources, Winstedt demonstrates to his Malay readers how to read Malay sources factually as historical documents. In the preface to *Tawarikh Melayu*, for instance, he notes that Malay manuscripts were copies of the original and have, over the years, been adapted by succeeding copyists to suit their needs and agendas, as well as those of their royal patrons.[399] He highlights the mythical elements of the *Sejarah Melayu*, which is his main Malay source on the region's history, and points out to his readers that some of their contents, such as the *Sejarah Melayu's* narrative of Alexander the Great's ancestry, do not

---

[397] Zainal Abidin bin Ahmad, "Modern Developments," an Additional Chapter to R.O. Winstedt "A History of Malay Literature": 151.

[398] Richard O. Winstedt, *Kitab Tawarikh Melayu*, 22–23.

[399] Ibid. i.

make factual sense and should, therefore, be read with caution.[400] In his narrative, Winstedt compares the information found in *Sejarah Melayu* with Portuguese, Chinese, and other local sources such as the *Hikayat Hang Tuah*, *Hikayat Acheh*, and the *Hikayat Merong Mahawangsa* to establish what happened, encouraging the intertextual comparison of sources by his Malay readers.[401]

Given its role as a school textbook, *Tawarikh Melayu* would have been influential at least among the educated portions of the Malay population in Malaya. Za'ba's recognition of its significance to Malay scholarship is an indication that its influence must have been notable. The influence of *Tawarikh Melayu* could also be observed in Abdul Hadi bin Haji Hassan's *Sejarah Alam Melayu*. Winstedt's diffusionist interpretation of Malay culture and history as a byproduct of Indian culture is noticeable, for example, in Abdul Hadi's remark on the history of Malay conversion to Islam: 'When the Malays embraced Islam, the names of their previous Hindu Gods were changed to Allah, the prophets and Angels of Islam.'[402] As Soda has pointed out, *Tawarikh Melayu* played an important role in the localization of colonial discourse on the region.[403]

Constructing a Malay History of Tanah Melayu Built on the Legacies of the Melaka-Johor Sultanate

In terms of its geographical scope, *Tawarikh Melayu* is intended to speak for the history of all the states in the Malay Peninsula that came under direct or indirect British control by the time it was published, which is (excluding Singapore) essentially the same as

---

[400] Ibid. 11, 21–23.

[401] See, for example, Ibid. 24–25, 40, 48–51, 54–55, 59.

[402] Abdul Hadi bin Haji Hasan, *Sejarah Alam Melayu*, 1947 reprint, vol. 2 (Singapore: Malaya Publishing House, 1926), 49.

[403] Naoki Soda, *Conceptualizing the Malay World*, 1, 3, 40, 53, 55, 81, 83.

Peninsular Malaysia today.[404] The scope is indicated in the book's concluding pages, which deal with the states of Perak, Pahang, Selangor, Negeri Sembilan, Pahang, Kedah, Perlis, Kelantan, and Terengganu coming under British rule, with Siam ceding the latter three states to Britain in 1909.[405] Given its territorial focus, it can be said that *Tawarikh Melayu* was the first work to construct Malaya's or Tanah Melayu's history in a way that captures the national boundaries of the post-colonial state of the Federation of Malaya or Persekuatan Tanah Melayu.[406] This aspect of *Tawarikh Melayu* is what makes it stand out from earlier histories of the region, such as the abovementioned works of Swettenham and Wilkinson. Although *Tawarikh Melayu* claims to speak for the history of Tanah Melayu, very little is said of the histories of the northern Malay states of Kelantan, Terengganu, and Perlis other than passing remarks, such as that Terengganu and Kelantan were possibly once under the control of Palembang.[407] These states are also mentioned at the close of *Tawarikh Melayu*, when they came under British protection in 1909.[408] Most of the historical focus of *Tawarikh Melayu* is on the Melaka-Johore Sultanate.

Winstedt gives the impression in the opening chapter of his book on Tanah Melayu's pre-history that there is nothing significant to note, claiming that Malay history during this period is obscure.[409] He acknowledges in this chapter that the earliest inhabitants were the indigenous Aslian tribes (today collectively known as the Orang Asli), the 'dark skinned' Semang and the Sakai in particular.[410] He asserts that they were first in the region

---

[404] Richard O. Winstedt, *Kitab Tawarikh Melayu*, 12–13.

[405] Ibid. 88–89.

[406] Ibid. 13, 26, 40–41, 44–45, 47, 55, 67.

[407] Ibid. 26.

[408] Ibid. 88.

[409] Ibid. 13.

[410] Ibid. 1. The term 'Sakai' is seen by the Orang Asli as a degrading Malay term and has been replaced by the more respectable 'Senoi'. See Kirk Endicott,

because if the Malays had been in the Malay Peninsula earlier, they would have been able to overcome any colonizing attempts by such a '*lemah*' (weak) and '*bebal*' (stupid) people.[411] According to Winstedt, there were kingdoms that emerged in the north of Tanah Melayu during the early period of its history, but it is not clear whether they were Malay.[412] As for the south, Winstedt claims that there were no eminent political entities until the Melaka Sultanate was established, therefore giving the Melaka Sultanate a founding role in Tanah Melayu's history.[413]

The way *Tawarikh Melayu* is organized emphasises the centrality of the Melaka Sultanate in the history of Tanah Melayu. The chapter on 'The Coming of the Sumatrans' marks the end of Winstedt's coverage of pre-history and signals the beginning of Malay history proper in Tanah Melayu with the establishment of the Melaka Sultanate. As the chapter's title suggests, Winstedt argues that the ancestors of the Malays of the present day came from Sumatra.[414] The chapter begins with an outline of the portion of the *Sejarah Melayu* that covers the ancestral story of Melaka's founder, Parameswara, and his flight from Palembang in Sumatra to Singapore and finally to Melaka, where he established the great Malay kingdom in Tanah Melayu.[415] According to Winstedt, the adat (Malay customs) of the Sultanates in the then Tanah Melayu were based on the customs of the Melaka Sultanate, the political influence of which is said to have spread throughout the region at the height of

---

"Introduction," in *Malaysia's Original People: Past, Present and Future of the Orang Asli*, ed. Kirk Endicott (Singapore: NUS Press, 2016), 1–2; Geoffrey Benjamin, "On Being Tribal in the Malay World," in *Tribal Communities in the Malay World: Historical, Cultural and Social Perspectives*, ed. Geoffrey Benjamin and Cynthia Chou (Singapore: Institute of Southeast Asian Studies, 2003), 13.

[411] Richard O. Winstedt, *Kitab Tawarikh Melayu*, 1.

[412] Ibid. 13.

[413] Ibid. 13–14.

[414] Ibid. 5.

[415] Ibid. 14–32.

its power.[416] Winstedt, therefore, gives the impression that the Melaka Sultanate helped spark a Malay historical and cultural renaissance that transformed the region. He also highlights the leading role played by the sultans of Melaka and their successors in Johor in establishing and spreading Islam in the region, for example in Pahang, Kampar, and Indragiri.[417]

There are some similarities between Winstedt's treatment of the Melaka Sultanate as a founding narrative and turning point in the region's history and the treatment of the Norman Conquest in British historiography, where the invasion and the establishment of Norman rule in Britain marked a new historical era in British history, notwithstanding that the Normans were foreign invaders. Their conquest, for instance, is often seen to have sparked significant transformations in the laws, property, and government of England.[418] Any coverage given to their history in Europe is done in the background of British history and is mostly limited to the purpose of establishing their roots and how they eventually founded a crucial dynasty in England through their conquest. Winstedt follows this practice of Western state histories in *Tawarikh Melayu* by only giving attention to Sumatra out of necessity—to provide background coverage to Melaka's founder because he was a Sumatran prince from Palembang. Given that the Melaka-centric history of Tanah Melayu is the main emphasis of *Tawarikh Melayu,* any historical events in Sumatra and Java not connected to Melaka's founder are considered irrelevant and, therefore, ignored. Other regions are mentioned only when needed and done, like his coverage of Sumatra, as a back story

---

[416] Ibid. 49. For example, see his comment: '*Maka di-dalam hikayat Melayu benarlah yang Raja Peramisura itu masok Islam, dan diubahi gelaran-nya iai-tu Sultan Muhammad Shah. Makai ia-lah yang pertama-tama meletakkan adat larangan raja-raja Melayu pada zaman purba kala.*'

[417] Ibid. 37, 39.

[418] Michael Bentley, "British Historical Writing," in *The Oxford History of Historical Writing: 1800-1945*, ed. Daniel Woolf, vol. 4 (Oxford, New York: Oxford University Press, 2011), 207.

to Tanah Melayu's history. The historical separation between the Malay Peninsula and the neighbouring regions of Sumatra and Java is marked by Winstedt's claim in *Tawarikh Melayu* that the link between Palembang and Temasek (Singapore) was broken in the thirteenth century after the latter became independent.[419] Its independence, according to him, signalled the end of Palembang's rule in the Malay Peninsula, which he likens to a severed umbilical cord between a mother and her baby.[420]

The glories and accomplishments of the Melaka Sultanate are emphasized by Winstedt in *Tawarikh Melayu*. For example, when citing the *Sejarah Melayu*, he notes that under the *gagah perkasa* (mighty) Sultan Mansor Shah, Melaka flourished, the number of his subjects grew, and many traders flocked to the city.[421] Most of Winstedt's attention in *Tawarikh Melayu* is devoted to the Melaka Sultanate and its successor, the Johor Sultanate.[422] Compared to the histories of the other sultanates of the region, the histories of Melaka and Johor are explained in greater detail and also include genealogies of their rulers, which reveals their connection to the ruler of Melaka.[423] The family connection of the rulers of the Sultanates of Perak, Kelantan, and Pahang to the Melaka Sultanate is also stressed in the genealogies.[424] There is a sense of continuity with Melaka in Winstedt's narrative even when he covers the European powers in the region after the fall of the sultanate at the hands of the Portuguese in 1511. Melaka and Johor continue to be his focus when discussing Dutch and British

---

[419] Richard O. Winstedt, *Kitab Tawarikh Melayu*, 27.

[420] Ibid.

[421] Ibid. 55.

[422] Richard O. Winstedt, *Kitab Tawarikh Melayu*, 48–80. See page 39 for Winstedt's reference to the current rulers of the Johor Sultanate as descendants of the Melaka Sultans.

[423] For genealogies, see: Ibid., 28, 29, 54, 68.

[424] Ibid. 54, 67–68.

involvement in the region.[425] He mentions in these chapters the histories of other local political entities or communities in the Malay Archipelago, such as Acheh and the Bugis, but only does so when they involve the Melaka and Johor sultanates.[426]

In contrast to the attention given to the history of the Melaka and Johor sultanates in *Tawarikh Melayu*, not much is said about the histories of the other polities in Tanah Melayu other than the occasional side remark, such as regarding their connection and engagement with the Melaka Sultanate, as in the case of Pahang and Perak.[427] As discussed above, the histories of the northern peninsular states of Kelantan, Terengganu, and Perlis are disregarded. The only time these states receive significant attention in *Tawarikh Melayu* is in the closing section, which covers British political expansion into these northern states in 1909.[428] About sixty-six out of *Tawarikh Melayu's* 107 pages are related to the Melaka Sultanate and, after Melaka's fall, to the Johor Sultanate.[429] With its emphasis on Melaka-Johor, the book brings the Melaka Sultanate to the forefront of the history of the region. In doing so, Winstedt was encouraging his Malay readers across Tanah Melayu to identify with the history of Melaka instead of the history of the states and the sultanates that they personally came from. Winstedt thus equates the development of the Malay history of Tanah Melayu to the development of the Melaka and, later, the Johor Sultanates.

While the multicultural aspect of Malaysia's history has been acknowledged by leading historians of the region, Winstedt's *Tawarikh Melayu* is predominantly a Malay-centric account that

---

[425] Ibid. 62–65, 68–81, 87–89.

[426] See, for example, ibid. 74–77.

[427] See Ibid. 55, 67–68.

[428] Ibid. 88–89.

[429] Ibid. 14–30, 32–36, 37, 38, 39, 40–41, 48–79, 97–106.

disregards the historical presence of other cultural groups.[430] The indigenous Orang Asli only occupy the first two opening pages of the section on pre-history.[431] They quickly disappear into the backdrop of pre-history once Winstedt covers the arrival of the Malays into the Malay Peninsula, displacing the Orang Asli, thereby giving the impression that history in Tanah Melayu or Malaya starts with the Malays. Other ethnic groups such as the Chinese are mentioned only out of necessity in the broader context of the Malay history of the region. An example of this can be seen in Winstedt's discussion of British intervention in the Malay Peninsula in the nineteenth century, in which he points to the *huru-hara* (chaos) that arose from infighting caused by Chinese miners in Perak, which forced Britain to intervene politically to restore peace in the region.[432] The Malay-centric aspect of *Tawarikh Melayu* promotes the image of a Tanah Melayu and Malaya that is historically and culturally Malay, with the Malay sultans playing a central role in the region's history.[433]

An Alternative Interpretation of Tanah Melayu History

The constructive feature of Winstedt's Tanah Melayu and its history can be understood through the way the region is framed in other Malay historical narratives of the region. One such alternative historical work is none other than Abdul Hadi Hassan's (1900–1937) *Sejarah Alam Melayu* (History of the Malay World), its first volume published in 1925 and the final fifth volume in 1940.

---

[430] See, amongst others: Andaya and Andaya, *A History of Malaysia*; Boon Kheng Cheah, *Malaysia: The Making of A Nation* (Singapore: ISEAS, 2002).

[431] Richard O. Winstedt, *Kitab Tawarikh Melayu*, 1–7.

[432] Ibid. 88.

[433] One example of the kerajaan or monarchy-centric interpretation of Malay history can be seen in his coverage of the Dutch dealing with the Malay rulers or rajas. Rather than framing his argument as a political engagement with the Malays in general, he chose to position it specifically as carried out with the Malay rulers only: Richard O. Winstedt, *Kitab Tawarikh Melayu*, 69.

Khoo regarded *Sejarah Alam Melayu* as Malaya's first national history.[434] He was perhaps right if *Sejarah Alam Melayu* is seen within the context of an archipelagic pan-Indonesian or Malay world perspective of a nationalistic history. It was probably the first Malay history in Malay(si)a that was written solely by a Malay author using modern historiographical methods of evidence-based history.[435] Soda has also remarked that Abdul Hadi 'portrayed Malaya as a focal point of the Malay territories'.[436] A close examination of Abdul Hadi's work, however, reveals that Malaya or Tanah Melayu was not his emphasis. Although he may have been writing a Malay national history, Abdul Hadi was not interested in creating a Malay nation that was politically centred on Tanah Melayu. To him, Tanah Melayu was never a political entity or a nation at all, but merely a geographical region within the broader Malay World. His geographical treatment of the region can be seen in his definition of Tanah Melayu as 'a piece of land that is protruding far into the southern direction of the sea from the Asian continent [. . .] as if it is a bridge connecting the mainland [Asian continent] with the Malay Archipelago.'[437]

Abdul Hadi's work is about the history of the *bangsa Melayu* (Malay people or race) in the Malay World. His focus widens the geographical reach of his history, which includes, besides the Malay Peninsula, present-day Indonesia, parts of Thailand, and the Philippines. Whenever he mentions the *negeri-negeri Melayu*

---

[434] Khoo, "Local Historians and the Writing of Malaysian History in the Twentieth Century," 304–305.

[435] Arrifin Omar, *Bangsa Melayu: Malay Concepts of Democracy and Community, 1945-1950*, Second edition (Petaling Jaya: SIRD, 2015), 22.

[436] Naoki Soda, *Conceptualizing the Malay World*, 125.

[437] Abdul Hadi bin Haji Hasan, *Sejarah Alam Melayu*, vol. 1 (Singapore: Malaya Publishing House, 1925), 1. '*Bahawa ada pun Tanah Mĕlayu kit aini ia-lah sa-kĕping tanah yang mĕnganjor jauh ka-laut arah ka-sĕlatan Bĕnua Asia, sa-olah-olah sa-umpama titian yang mĕnyambong tanah besar (Bĕnua Asia, sa-olah-olah sa-umpama titian yang mĕnyambong tanah besar (Bĕnua Asia) itu dĕngam Pulau-Pulau Melayu yang bergugus-gugus itu.*'

(Malay states) in his work, he is referring to the Malay World and not merely the Malay Peninsula.[438] This Malay World focus can be observed in how he positions Melaka in his history when discussing the spread of Islam in the region. He acknowledges the Melaka Sultanate as an important centre for the religion, promoting its spread to the Malay Peninsula and Sumatra.[439] After the fall of Melaka in 1511, however, his attention shifts to the history of Islam in Sumatra and Java.[440] Abdul Hadi also demonstrates that there were other important Islamic centres in the Malay World, such as Tidore and Ternate.[441] In contrast to the central importance that Winstedt accorded the Melaka Sultanate, Abdul Hadi regards Melaka as simply 'a trading centre in the Malay World'—one among several other important Malay polities in the region.[442]

Abdul Hadi's inclusion of the Christian inhabitants of the Philippines, Ambon, and Timor as part of his history of the Malay World is an indication of the broader regional scope of his work and his more inclusive definition of Malay identity. This includes non-Muslims and even regards the Chinese Peranakan (Chinese born of Malay mothers) community as indigenous, or *bumiputera* (sons of the soil).[443] On the contrary, in *Tawarikh Melayu*, Winstedt sees the Malays, except in the pre-Melaka Sultanate period, more narrowly as comprising only Muslims in a way that reflects how Malay identity is officially seen in Malaysia today. The Malay World and the Malay people were Abdul Hadi's national focus, not Tanah Melayu. Placing the historical focus on Tanah Melayu would have undermined the broader orientation of Abdul Hadi's

---

[438] Abdul Hadi bin Haji Hasan, *Sejarah Alam Melayu*, 1949 edition, vol. 3 (Singapore: Malaya Publishing House, 1929), 34.

[439] Abdul Hadi, *Sejarah Alam Melayu*. 5 vols. Vol. 2 (Singapore: Malaya Publishing House,1926), 91.

[440] Ibid. 91–97.

[441] Ibid. 122.

[442] Ibid. 202–203.

[443] Abdul Hadi, *Sejarah Alam Melayu*, 3, 49, 111.

history.[444] Winstedt's *Tawarikh Melayu*, in contrast, has more of a national orientation in his historical coverage of British Malaya-centred Tanah Melayu. This is especially the case with the way the author speaks as if he was a Malay inhabitant and his attempt to collectively link Malay culture and history to the Melaka-Johor Sultanate. Pre-twentieth century Malay-language classical texts on the region, such as Kedah's *Hikayat Merong Mahawangsa*, can also provide an alternative narrative of its history to the one afforded by Winstedt's Melaka-centric *Kitab Tawarikh Melayu*. Hendrik Maier has reasonably charged Winstedt with failing to pay enough attention to the *Hikayat Merong Mahawangsa* in his histories, despite the source's historical value.[445] Regardless of whether or not Winstedt's omission was deliberate, the *Hikayat Merong Mahawangsa* does not support his Melaka-centric interpretation of the region's history because it places Kedah at the heart of its narrative. It also emphasizes the state's political and historical links to the Kingdom of Siam and the northern Malay states that were, at the time when Winstedt was writing, located within Siam's borders.

The *Hikayat Merong Mahawangsa* does not link Kedah to the Sultanate of Melaka, which challenges Winstedt's Melaka-centric narrative of the region's history. According to the Kedah text, the grandson of Merong Mahawangsa, who the author claims was descended from the line of Alexander the Great, founded the Kedah Sultanate. His descendants, it is claimed, went on to establish polities in the Malay Peninsula such as Perak and Pattani and elsewhere within Siam.[446] The focus on Kedah in the founding narrative of the northern Malay states shifts the historical centre of gravity away from the Sultanate of Melaka, and even undermines Winstedt's claim that the Sultanate of Perak

---

[444] Ibid. 110–111.

[445] Hendrik M.J. Maier, *In the Center of Authority: The Malay Hikayat Merong Mahawangsa* (New York: Southeast Asia Program, 1988), 63, 65, 67.

[446] Ibid. 49–50, 52–59.

was founded by descendants of the Melaka Sultanate.[447] While no mention is made of Kedah's links with the Melaka Sultanate, the *Hikayat Merong Mahawangsa* highlights the close family ties between the rulers of Kedah and of Siam, which draws historical attention to the Malay states favourably towards Siam, Britain's regional competitor at the time of Winstedt's writing.[448] Winstedt's method of placing the Melaka Sultanate centrally in the founding narrative of Tanah Melayu was strategically ideal in writing a history of a Malay nation based along British colonial lines, with Melaka having been under Britain's political control since the nineteenth century. Endorsing Siam's historical links to the region would have undermined this purpose. The *Sejarah Melayu*, which Winstedt cites often, contains useful information that enabled him to build a Melaka-centric history of Tanah Melayu.[449]

Much of the contents of the *Sejarah Melayu*, however, concern events outside of the Melaka Sultanate and the Malay Peninsula. Even in the *Hikayat Hang Tuah*—a text widely celebrated in Malaysia for its valuable information on the Melaka Sultanate—locates the political and cultural centre of the Malay rajas in Bukit Seguntang (Palembang), rather than the Melaka Sultanate. The text often situates the narrative of the Melaka monarchs in relation to events in Bukit Seguntang and other monarchs in the region who had ancestral links to this polity, which demonstrates the political and cultural reverence given by Melaka to Bukit Seguntang.[450] The Malay rajas are shown in the *Hikayat Hang*

---

[447] On the rulers of Perak being the descendants of the sultans of Melaka, see: Richard O. Winstedt, *Kitab Tawarikh Melayu*, 20.

[448] Syed Nasir bin Ismail, ed., *Hikayat Merong Mahawangsa* (Kuala Lumpur: Dewan Bahasa dan Pustaka, 1968), 56–57.

[449] See for example: Richard O. Winstedt, *Kitab Tawarikh Melayu*, 36, 55, 70. For an example of Winstedt's selective use of Malay manuscripts such as the *Sejarah Melayu* to build a Melaka-centric founding narrative for his Tanah Melayu history, see: 14–24.

[450] Hassan Ahmad, ed., *Hikayat Hang Tuah*, Second edition (Kuala Lumpur: Yayasan Karyanan dan Dewan Bahasa dan Pustaka, 2008), 70, 83, 95.

Tuah to be wary of committing *derhaka* (treason) against Bukit Seguntang or acting against the will of its ruler.[451] Melaka is also treated as a political extension of the dynasty of Bukit Seguntang, and the leaving of a good nama or reputation with the dynasty is seen as important.[452] The *Hikayat Hang Tuah* stresses continuity between the rulers of Malay polities with Bukit Seguntang. By contrast, in *Tawarikh Melayu*, Winstedt emphasizes the historical continuity of the Melaka-Johor Sultanate. As mentioned earlier, Winstedt severs Melaka's link to Bukit Seguntang at the time the Melaka Sultanate was established. When using Malay manuscripts as historical sources, he was selective and only focused on the parts that were useful for his Melaka-centric Malaya and Tanah Melayu histories.

Winstedt's Construction of Tanah Melayu in the Post-Colonial Period

The Melaka-centric narrative of Tanah Melayu that Winstedt projected in his 1918 Malay history remains influential in the nation-state narrative of post-colonial Malaysia, demonstrating its continuing appeal as a nation-building narrative for the country. The legacy of his Melaka-Johor Sultanate-centric discourse can be observed in the contents of a 2014 Form 1 Malaysian secondary school history textbook. It emphasizes that the nation is built on the historical legacies of the Malay sultanates of Melaka and Johor. The chronological order in which the history is structured—pre-history, the founding of the Melaka Sultanate, the fall of Melaka, the Johor Sultanate, and the legacies of the Melaka Sultanate in the Malay Peninsula—is similar to how Winstedt structured *Kitab Tawarikh Melayu* and his other general histories of

---

[451] Ibid. 70, 83, 92, 95.

[452] Ibid. 95.

Malaya.[453] Unsurprisingly, his works are cited as a key reference in the textbook's bibliography.[454] This is a historical narrative that Malaysian students are expected to remember. In one of the questions on the 2019 year-end Form 5 secondary school history exam, students are asked to 'prove that Malaysia and its people are built on the legacies of the Sultanate of Melaka'.[455] The same Melaka-Johor Sultanate-centred national narrative is now continued as part of Malaysia's Form 2 secondary school history syllabus.[456] With its focus on Tanah Melayu and its emphasis on the Melaka-Johor Sultanate as its founding narrative, Winstedt's *Tawarikh Melayu* is considered well suited as a nation-building narrative for post-colonial Malaysia. Abdul Hadi's Malay World-orientated *Sejarah Alam Melayu*, by contrast, is more suited for building a pan-Malay nation across the archipelago.

An examination of the recent edition of Singapore's Secondary 1 history textbook shows that its contents remain centred around Mills' and Turnbull's construction of the region's history due to its greater emphasis on the non-Malay communities. There is an attempt in the textbook to address Singapore's past as a Malay polity when it covers the pre-colonial period, going back to 1299 CE.[457] It must be stressed, however, that the word 'Malay' is only used when referring to the *Sejarah Melayu* or *Malay Annals* as a

---

[453] Ahmad Fawzi bin Mohd. Basri, Mohd. Fo'ad bin Sakdan, and Azami bin Man, *Sejarah Tingkatan 1*, ed. Wan Norliani binti Wan Jusoh and Nazri bin Mohamad Don, Kurikulum Bersepadu Sekolah Menengah (Kuala Lumpur: Dewan Bahasa dan Pustaka, 2014), 20–176.

[454] Ibid. 210.

[455] 'Sijil Pelajaran Malaysia 2019. Sejarah. Kertas 3' (Lembaga Peperiksaan Malaysia, November 2019).

[456] Suffian bin Mansor, Mardiana binti Nordin, and Ahmad Salehee bin Abdul Ishak bin Saidoo, *Sejarah Tingkatan 2*, ed. Abdul Ghani bin Abu and Md Shukuri bin Hamzah, Kurikulum Standard Sekolah Menengah (Kuala Lumpur: Dewan Bahasa dan Pustaka, 2022), 8–13.

[457] *Singapore: The Making of a Nation-State, 1300-1975. Textbook. Secondary One* (Singapore: Curriculum Planning & Development Division, Ministry of Education, 2014), 8–42. I am grateful to Peter Borschberg for his help in this

historical source and is never again mentioned in the chapter even when discussing the Melaka and Johor sultanates. Despite this inclusion, most of the textbook remains focused on the post-1819 colonial period. Only thirty-four out of its 205 pages cover the pre-colonial period.[458] The textbook's structure gives the impression that Singapore is built on the legacies of colonial state-building, and the contributions and experiences of the different ethnicities or communities that have established themselves on the island. This narrative, as it seems, gives the impression of multiculturalism because of its focus on the different races and is, therefore, suited for promoting Singapore's national image of diversity.[459] The pre-colonial period remains a prelude or a footnote, a memory of a bygone era. The impression is given at the end of the pre-colonial chapter that Singapore declined and faded into obscurity, marking the end of a period until the British gave it a new beginning in 1819.[460] The colonial period was what shaped Singapore into the modern state that it is today.

The legacy of Winstedt's historical construction of Tanah Melayu, however, can be seen in Singapore's Secondary 1 history textbook. The pre-1819 section of the textbook follows the structure of Winstedt's Melaka- and Johor-centric history in the way it discusses Singapore's link to the Sumatran-based empire of Srivijaya before transitioning to the Melaka and Johor sultanates, which Singapore was part of.[461] Singapore's place as an important port for trade in the region is also discussed in the pre-1819 section of the textbook.[462] Significant coverage is given to the Melaka and Johor sultanates, which serves as a reminder of how

---

chapter on Singapore's history. The insights on Singapore's national narrative, however, are my own.

[458] *Singapore: A Journey Through Time, 1299-1970s* (Singapore: Star Publishing Pte Ltd, 2021), 8–42.

[459] Ibid. 72.

[460] Ibid. 9, 30–37.

[461] Ibid. 21–39.

[462] Ibid. 11, 16–17, 20–24.

Singapore's history can be constructed in a way that connects it to Tanah Melayu or, in today's words, Malaysia.[463] This approach to Singapore's history may seem counterproductive and awkward for its nation-building because it brings Singapore closer to Malaysia's national narrative. From a geopolitical context, focusing on the Melaka and Johor Sultanates also places the historical, political, and cultural centre on Malaysia rather than Singapore. However, an analysis of how the narrative of Tanah Melayu is positioned within the Secondary 1 textbook shows that it is done in a way that strengthens rather than undermines Singapore's state narrative. Turnbull's approach of emphasising 1819 as the starting point of Singapore's history is a core weakness of the state's national narrative and, as discussed above, has come under scrutiny by scholars. Including the Melaka- and Johor-centric construction of Tanah Melayu's, or Malaysia's, history into Singapore's national narrative addresses this issue (and its critics) by giving Singapore a longer existence that predates the colonial period. Longevity is an important aspect of nation-state histories because it gives a state a sense of legitimacy, an existence that predates the colonial establishment of 1819 in the case of Singapore.[464]

The periods of the Melaka and Johor sultanates in Singapore's history are presented in the textbook in a way that strategically marks a transition, creating a clear boundary between Singapore's past and that of Tanah Melayu, or Malaysia. As noted earlier, the pre-1819 chapter concludes with the decline of both sultanates—and, by extension, Singapore—reflecting how the island's fate was closely linked to theirs. The subsequent chapter, which starts in 1819 when Britain established Singapore as a trading post, marks

---

[463] Ibid. 25–40.

[464] Stefan Berger, "The Invention of European National Traditions in European Romanticism," in *The Oxford History of Historical Writing: 1800-1945*, ed. Stuart Macintyre, Juan Maiguashca, and Attila Pók, vol. 4 (Oxford: Oxford University Press, 2011), 32.

a new historical beginning for Singapore.⁴⁶⁵ As noted in the first page of the textbook's chapter on the colonial period, Singapore 'would regain prominence later in the nineteenth century as a British trading post and port city.'⁴⁶⁶ In the chapters covering the colonial period, Singapore's history is constructed in a way that gives the impression that it began to develop differently from Tanah Melayu, effectively separating Singapore from the region. Singapore becomes the main focus of these chapters. Its pre-1819 past along with its historical links with Tanah Melayu was prehistory or old Singapore. The colonial period was when the history of modern Singapore as a city-state truly began, as the island experienced significant transformations during this time. This learning outcome is one of the stated objectives of the colonial period section of the textbook, which is 'to study the changes in Singapore under British rule' and learn about the 'experiences of the various groups of people living in Singapore [...] the challenges they faced and their contributions up to the fall of Singapore in 1942.'⁴⁶⁷

As seen, Winstedt's Melaka-centric construction of the region's history has been used to serve the national narratives of both Malaysia and Singapore and remains crucial in the historical discourse of both nations.

The Legacies of Winstedt and the Colonial Construction of Tanah Melayu in Malaysia's and Singapore's Histories

Within the context of Malaysia's historiography, *Tawarikh Melayu*'s distinctiveness and importance lay in the historical foundation

---

⁴⁶⁵ See, for example, the opening of the colonial period chapter in *Singapore: A Journey Through Time, 1299-1970s* (Singapore: Star Publishing Pte Ltd, 2021), 43.
⁴⁶⁶ Ibid. 43.
⁴⁶⁷ Ibid. 72.

it provided for envisioning Tanah Melayu as a nation and, as a Malay history, its placing of the Melaka Sultanate as the founding narrative of the region's history. It was the first history of its kind to reflect the structure of Malaysia's post-colonial Melaka-centric national narrative and helped reify the present boundaries of Tanah Melayu. The historical consciousness that Winstedt's *Tawarikh Melayu* helped cultivate amongst its readers is an example of British colonialism's far-reaching intellectual transformation of the historical consciousness of the people in the region, as acknowledged by Za'ba.

The continued legacy of Winstedt's Melaka-centric interpretation of Tanah Melayu or Malaya's history can be observed in Malaysia's national narrative, which speaks broadly about colonialism in the historical discourse of post-colonial societies. Malaysia's current secondary school history textbook, for example, positions the Melaka-Johor Sultanate at the centre of Malaysia's pre-twentieth century history, as Winstedt had done in *Tawarikh Melayu* and his other historical works. His works are also referenced in the bibliography of Malaysia's secondary school history textbook, demonstrating the importance his work continues to enjoy in Malays(si)a's national narrative. The Malay- and Melaka-centric narrative that Winstedt features in *Tawarikh Melayu* gives a unifying founding narrative to the nation—built on the foundations of the Melaka-Johor Sultanate. His focus on the Malay monarchs as the central force of Malay history also complements Malay(si)a's postcolonial nation-building narrative of a country that comprises a federation of sultanates that are somehow linked back to Melaka.[468] His sketch of Tanah Melayu as culturally and historically Malay, disregarding the minorities with a historical presence in the region, furthermore suits Malaysia's postcolonial nation-state narrative well, which remains Peninsular- or Tanah

---

[468] Anthony Milner and Wilbert W. W. Wong, "Winstedt, Colonialism and the Malaysian History Wars," *Indonesia and the Malay World* 52, no. 133 (2024): 7.

Melayu-centric. The legacies of Winstedt's interpretation of Tanah Melayu history in Malaysia's state narrative reveal the irony of how both nationalist and colonial discourses can operate in a common narrative.[469]

In Malaysia, Winstedt's works such as *Kitab Tawarikh Melayu* provide historical endorsement to a unifying Malay-centric kerajaan history that is ideal for nation-building. In Singapore, his Malay-centric histories have been used to challenge the pluralistic narrative of Singapore's history, a narrative which has been charged with favouring the Chinese and disregarding the Malays' historical presence on the island. Singapore falls within the scope of Winstedt's Tanah Melayu. His historical construction of Tanah Melayu challenges Singapore's postcolonial state narrative because it serves as a model for bringing Malays to the forefront of Singapore's history. This can be seen in how his works have been recently used to criticize Singapore's historiography for its failure to acknowledge its Malay past. In Winstedt's Tanah Melayu, Singapore was part of a Malay kerajaan that had historical and cultural links to the Melaka-Johor Sultanate. This narrative, however, has been at least partially adapted into Singapore's nation-state history as the contents of the recent edition of Singapore's Secondary 1 history textbook have shown. The inclusion of Singapore as part of the histories of Srivijaya and, later, the Melaka and Johor sultanates, helps give the impression that Singapore has a long continuous historical existence that predates the colonial period. This complements the state's narrative because it shows Singapore's older historical and traditional roots. This inclusion also addresses some criticisms that have been levelled against Singapore's state history for starting only in 1819. It is possible to reconcile Singapore's past to Tanah Melayu in a strategic way that complements its national narrative while doing justice to Singapore's diverse, multicultural past.

---

[469] Ibid. 16; Partha Chartterjee, *Nationalist Thought and the Colonial World* (New York: Zed, 1986), 38.

Including the Melaka- and Johor-centric narrative of Tanah Melayu in Singapore's historiography also helps to furnish Singapore with a distinct national identity. The Melaka and Johor sultanates were shown to have gone into decline at the end of the prehistory section of Singapore's textbook. The colonial period was a turning point that gave Singapore a new beginning and helped define its character as a modern nation-state. From this point onward, Singapore started to diverge from Tanah Melayu (or Malaysia) in its historical development due to the initiatives of colonial state-building. Singapore's new identity made it distinct from the region despite shared historical roots.

The use of Winstedt's historical construction of Tanah Melayu to both undermine and complement Singapore's national narrative points to the legacy of his historical construction of the region in the nation-state historiographies of both Singapore and Malaysia.

Bibliography

Prologue

Kratoska, Paul H., Remco Raben, and Henk Schulte Nordholt. *Locating Southeast Asia: Geographies of Knowledge and Politics of Space*. Singapore: NUS Press, 2005.

Wang, Gungwu. "Before Southeast Asia: Passages and Terrains." In *ISEAS at 50: Understanding Southeast Asia Past and Present*, by Lee Hsien Loong, Leonard Y. Andaya, and Wang Gungwu. Singapore: ISEAS–Yusof Ishak Institute, 2018.

Wang, Gungwu. "From Nusantara Local to Maritime Global." Asian Civilisations Museum, 2023.

White, Hayden. *Metahistory: The Historical Imagination in Nineteenth-Century Europe*. Baltimore, Maryland: JHU Press, 2014.

The Dialogue between Past and Present in the Reimagining of Pre-Colonial Singapore

Bonny, Tan. "Constance Mary Turnbull." In Singapore Infopedia. Singapore: National Library Board, 2016.

Borschberg, Peter. "Singapore in the Cycles of the Longue Durée." *Journal of the Malaysian Branch of the Royal Asiatic Society* 90, no. 1 (2017): 29–60.

Borschberg. "Singapore's Longer History." *Jahrbuch Für Europäische Überseegeschichte* 19 (2019): 35–57.

Borschberg, Peter, and Benjamin J.Q. Khoo. "Singapore as a Port City, c.1290–1819: Evidence, Frameworks and Challenges."

Journal of the Malaysian Branch of the Royal Asiatic Society 91, no. 314 (2018): 1–27.

Delaye, Karine, Karl Hack, and Jean-Louis Margolin, eds. *Singapore from Temasek to the 21st Century: Reinventing the Global City*. NUS Press, 2010. https://doi.org/10.2307/j.ctv1qv3pw.

Hannigan, Tim. "The Myth and the Man: Bringing Singaporean History Out of Stamford Raffles' Shadow." Asian Civilisations Museum, 2023.

Heng, Derek. "Casting Singapore's History in the Longue Durée." In *Singapore from Temasek to the 21st Century: Reinventing the Global City*, edited by Karine Delaye, Karl Hack, and Jean-Louis Margolin. NUS Press, 2010. https://doi.org/10.2307/j.ctv1qv3pw.

Kheng, Cheah Boon. "*Review of The Makers and Keepers of Singapore History*, edited by Loh Kah Seng and Liew Khai Khiun." *Journal of the Malaysian Branch of the Royal Asiatic Society* 84, no. 1 (300) (2011): 109–111.

Khoo, Benjamin J.Q. and Peter Borschberg. *Knowing Singapore: The Evolution of Published Information in Europe, c.1500–1819*. Malaysian Branch of the Royal Asiatic Society, 2023.

Kwa, Chong Guan. "Editorial Foreword: The Singapore Bicentennial as Public History." *Journal of Southeast Asian Studies* 50, no. 4 (2019): 469–475. https://doi.org/10.1017/S0022463420000120.

Kwa, Chong Guan, ed. *1819 & Before: Singapore's Pasts*. Singapore: ISEAS Publishing, 2021.

Kwa. *Singapore Chronicles: Pre-Colonial Singapore*. Singapore: Straits Times Press, 2017.

Kwa. *Shipwrecks and the Maritime History of Singapore*. Singapore: ISEAS Publishing, 2023.

Kwa, Chong Guan, and Peter Borschberg, eds. *Studying Singapore before 1800*. Singapore: NUS Press, 2018.

Kwa, Chong Guan, and Chi Tim Ho. "Archival Records in the Writing of Singapore History: A Perspective from the

Archives." In *The Makers and Keepers of Singapore History*, edited by Kah Seng Loh and Kai Khiun Liew. Singapore: Ethos Books, 2010, 48–64.

Kwa, and Ho. "Archives in the Making of Post-Colonial Singapore." In *Colonial Legacy in South East Asia: The Dutch Archives*, edited by C. Jeurgens, T. Kappelhof, and M. Karabinos. The Hague: Stichting Archiefpublicaties, 2012, 125–150.

Kwa, Chong Guan, Derek Heng, Peter Borschberg, and Tan Tai Yong. *Seven Hundred Years: A History of Singapore*. Singapore: National Library Board and Marshall Cavendish Editions, 2019.

Loh, Kah Seng, Ping Tjin Thum, and Jack Meng-Tat Chia, eds. *Living with Myths in Singapore*. Singapore: Ethos Books, 2021.

Miksic, John N. *Singapore & the Silk Road of the Sea, 1300–1800*. Singapore: NUS Press, 2013.

Sa'at, Alfian, Faris Joraimi, and Siew Min Sai, eds. *Raffles Renounced: Towards a Merdeka History*. Singapore: Ethos Books, 2021.

Sinnathamby Rajaratnam. "Speech by Mr S Rajaratnam, Second Deputy Prime Minister (Foreign Affairs), at a Seminar on 'Adaptive Reuse: Integrating Traditional Areas Into The Modern Urban Fabric' Held at the Shangri-La Hotel on Saturday, 28 April 1984 at 10.30 A.M." June 13, 1984, Archives & Oral History Department Singapore, https://www.nas.gov.sg/archivesonline/speeches/record-details/79c7d80b-115d-11e3-83d5-0050568939ad.

Singapore Bicentennial Office. "About the Singapore Bicentennial." The Singapore Bicentennial, 2020. https://www.sg/sgbicentennial/about/.

Singapore: The Making of a Nation-State, 1300-1975. Textbook. Secondary One. Singapore: Curriculum Planning & Development Division, Ministry of Education, 2014.

Syed, Farid Alatas. "Introduction." In *Thomas Stamford Raffles: Schemer or Reformer?*, by Syed Hussein Alatas. Singapore: National University of Singapore Press, 2020.

The Straits Times. "Raffles: How He Nearly Came off His Empress Place Pedestal." August 7, 1969.

Tregonning, Kennedy Gordon. "The Historical Background." In *Modern Singapore*, edited by Hai Ding Chiang and Jin-Bee Ooi. Singapore: Singapore University Press, n.d.

Wang, Gungwu. "From Nusantara Local to Maritime Global: Singapore and the Reimagining of Southeast Asia." Asian Civilisations Museum, 2023.

Wong, Lin Ken. "A View of Our Past." In *Singapore in Pictures, 1819-1945*, edited by Yik Lee and C.C. Chang. Singapore: Sin Chew Jit Poh and Ministry of Culture, 1981.

Chapter 1: Sources for the Study of Singapore before 1800

Maps and Manuscripts

Canberra: National Library of Australia, Ms. 10724. Bremond, 1687–1688. "Journal of a voyage from Brest to Siam in l'Oiseau".

Lisbon, *Codex Castelo Melhor*, private collection of Francisco Vasconcelos e Sousa.

Munich, Bayerische Staatsbibliothek, Ms. Cod. Icon. 138, Robert Dudley, *Arcano del Mare* (1636), vol. I.

Paris, Bibliothèque Nationale de France (BNF), GE SH 18 PF 199 DIV 3 P 1 D, Anonymous, *Carte de l'isle Thimon en Malacca: corrigée sur les lieux en passant sur le vaisseau du roi l'loyseau ou la trace dudit vaisseau est marquée pars de points rouges et le mouillages comme cy après* (Map of the island Tioman at the Melaka [Peninsula]: corrected on-site while passing on the [French] king's ship *l'Oyseau,* where the path of the said ship is marked by red dots together with the anchorages), 1687.

Paris, BNF, Collection d'Anville, 07101 B, Bellin, *Carte du Detroit de Malacca* (Map of the Melaka Strait), 1760.

Printed studies and sources

Albuquerque, B. de, *Comentarios de Afonso d'Albuqerque*, edited by J.V. Serrão, text of the 2nd edition of 1576, 2 vols. (Lisbon: Imprensa Nacional–Casa de Moeda, 1973).

Albuquerque, *Commentaries of the Great Afonso Dalboquerque, Second Viceroy of India: Translated from the Portuguese Edition of 1774*, edited and translated by W. de Gray Birch, 4 vols. (London: Hakluyt Society, 1875–1884).

Andaya, L.Y., *The Kingdom of Johor 1641–1728: Economic and Political Developments* (Kuala Lumpur: Oxford University Press, 1975).

Barros, J. de, *Décadas da Ásia* (Lisbon: Sá da Costa Editora, 1945–1946).

Borschberg, P., *Admiral Matelieff's Singapore and Johor (1606–1616)* (Singapore: NUS Press, 2016).

Borschberg, "Alatas' Raffles. A Review of Syed Hussein Alatas' Thomas Stamford Raffles", *Singapore Journal of Tropical Geography*, 43, 1 (2022): 110–112.

Borschberg, *Jacques de Coutre's Singapore and Johor (c.1594-1625)* (Singapore: NUS Press, 2015).

Borschberg, "Jacques de Coutre as a Source for the Early 17th Century History of Singapore, the Johor River, and the Straits", *Journal of the Malaysian Branch of the Royal Asiatic Society*, 81, 2 (2008): 71–97.

Borschberg, *Mapping Singapore Before 1819* (Singapore, NUS Press, forthcoming).

Borschberg, "Portuguese and Dutch Records for Singapore before 1819: An Overview", in *1819 & Before: Singapore's Pasts*, edited by Kwa Chong Guan (Singapore: ISEAS Publishing, 2021), 88–99.

Borschberg, *Reconstructing Singapore, c.1500-1800* (Singapore: NUS Press, forthcoming).

Borschberg, *The Singapore and Melaka Straits: Violence, Security and Diplomacy in the 17th Century* (Singapore and Leiden: NUS Press and KITLV Press, 2010).

Borschberg, "Singapura in Early Modern Cartography: A Sea of Challenges", in *Visualising Space: Maps of Singapore and the Region. Collections from the National Archives and National Library of Singapore* (Singapore: National Library Board, 2015), 6–33.

Borschberg, "Urban Impermanence on the Southern Malay Peninsula: The Case of Batu Sawar Johor (c.1587-1615)", *Journal of East Asian Urban History* 3, 1 (2021): 57–82.

Carey, Daniel, and Claire Jowitt, eds. *Richard Hakluyyt and Travel Writing in Early Modern Europe* (Abingdon: Routledge, 2016).

Chew, E.C.T., and E. Lee, eds. *A History of Singapore* (Singapore: Oxford University Press, 1991).

Chew and Syed Hussein Alatas, "A controversy on Raffles", *Suara University* 3 (1972): 49–61.

Coleridge, Henry J., ed. *The Life and Letters of St. Francis Xavier*, 2 vols. (London: Burns and Oates, 1872–1876).

Coutre, J. de, *Journal, Memorials and Letters of Cornelis Matelieff de Jonge: Security, Diplomacy and Commerce in 17th-century Southeast Asia*, edited by P. Borschberg and translated by R. Roy (Singapore: NUS Press, 2014).

Crawfurd, John, *Descriptive Dictionary of the Indian Islands and Adjacent Countries* (London: Bradbury and Evans, 1856).

Cruysse, Dirk van der, *Louis XIV et le Siam* (Paris: Fayard, 1991).

Cruysse, *Siam and the West, 1500–1700* (Chiang Mai: Silkworm Books, 2002).

Defoe, Daniel, *The Life, Adventures, and Pyracies, of the Famous Captain Singleton* (London: Printed for J. Brotherton, 1720).

Gibson-Hill, C.A., "Singapore: Notes on the History of the Old Strait, 1580–1850", *JMBRAS* 27, 1: 175–176.

Gibson-Hill, "Singapore Old Strait and New Harbour, 1300-1870", *Memoirs of the Raffles Museum,* no. 3 (1956): 11–115, reproduced in KBSS, 211–308.

Han Wai Toon, "A Study on Johore Lama", *Journal of the South Seas Society* 5 (1948): 17–35 (in English) and ibid., 5–25 (in Chinese).

Hassel, J.G.H., *Geographisch-Statistisches Handwörterbuch: nach den neuesten Quellen und Hülfsmitteln*, 2 vols. (Weimar: Im Verlage des geographischen Instituts, 1817).

Hsü Yün-T'siao, "Notes on the Malay Peninsula in ancient voyages", *JSSS* 5 (1948): 1–16 (in English) and ibid., 25–39 (in Chinese).

Hsü Yün-T'siao, "Singapore in the Remote Past", *Journal of the Malaysian Branch of the Royal Asiatic Society (JMBRAS)* 45, 1 (1972): 1–9, or its reprint in KBSS, 38–52.

Khoo, Benjamin J.Q., "The Changing Fortunes of the Raja Negara and the Orang Laut of Singapore in the 18th Century", *Temasek Working Papers Series,* no. 7 (2024): 1–32.

Khoo, Benjamin J.Q., and P. Borschberg, *Knowing Singapore. The Evolution of Published Information in Europe, c.1500–1819* (Kuala Lumpur: Malaysian Branch of the Royal Asiatic Society, 2023).

Khoo Chun Yok, Jeff, "French encounters with the Straits Entrepot, 1680-1787" (doctoral dissertation, Department of History, National University of Singapore, 2024).

Kwa, Chong Guan, *Singapore Chronicles: Precolonial Singapore* (Singapore: Straits Times Press, 2017).

Kwa, "Raffles and the writing of Asia-Centric History. A review of Syed Hussein Alatas, *Thomas Stamford Raffles*", *Singapore Journal of Tropical Geography,* 43, 1 (2022): 116–119.

Kwa, Chong Guan, Derek T.S. Heng, and Tan Tai Yong, *Singapore, a 700-Year History from Early Emporium to World City* (Singapore: National Archives of Singapore, 2009).

Kwa, Chong Guan and P. Borschberg, eds. *Studying Singapore before 1800* (Singapore: NUS Press, 2018).

Kwa, Chong Guan, Derek Heng, P. Borschberg, Jeff C.Y. Khoo, and Tan Tai Yong, *Seven Hundred Years: A History of Singapore*, rev. ed. (Singapore: National Library of Singapore, 2026).

Lim, Arthur J.J., "The Geography and Early History of Singapore", in *A History of Singapore,* edited by E.C.T. Chew and E. Lee (Singapore: Oxford University Press, 1991).

Linschoten, J.H. van, *The voyage of John Huyghen van Linschoten to the East Indies: from the old English translation of 1598,* edited by A.C. Burnell and P.A. Tiele, 2 vols. (London: Hakluyt Society, 1874, reprint 1885).

Linschoten, *Voyage ofte schipvaert van Jan Huygen* van Linschoten *naer Oost ofte Portugaels Indiën, 1579–1592, vierde deel: Reys-Gheschrift vande Navigatiën der Portugaloysers,* edited by J.C.M. Warnsinck and Linschoten Vereeniging (The Hague: Martinus Nijhoff, 1939), vol. IV, 97–99.

Macgregor, Ian A., "Johore Lama in the Sixteenth Century", *JMBRAS* 28, 2 (1955): 48–125.

Macgregor, "Notes on the Portuguese in Malaya", *JMBRAS* 28, 2 (1955): 4–47.

Macgregor, "Johore Lama in the Sixteenth Century", *JMBRAS* 28, 2 (1955): 48–125, and its reprint in KBSS, 206–220.

Manguin, P.Y., "A mid-17th century collection of roteiros for Asian waters", *Studia,* 48 (1989): 187–212.

Marks, Harry, *The First Contest for Singapore* (The Hague: Martinus Nijhoff, 1959).

Matos, L.J., "Roteiros e rotas portuguesas do oriente nos séculos XVI e XVII" (doctoral dissertation, University of Lisbon, 2016).

Miksic, J.N., *Singapore and the Silk Road of the Sea* (Singapore: NUS Press, 2013).

Netscher, E., *De Nederlanders in Djohor en Siak, 1602–1867* (Batavia: Bruining & Wijt, 1870).

Schürhammer, Georg, ed. *Francisco Javier: su vida y su tiempo,* 4 vols. (Pamplona: Gobierno de Navarra, 1992).

Syed Hussein Alatas, *Thomas Stamford Raffles: Schemer or Reformer?,* reprint with a foreword by Farid Alatas (National University of Singapore Press, 2020).

Temple, Richard C., "Some Discursive Comments on Barbosa", *The Indian Antiquary: A Journal of Oriental Research, etc,* 52 (1923): 130–139.

Tibbetts, Gerard R., *A Study of the Arabic Texts Containing Material on South-East Asia* (London and Leiden: E.J. Brill, 1979).

Tregonning, Kennedy G., "The Historical Background", in *Modern Singapore,* edited by O. Jin-Bee and C.H. Ding (Singapore: Singapore University Press, 1969).

Turnbull, C.M., *A History of Modern Singapore, 1819–2005* (Singapore: NUS Press, 2009).

Turnbull, *A History of Singapore, 1819–1975* (Kuala Lumpur: Oxford University Press, 1977).

Urville, D.S.C. Dumont de, and C.A. Vicendo-Dumoulin, *Voyage au Pôle Sud et dans l'Océanie sur les corvettes Astrolabe et La Zélée par ordre du roi pendant les années 1837, 1839, 1840*, 10 vols. (Paris: Gids & C.ie, 1841–1846).

Wheatley, Paul, *Impressions of the Malay Peninsula in Ancient Times* (Singapore: Eastern Universities Press, 1964).

Wheatley, *The Golden Khersonese: Studies in the Historical Geography of the Malay Peninsula before A.D. 1500*. (Kuala Lumpur: University of Malaya Press, 1961).

Winius, George D., and C.C. Chorba, "Literary Invasions in La vida de Jaques de Coutre: do they prejudice its value as an historical source?", in *A Carreira da Índia e as Rotas dos Estreitos: Actas do VIII Seminário Internacional de História Indo Portuguesa*, edited by Arturo Teodoro de Matos and Luís Filipe Reis Thomaz (Angra do Heroísmo: Barbosa & Javier, 1998), 709–719.

Wong, L.K., "The Trade of Singapore, 1819–1869", *JMBRAS* 33, 4 (1960): 4–315.

Wong, "Singapore: Its Growth as an Entrepot Port, 1819–1941", *Journal of Southeast Asian Studies (JSEAS)* 9, 1 (1978): 50–84.

Won Lin Ken, "A View of Our Past", in *Singapore in Pictures, 1819-1945*, edited by Lee Yik and C.C. Chang (Singapore: Sin Chew Jit Poh and Ministry of Culture, 1981).

Zedler, J.H., *Grosses vollständiges Universal-Lexicon aller Wissenschafften und Künste*, 64 vols. (Leipzig and Halle: Verlag Heinrich Zedler, 1732–54). This publication is freely accessible at www.zedler-lexikon.de (accessed on 17 Aug. 2024).

Chapter 2: Archaeology in the Writing of Singapore's History

Abdul Rahman, N.H.S.N., "Current issues on prehistory and protohistory in Malaysian archaeology", *JMBRAS* 80, no. 1 (2007): 41–57.

Abdul Rahman, and Zuliskandar Ramli, eds. *Prasejarah dan Protosejarah Tanah Melayu; Sejarah Nasional Malaysia* (Kuala Lumpur: Dewan Bahasa dan Pustaka, 2021).

Anon, Fourth Intra-ASEAN Archaeological and Conservation Workshop Singapore, 1–21 November 1987, *Report* deposited in https://eservice.nlb.gov.sg/item_holding.aspx?bid=5295851.

Anon, *Hoard of Chinese Porcelain (A Rare Discovery from Firoz Shah Kotla)* (New Delhi: Archaeological Survey of India, 2017).

Bellina, B., "Was there a Late Prehistoric Integrated Southeast Asia Maritime Space? Insight from Settlements and Industries", in *Spirits and Ships: Cultural Transfers in Early Monsoon Asia*, edited by A. Acri and others (Singapore: ISEAS–Yusof Ishak Institute, 2017), 239–272.

Caple, C., *Objects: Reluctant Witnesses to the Past* (London: Routledge, 2006).

Chasen, F.N., and M.W.F Tweedie, eds. *Proceedings of the Third Congress of Prehistorians of the Far East, Singapore, 24th January – 30th January 1938* (Singapore: Government Printers/ Washington D.C.: U.S. Government Printing Office, 1940).

Chia, S., "A history of Archaeology in Malaysia", in *Handbook of East & Southeast Asian Archaeology*, edited by Junko Habo and others (New York: Springer, 2017), 125–141.

Chia, and Velat Bueng, eds. *Arkeologi di Malaysia: Sejarah, Warisan dan Kebudayaan* (Kuala Lumpur: Dewan Bahasa dan Pustaka, 2020).

Choo-Avieropoulou, A., *Report on the Excavation at Fort Canning Hill* (Singapore: National Museum, 1986).

Choo-Avieropoulou, *Archaeology; A Guide to the Collections, National Museum Singapore* (Singapore: National Museum of Singapore, 1987).

Clinnick, D., and S. Lim, "In search of prehistoric Singapore", *MuseSG* 10 no. 36, issue 2 (Singapore: National Heritage Board, 2018): 40–42.

Collins, H.D., "Recent finds of Iron Age sites in southern Perak and Selangor", *Bulletin of the Raffles Museum* series B, 1 pt. 2 (1937): 75–92.

Cooke Jr., S., *Global Objects: Toward a Connected Art History* (Princeton: Princeton University Press, 2022).
Denham, T., "Domestic dispersal, human agency and connectivity in Island Southeast Asia during the Holocene", in *Globalization in prehistory: Contact, exchange and the 'People Without History'*, eds. N. Boivin and M.D. Frachetti (Cambridge: Cambridge University Press, 2018), 81.
Foo Shu Teng, "Hoabinhian rocks: An examination of Guar Kepah artifacts from the Heritage Conservation Centre in Jurong" (MA Thesis, National University of Singapore, 2010), DOI:10.13140/RG.2.2.28005.29929).
Gerritsen, A., *The City of Blue and White; Chinese Porcelain and the Early Modern World* (Cambridge: University Press, 2020).
Gibson-Hill, C.A., "Johore Lama and other ancient sites on the Johore River", *JMBRAS* 28, part 2 (1955): 126–197.
Heng, D., "Temasik as an International and Regional Trading Port in the Thirteenth and Fourteenth Centuries: A Reconstruction Based on Recent Archaeological Data", *JMBRAS* 72, no. 1 (1999): 113–124.
Heng, D., "Reconstructing Banzu: a Fourteenth Century Port Settlement in Singapore", *JMBRAS* 75, no. 1 (2002): 69–90.
Heng, "Regional Influences, Economic Adaption and Cultural Articulation: Diversity and Cosmopolitism in Fourteenth-century Singapore", *Journal of Southeast Asian Studies* 50, no. 4 (2019): 476–488. DOI: https://doi.org/10.1017/S0022463420000016.
Heng, "Urban Demographics along the Asian Maritime Silk Road", in *The Maritime Silk Road: Global Connectivities, Regional Nodes, Localities*, edited by F. Billé and others (Amsterdam: Amsterdam University Press, 2022), 215–241.
Kwa, C.G., "16th century underglazed blue porcelain sherds from the Kallang estuary", in *Early Singapore 1300s-1819: Evidence in maps, text and artefacts*, edited by J.N. Miksic and C.A. Low Mei Gek (Singapore: Singapore History Museum, 2004), 86–94.
Kwa, "A Seventeenth-Century Port Settlement in the Kallang Estuary", in *Shipwrecks and the Maritime History of Singapore*,

edited by Kwa Chong Guan (Singapore: ISEAS–Yusof-Ishak Institute, 2023), 70–79.

Kwa, ed. *Shipwrecks and the Maritime History of Singapore* (Singapore: ISEAS–Yusof Ishak Institute, 2023).

Luyt, B., "Collectors and collecting for the Raffles Museum in Singapore 1920–1940", *Library & Information History* 26, no. 3 (2013): 183–195, DOI: 10.1179/175834810X12731358995235.

Macgregor, I.A., "Johore Lama in the sixteenth century", *JMBRAS* 28, part 2 (1955): 48–125.

Masihi, A., *Seramik empayar Johor: Abad 11–19* (Kuala Lumpur: Jabatan Muzium Malaysia, 2012).

Miksic, J.N., *Archaeological Research on the "Forbidden Hill" of Singapore: Excavations at Fort Canning, 1984* (Singapore: National Museum, 1986).

Miksic, J.N., *Singapore & the Silk Road of the Sea, 1300–1800* (Singapore: NUS Press, 2013), 222–229.

Movius Jr., H.L., "Palaeolithic archaeology in Southern and Eastern Asia, exclusive of India", *Cahiers d'histoire Mondiale* 2/iii (1955): 511–512.

Muhamazd, A., ed. *Arkeologie di Malaysia dahulu dan kini* (Bangi: Penerbit Universiti Kebangsaan Malaysia, 2018).

Pearson, N., *Belitung: The Afterlives of a Shipwreck* (Honolulu: University of Hawai'I Press, 2023).

Pope, J.A., *Chinese Porcelains from the Ardebil Shrine* (London: Sotheby Parke Bernet,1981, 2nd edn.).

Sieveking, G. de G., "Excavations at Gua Cha, Kelantan, 1954, Part 1", *Federation Museums Journal* 1–2 (1954–1955): 75–138.

Sieveking, "The fortified city of Johore Lama, and the use of archaeological evidence", *JMBRAS* 28, part 2 (1955): 198–199.

Sieveking, G. de G., P. Wheatley, and C.A. Gibson-Hill, "Archaeological discoveries in Malaya (1953): The excavations at Johore Lama", *Journal of the Malayan Branch of the Royal Asiatic Society* [*JMBRAS*] 27, part 2 (1954): 224–233.

Taha, A.H., "Archaeology in Peninsula Malaysia: Past, Present and Future", *Journal of Southeast Asian Studies* 18, issue 2 (1987): 205–211.

Taha, ed. *Tamadun Prasejarah Malaysia/Prehistoric Civilization of Malaysia*, revised edition (Kuala Lumpur: Muzium Negara, 2022).

Wai-yee Wong, S., "A Case Report on the Function(s) of the 'Mercury jar': Fort Canning, Singapore, in the 14th Century", *Archaeological Research in Asia* 7 (2016): 10–17.

Williams-Hung, P.D.R., "Recent archaeological discoveries in Malaya (1845–1950)", *JMBRAS* 24, no. 1 (1951): 191.

Zaini, S.A., "Metal Production and Social Organization in Fourteenth Century Singapore", *Journal of Southeast Asian Studies* 59, no. 4 (2019): 489–506. DOI: https://doi.org/10.1017/S0022463420000028.

Chapter 3: Confronting 'The Singapore Story': Colonial Rule And The Power Of History-Making

Benedict, A., *Imagined Communities: Reflections on the Origin and Spread of Nationalism* (London: Verso, 2006).

Barr, M., "Background figures in a British portrait: the Johor royal family in nineteenth-century Singapore", *History Australia* 18, no. 2 (2021): 283–301.

Barr, M., "Singapore Comes to Terms with its Malay Past: The Politics of Crafting a National History", *Asian Studies Review* 46, no. 2 (2022): 350–368.

Bayly, C.A., *Empire and Information: Intelligence Gathering and Social Communication in India, c1780–1870* (Cambridge: Cambridge University Press, 1996).

Biggar, N., *Colonialism: a Moral Reckoning* (London: William Collins, 2023).

Bloxham, D., *Why history: a history* (Oxford: Oxford University Press, 2020).

Burke, E., *The Project Gutenberg EBook of The Works of the Right Honourable Edmund Burke*, Vol. X. (of 12), 2006.

Chong, T., "The Bicentennial Commemoration: Imagining and Re-imagining Singapore's History", *Southeast Asian Affairs*, no. 1 (2020): 323–334.

Cohn, B.S., *Colonialism and its forms of knowledge: the British in India* (London: Princeton University Press, 1996).

Colley, L., *The Gun, the Ship and the Pen: Warfare, Constitutions and the Making of the Modern World* (London: Profile, 2021).

Crawfurd, J., *Journal of an Embassy from the Governor-General of India to the Courts of Siam and Cochin China, Exhibiting a View of the Actual State of Those Kingdoms*, 2nd ed. (London: Henry Colburn and Richard Bentley, 1830).

Crawfurd, *History of the Indian Archipelago: Containing an Account of the Manners, Art, Languages, Religions, Institutions, and Commerce of Its Inhabitants* (Cambridge University Press, 2013).

Hagerman, C.A., *Britain's Imperial Muse: The Classics, Imperialism, and the Indian Empire, 1784–1914* (New York: Palgrave Macmillan, 2013).

Harper, T., *The End of Empire and the Making of Malaya* (Cambridge: Cambridge University Press, 1999).

Hingley, R., *Roman Officers and English Gentlemen: The Imperial Origins of Roman Archaeology* (London: Taylor & Francis, 2013).

Knapman, G., "Unencumbered by the Scruples of Justice and Good Faith", *in The Colonial Achievements of Raffles in Southeast Asia, The Truth About Empire: Real Histories of British Colonialism*, edited by A. Lester (London: Hurst & Company, 2024), 121–146.

Knapman, "Uninhabited Islands in the Bay of Bengal, Penang, Singapore and Botany Bay: What Did Terra Nullius Mean in British Colonial Thinking?", *Australian Historical Studies*, vol. 55, no. 3, 2 (2024): 444–463.

Knapman, *Race and British Colonialism in Southeast Asia, 1770–1870: John Crawfurd and the Politics of Equality* (London: Taylor & Francis, 2016).

Knapman, G., and S. Boonstra, "Plunder and Prize in 1812 Java: The Legality and Consequences for Research and Restitution of the Raffles Collections", *Art, Antiquity & Law* 28, no. 3 (2023).

Kwa, C.G., and P. Borschberg, eds. *Studying Singapore before 1800* (Singapore: NUS Press, 2018).

Leyden, J., with an introduction by Stamford Raffles, *Malay Annals (Sejarah Melayu)* (London: Longman, Hurst, Rees, Orme and Brown, 1821).

Lester, A., ed. *The Truth About Empire: Real Histories of British Colonialism* (London: Hurst, 2024).

Metcalf, T.R., *Ideologies of the Raj* (London: Cambridge University Press, 1997).

Mill, J., *History of British India*, 10 vols. (including Horace Hayman Wilson's continuation to 1835) (London: Routledge, 1997).

Miksic, John N. *Singapore & the Silk Road of the Sea, 1300–1800* (Singapore: NUS Press, 2013).

Milner, A., and Wilbert W. W. Wong, "Winstedt, Colonialism and the Malaysian History Wars", *Indonesia and the Malay World* 52 (153): 179–198. doi:10.1080/13639811.2024.2351280.

Noor, Farish A., *Data-Gathering in Colonial Southeast Asia 1800–1900: Framing the Other* (Amsterdam: AUP, 2022).

Noor, *The Discursive Construction of Southeast Asia in 19th Century Colonial-Capitalist Discourse* (Amsterdam: AUP, 2016).

Raffles, T.S., *A History of Java of Cambridge Library Collection–East and South-East Asian History* (Cambridge: Cambridge University Press, 2010).

Satia, P., *Times Monster: History, Conscience and Britain's Empire* (London: Allen Lane, 2020).

Seeley, J.R., *The Expansion of England; Edited and Introduced by John Gross* (Chicago: University of Chicago Press, 1971).

Tarling, Nicholas, ed. *Studying Singapore's Past: C.M. Turnbull and the History of Modern Singapore* (Singapore: NUS Press, 2012).

Vasunia, P., "Memories of Empire: Literature and Art, Nostalgia and Trauma", in the *Oxford World History of Empire, vol. 1: The Imperial Experience*, edited by Peter Fibiger Bang, C. A. Bayly, and Walter Scheidel (Oxford, 2021), 497–522.

Vasunia, "Ethiopia and India: Fusion and Confusion in British Orientalism", in *Les Cahiers d'Afrique d'Est*, No. 51 (2016), 21–43.

Vasunia, "Barbarism and Civilization: Political Writing, History, and Empire", in the *Oxford History of Classical Reception in English Literature, vol. 4: 1790–1880*, edited by Norman Vance and Jennifer Wallace (Oxford: Oxford University Press, 2015), 131–158.

Wilbert W. W. Wong, "Sir Richard Olaf Winstedt and the Historical Creation of 'Malaya' and 'Tanah Melayu'", PhD dissertation, The Australian National University (Australia), 2021.

Chapter 4: Marginal Notes to a Treaty: The Quibble of the Malay Princes

Archival Sources

2.21.007.57, Stukken betreffende Riouw en Malakka. (Oude inv., no. 24 Be.) 1818–1825, Nationaal Archief, The Hague.

NAB 1668, National Archives of Singapore, Singapore.

NAB 1673, National Archives of Singapore, Singapore.

Published Sources

Abdullah bin Abdul Kadir, *The Hikayat Abdullah*, translated by A.H. Hill (Kuala Lumpur: Oxford University Press, 1970).

Aitchison, C.U., *A Collection of Treaties, Engagements, and Sunnuds, Relating to India and Neighbouring Countries*, Vol. 1 (Calcutta: Foreign Office Press, 1876).

Amirell, S., "International Treaties: The Foundations of Colonial Rule in Southeast Asia", *The Newsletter*, no. 95 (2023). Accessed at: https://www.iias.asia/the-newsletter/article/internationaltreaties-foundations-colonial-rule-southeast-asia.

Anon., *Minutes of Evidence Taken Before the Select Committee on the Affairs of the East India Company*, Vol. 14 (London: House of Commons, 1832).

Bastin, J., "Problems of Personality and the Reinterpretations of Modern Malaysian History", in *Malayan and Indonesian*

Studies: Essays Presented to Sir Richard Winstedt on His Eighty-Fifth Birthday, edited by J.S. Bastin and R. Roolvink (Oxford: Clarendon Press, 1964), 141–153.

Braddell, T., "Notices of Singapore", *The Journal of the Indian Archipelago and Eastern Asia*, Vol. VII (1855): 349–354.

Buckley, C., *An Anecdotal History of Old Times in Singapore, etc.*, Vol. 1 (Singapore: Fraser and Neave, 1902).

Frost, M., and Yu-Mei Balasingamchow, *Singapore: A Biography* (Singapore: Didier Millet, 2009).

Khoo, J.Q.B., "The Changing Fortunes of the Raja Negara and the Orang Laut of Singapore", *Temasek Working Paper Series* 7 (2024).

Khoo, K., "A Treaty Most Unfriendly" in *50 Records from History: Highlights of the National Archives of Singapore* (Singapore: National Archives of Singapore, 2019), 20–21.

Knapman, G., "Settler Colonialism and Usurping Malay Sovereignty in Singapore", *Journal of Southeast Asian Studies* 52, no. 3 (2021): 418–440.

Milner, A., *The Malays* (Chichester: Wiley-Blackwell, 2008).

National Archives of Singapore (NAS), IOR/H/641, manuscript copy of the 1824 Treaty, dated September 1841, 547–556.

Trocki, C., *Prince of Pirates: The Temenggongs and the Development of Johor and Singapore, 1784–1885* (Singapore: NUS Press, 2007).

Turnbull, C.M., *A History of Modern Singapore, 1819–2005* (Singapore: NUS Press, 2009).

Wake, C.H., "Raffles and the Rajas: The Founding of Singapore in Malayan and British Colonial History", *Journal of the Malaysian Branch of the Royal Asiatic Society* 48, no. 1 (1975): 47–73.

Chapter 5: Raffles and the Coloniality of History

Aas, Katja F., "Visions of Global Control: Cosmopolitan Aspirations in a World of Friction", in *What is Criminology?*, edited by M. Bosworth and C. Hoyle (Oxford: Oxford University Press, 2011).

Aas, "The Earth is One but the World is Not: Criminological Theory and its Geopolitical Divisions", *Theoretical Criminology* 16, 1(2012): 5–20.

Ahmat A. *Letters of Sincerity: The Raffles Collection of Malay Letters (1780–1824). A Descriptive Account with Notes and Translation* (Kuala Lumpur: Malaysian Branch of the Royal Asiatic Society, 2009).

Alatas, Syed F., "Knowledge hegemonies and autonomous knowledge", Third World Quarterly (2022): 1–18. https://doi.org/10.1080/01436597.2022.2124155.

Alatas, S.H., "Theoretical Aspects of Southeast Asian History: John Bastin and the Study of Southeast Asian History", *Asian Studies* 2, 2 (1964): 247–260.

Alatas, *Thomas Stamford Raffles: Schemer or Reformer* (Sydney: Angus & Robertson, 1971).

Alatas, *The Myth of the Lazy Native: A Study of the Image of the Malays, Filipinos and Javanese from the 16th to the 20th Century and its Function in the Ideology of Colonial Capitalism* (London: Frank Cass, 1977).

Alatas, *Thomas Stamford Raffles: Schemer or Reformer* (Singapore: National University Press, 2020).

Aveling, H., "1819: Isa Kamari on the Foundation of Singapore", *Asiatic* 8, 2 (2014): 88–108.

Bastin, J., "The Study of Modern Southeast Asian History: An Inaugural Lecture delivered in the University of Malaya in Kuala Lumpur on 14 December 1959, Kuala Lumpur", University of Malaya, 1959.

Bastin, J., "The Western Element in Modern Southeast Asian History", Papers on Southeast Asian Subjects, no. 2 (Kuala Lumpur: Department of History, University of Malaya, 1960).

Carey, P., *The Power of Prophecy: Prince Dipanagara and the End of an Old Order in Java, 1785–1855* (Leiden: Brill, 2007).

Carrington, K., R. Hogg, and M. Sozzo, "Southern Criminology", *British Journal of Criminology* 56 (2016): 1–20

Césaire, A., *Discourse on Colonialism* (New York & London: Monthly Review, 1972).

Derks, H., *History of the Opium Problem: The Assault on the East, Ca. 1600 – 1950* (Leiden: Brill, 2012).

Farish, N.A., "Don't Mention the Corpses: The Erasure of Violence in Colonial Writings on Southeast Asia", *Biblioasia*, 15, 2 (2019).

Furnivall, J.S., *Colonial Policy and Practice: A Comparative Study of Burma and Netherlands India* (New York: New York University Press, 1956).

Hahn, E., *Raffles of Singapore: a Biography* (Kuala Lumpur: University of Malaya Press, 1968).

Hill, A. H., "The Hikayat Abdullah", *Journal of the Malayan Branch of the Roya Asiatic Society* 28, pt. 3 (1955).

Kamari, I., *Duka Tuan Bertakhta (Sadly You Rule)* (Kuala Lumpur: Al-Ameen Serve Holdings, 2011).

Kamari, *1819*, translated by R. Krishnan (Kuala Lumpur: Silverfish, 2013).

Khaldun, Ibn, *Ibn Khaldûn: The Muqadimmah - An Introduction of History*, 3 vols., translated from the Arabic by Franz Rosenthal (London: Routledge & Kegan Paul, 1967).

Kwa C.G., "Introduction", in *Studying Singapore Before 1800*, edited by Kwa Chong Guan & Peter Borschberg (Singapore: NUS Press, 2018), 1–26.

Kwa, "From Temasek to Singapore: Locating a Global City-State in the Cycles of Melaka Straits History", in *Studying Singapore Before 1800*, edited by Kwa Chong Guan & Peter Borschberg (Singapore: NUS Press, 2018), 179–205.

Kwa C.G., D. Heng, and T.T. Yong, *Singapore: A 700-Year History - From Early Emporium to World City* (Singapore: National Archives, 2009).

Markasan, S., "Balada Seorang Lelaki di Depan Patung Raffles - The Ballad of a Man Before the Statue of Raffles", in *Suratman Markasan: Puisi-puisi Pilihan - Selected Poems of Suratman Markasan* (Singapore: NLB, 2014), 18–29.

Moosavi, L., "Decolonising Criminology: Syed Hussein Alatas on Crimes of the Powerful", *Critical Criminology* 27 (2019): 229–242. https://doi.org/10.1007/s10612-018-9396-9.

Multatuli [Eduard Douwes Dekker], *Max Havelaar: or The Coffee Auctions of a Dutch Trading Company* (London: Penguin Books, 1987).

Raffles, T.S., *The History of Java*, 2 vols. (London: Printed for Black, Parbury, and Allen, Booksellers to the Hon. East-India Company and John Murray, 1817).

Rajaratnam, S., "Raja Tells Why We Still Honour Raffles' Name", *The Straits Times*, 25 May 1983.

Rajaratnam, "Untitled Speech", in *The Prophetic and the Political: Selected Speeches and Writings of S. Rajaratnam*, edited by Chan Heng Chee & Obaid Ul Haq (Singapore: Graham Brash, 1987).

Rajaratnam, "S'pore's Future Depends on Shared Memories, Collective Amnesia", *The Straits Times*, 20 June 1990.

Ricklefs, M. C., *A History of Modern Indonesia since c. 1200*, 4th ed. (Houndmills: Palgrave Macmillan, 2008).

Smail, John R. W., "On the Possibility of an Autonomous History of Modern Southeast Asia", *Journal of Southeast Asian History* 2, 2 (1961): 72–102.

Tregonning, K. G., "The Historical Background", in *Modern Singapore*, edited by Ooi Jin-Bee and Chiang Hai Ding (Singapore: Singapore University Press, 1969).

Trocki, C., *Singapore: Wealth, Power and the Culture of Control* (London: Routledge, 2006).

Wright, N., "Farquhar and Raffles: The Untold Story", *Biblioasia* 14, 4 (2019).

Yew, L.K., *From Third World to First: The Singapore Story, 1965-2000* (New York: HarperCollins, 2000).

Chapter 6: The Myth and the Man: Bringing Singapore's History Out of Stamford Raffles' Shadow

Alatas, Syed Hussein, *The Myth of the Lazy Native* (London: Frank Cass and Company, 1977).

Alatas, *Thomas Stamford Raffles, 1781–1826: Schemer or Reformer?* (Sydney: Angus & Robertson, 1971).

Appleyard, Janet, *Raffles Finds a Friend* (Singapore: EPB, 1992).

Barley, Nigel, *The Duke of Puddle Dock: Travels in the Footsteps of Stamford Raffles* (London: Henry Holt & Company, 1991).

Benner, Tom, "Pirate or hero? Raffles bicentennial fuels Singapore debate", *Al Jazeera*, 29 January 2019, available online at https://www.aljazeera.com/news/2019/1/28/pirate-or-hero-raffles-bicentennial-fuels-singapore-debate (accessed 17 January 2025).

Boulger, Demetrius Charles, *Life of Sir Stamford Raffles* (London: Horace Marshall & Son, 1897).

Collis, Maurice, *Raffles* (London: Faber & Faber, 1966).

Glendinning, Victoria, *Raffles and the Golden Opportunity* (London: Profile, 2012).

Grabsky, Phil, *The Lost Temple of Java* (London: Orion, 1999), 45.

Hahn, Emily, *Raffles of Singapore* (New York: Doubleday, 1946).

Ng Yi-Sheng, "Effigies", available online at https://www.facebook.com/groups/singpowrimo/posts/1664082880373623/, accessed 17 January 2025.

Noor, Farish A., *The Discursive Construction of Southeast Asia in 19th Century Colonial-Capitalist Discourse* (Amsterdam: Amsterdam University Press, 2016).

Raffles, Sophia, *Memoir of the Life and Public Services of Sir Thomas Stamford Raffles* (London: John Murray, 1830).

Randall, Lee, "Interview: Victoria Glendinning, author of Raffles and the Golden Opportunity", *The Scotsman*, 3 November 2012.

Sa'at, Alfian, Faris Joraimi, and Sai Siew Min, eds. *Raffles Renounced: Towards a Merdeka History* (Singapore: Ethos Books, 2021).

Said, Edward W., *Orientalism*, 3rd ed. (London: Penguin, 2003), 93.

Wurtzburg, C.E., *Raffles of the Eastern Isles* (London: Hodder and Stoughton, 1954).

Yimin, Zhou, *Stamford Raffles: Founder of Modern Singapore* (Singapore: Asiapac Books, 2002).

Chapter 7: Sultan Ali's Reign and the Impact of the 1855 Treaty: A Reassessment

The Singapore Free Press and Mercantile Advertiser. March 26, 1857. https://eresources.nlb.gov.sg/newspapers/digitised/article/singfreepressa18570326-1.2.4.

Straits Times. June 25, 1859. https://eresources.nlb.gov.sg/newspapers/digitised/article/straitstimes18590625-1.2.4.

Abdul Shukor Ismail, Dato' Haji. *Sejarah Ringkas Muar* (Muar: Penerbitan Toko Buku Manaf, 1984).

Abdullah Zakaria, Ghazali. *Istana Dan Politik Johor, 1835–1885* (Kuala Lumpur: Yayasan Penataran Ilmu, 1997).

Adil, Buyong. *Sejarah Johor* (Dewan Bahasa dan Pustaka, 1980). https://books.google.com.sg/books?id=351uAAAAMAAJ.

American and British Claims Arbitration. U.S. Government Printing Office, 1913. https://books.google.com.sg/books?id=5ygWAAAAYAAJ.

Andaya, Leonard Y. *Leaves of the Same Tree: Trade and Ethnicity in the Straits of Melaka* (Honolulu: University of Hawai'i Press, 2008).

Andaya. "The Makassar War". In *The Heritage of Arung Palakka: A History of South Sulawesi (Celebes) in the Seventeenth Century* (Brill, 1981), 73–99.

Aung-Thwin, Michael. "The British 'Pacification' of Burma: Order without Meaning". *Journal of Southeast Asian Studies* 16, no. 2 (1985): 245–261. http://www.jstor.org.proxy.lib.sg/stable/20070866.

Balfour, E. *The Cyclopædia of India and of Eastern and Southern Asia, Commercial Industrial, and Scientific: Products of the Mineral, Vegetable, and Animal Kingdoms, Useful Arts and Manufactures.* Bernard Quaritch, 1885. https://books.google.com.sg/books?id=vlsIAAAAQAAJ.

Basri, M. A. Fawzi, Haron Hasrom, and Malaysia. Muzium Negara. *Sejarah Johor Moden 1855–1940: Satu Perbicangan Dari Pelbagai Aspek.* Monograf Siri Pustaka Tinta Emas (Kuala Lumpur: Muzium Negara, 1978).

Borschberg, Peter. "The Seizure of the Sta. Catarina Revisited: The Portuguese Empire in Asia, Voc Politics and the Origins of the Dutch-Johor Alliance (1602-C.1616)". *Journal of Southeast Asian Studies* 33, no. 1 (2002): 31–62.

Favre, P.É.L. *An Account of the Wild Tribes Inhabiting the Malayan Peninsula, Sumatra, and a Few Neighbouring Islands: With a Journey in Johore and a Journey in the Menangkabaw States of the Malayan Peninsula.* Printed at the Imperial Printing-office, 1865. https://books.google.com.sg/books?id=W2hfAAAAcAAJ.

"Government Notification". *Singapore Chronicle and Commercial Register*, 18 March, 1837. https://eresources.nlb.gov.sg/newspapers/digitised/article/singchronicle18370318-1.2.2.

Graeber, D. *Debt: The First 5,000 Years, Updated and Expanded* (New York: Melville House, 2014).

Hall, K.R. *A History of Early Southeast Asia: Maritime Trade and Societal Development, 100–1500* (Rowman & Littlefield Publishers, 2010).

House of Lords. *Accounts and Papers* (London: n.p., 1855). https://books.google.com.sg/books?id=fhtcAAAAQAAJ.

"Inverted Umbrellas to Catch Gold Leaves at Funeral". *Straits Times*, November 20, 1938. https://eresources.nlb.gov.sg/newspapers/digitised/article/straitstimes19381120-1.2.97.

Journal of the Straits Branch of the Royal Asiatic Society. 1881. https://books.google.com.sg/books?id=y3icdojOauwC.

Journal of the Straits Branch of the Royal Asiatic Society. 1894. https://books.google.com.sg/books?id=RZnwqKpCQvcC.

Kathirithamby-Wells, Jeyamalar. "Hulu-Hilir Unity and Conflict: Malay Statecraft in East Sumatra before the Mid-Nineteenth Century". *Archipel-etudes Interdisciplinaires Sur Le Monde Insulindien* 45 (1993): 77–96.

Lister, M., "Malay Law in Negri Sembilan", *Journal of the Straits Branch of the Royal Asiatic Society* (Malaysian Branch of the Royal Asiatic Society) nos. 20–22 (1889): 301.

Logan, J.R. *The Journal of the Indian Archipelago and Eastern Asia.* Printed at the Mission Press, 1849. https://books.google.com.sg/books?id=UjJTAAAAcAAJ.

Logan. *The Journal of the Indian Archipelago and Eastern Asia*. Printed at the Mission Press, 1848. https://books.google.com.sg/books?id=RNBgAAAAcAAJ.

Matheson, Virginia. "Strategies of Survival: The Malay Royal Line of Lingga-Riau". *Journal of Southeast Asian Studies* 17, no. 1 (1986): 5–38.

Mills, J.V. "Eredia's Description of Malaca, Meridional India, and Cathay". *Journal of the Malayan Branch of the Royal Asiatic Society* 8, no. 1 (109) (1930): 1–288.

Milner, A. *The Malays* (London: Wiley, 2009).

"Moar State". *Straits Times*, August 18, 1877. https://eresources.nlb.gov.sg/newspapers/digitised/article/straitstimes18770818-1.2.5

"Muar". *The Singapore Free Press and Mercantile Advertiser*, July 31, 1858. https://eresources.nlb.gov.sg/newspapers/digitised/article/singfreepressa18580731-1.2.4.

Newbold, T.J. *Political and Statistical Account of the British Settlements in the Straits of Malacca, Viz: Pinang, Malacca, and Singapore* (John Murray, 1839). https://books.google.com.sg/books?id=2E0PAAAAMAAJ.

Pinto, Paulo Jorge de Sousa. *The Portuguese and the Straits of Melaka, 1575–1619: Power, Trade and Diplomacy* (Singapore, Kuala Lumpur: NUS Press, Malaysian Branch of the Royal Asiatic Society, 2012).

Rahman, Noor Aisha Abdul. *Colonial Image of Malay Adat Laws: A Critical Appraisal of Studies on Adat Laws in the Malay Peninsula During the Colonial Era and Some Continuities* (Brill, 2006).

Rahmat, H.B. *Abdullah Bin Abdul Kadir Munshi* in 2 vols. (Singapore: World Scientific, 2020).

Rasheed, Z.A., W.H. Zoohri, and N. Saat. *Beyond Bicentennial: Perspectives on Malays* (Singapore: World Scientific Publishing Company, 2020).

Read, W.H.M. *Play and Politics, Recollections of Malaya by an Old Resident* (London: W. Gardner, 1901).

"Recognition of the Sultan of Johore". *Straits Times*, February 13, 1855. https://eresources.nlb.gov.sg/newspapers/digitised/article/straitstimes18550213-1.2.18.

Speechley, S.T. *Malayan Classicism: From the Architecture of Empire to Asian Vernacular* (Bloomsbury Publishing, 2023).
Swettenham, F.S. *British Malaya: An Account of the Origin and Progress of British Influence in Malaya* (Taylor & Francis, 2018).
Taylor, A. *Lords of Misrule: Hostility to Aristocracy in Late Nineteenth and Early Twentieth Century Britain* (Palgrave Macmillan UK, 2004).
Trocki, C.A. *Prince of Pirates: The Temenggongs and the Development of Johor and Singapore, 1784–1885* (NUS Press, 2007).
Turnbull, C.M. *A History of Modern Singapore, 1819–2005* (Singapore University Press, 2009).
Wiener, Margaret J. *Visible and Invisible Realms: Power, Magic, and Colonial Conquest in Bali* (Chicago: University of Chicago Press, 1995).
Moor, J.H. *Notices of the Indian Archipelago & Adjacent Countries: Being a Collection of Papers Relating to Borneo, Celebes, Bali, Java, Sumatra, Nias, the Philippine Islands* (F. Cass & Company, 1837).
Tully, John. "A Victorian Ecological Disaster: Imperialism, the Telegraph, and Gutta-Percha". *Journal of World History* 20, no. 4 (2009): 559–579.

Chapter 8: Colonialism, the Historical Construction of 'Tanah Melayu', and its Significance to Malaysia's and Singapore's National Narratives

Abdul Hadi bin Haji Hassan. *Sejarah Alam Melayu*. Vol. 1. 5 vols. (Singapore: Malaya Publishing House, 1925).
Abdul Hadi bin Haji Hassan. *Sejarah Alam Melayu*. 1947 reprint. Vol. 2. 5 vols. (Singapore: Malaya Publishing House, 1926).
Abdul Hadi bin Haji Hassan. *Sejarah Alam Melayu*. 1949 edition. Vol. 3. 5 vols. (Singapore: Malaya Publishing House, 1929).
Afian Sa'at, Faris Joraimi, and Siew Min Sai, eds. *Raffles Renounced: Towards a Merdeka History* (Singapore: Ethos Books, 2021).
Ahmad Fawzi bin Mohd. Basri, Mohd. Fo'ad bin Sakdan, and Azami bin Man. *Sejarah Tingkatan 1*, edited by Wan Norliani

binti Wan Jusoh and Nazri bin Mohamad Don. Kurikulum Bersepadu Sekolah Menengah (Kuala Lumpur: Dewan Bahasa dan Pustaka, 2014).

Ahmad, Hassan, ed. *Hikayat Hang Tuah*. Second Edition (Yayasan Karyanan dan Dewan Bahasa dan Pustaka, 2008).

Ahmad, Kassim. "Introduction". In *Hikayat Hang Tuah*, edited by Hassan Ahmad, Second Edition (Kuala Lumpur: Yayasan Karyanan dan Dewan Bahasa dan Pustaka, 2008), xi–xxv.

Andaya, Barbara Watson, and Leonard Andaya. *A History of Malaysia*. Third Edition (London: Palgrave Macmillan, 2017).

Arrifin Omar. *Bangsa Melayu: Malay Concepts of Democracy and Community, 1945–1950*. Second Edition (Petaling Jaya: SIRD, 2015).

Barr, Michael D. "Background Figures in a British Portrait: The Johor Royal Family in Nineteenth-Century Singapore". *History Australia* 18, no. 2 (2021): 283–301.

Barr. "Singapore Comes to Terms with its Malay Past: The Politics of Crafting a National History". *Asian Studies Review* 46, no. 2 (2021): 350–368.

Barr. *Singapore: A Modern History* (London: Bloomsbury, 2019).

Benjamin, Geoffrey. "On Being Tribal in the Malay World". In *Tribal Communities in the Malay World: Historical, Cultural and Social Perspectives*, edited by Geoffrey Benjamin and Cynthia Chou (Singapore: Institute of Southeast Asian Studies, 2003), 7–76.

Bentley, Michael. "British Historical Writing". In *The Oxford History of Historical Writing: 1800–1945*, edited by Daniel Woolf (Oxford, New York: Oxford University Press, 2011), 4: 204–224.

Berger, Stefan. "The Invention of European National Traditions in European Romanticism". In *The Oxford History of Historical Writing: 1800–1945*, edited by Stuart Macintyre, Juan Maiguashca, and Attila Pók, Vol. 4 (Oxford: Oxford University Press, 2011).

Blackburn, Kevin, and ZongLun Wu. *Decolonizing the History Curriculum in Malaysia and Singapore* (Abingdon: Routledge, 2019).

Chartterjee, Partha. *Nationalist Thought and the Colonial World* (New York: Zed, 1986).

Chong, Terence. "The Bicentennial Commemoration: Imagining and Re-Imagining Singapore's History". *Southeast Asian Affairs*, 2020: 323–334.

Choy, Chee Meh (née Lum) et al. "History of the Malaysian Branch of the Royal Asiatic Society". *JMBRAS* 68, no. 2 (1995): 81–144.

Daniel, Padma. "A Descriptive Catalogue of the Books Relating to Malaysia in the Raffles Museum & Library Singapore". *JMBRAS* 19, no. 3 (1941): 1–125.

Endicott, Kirk. "Introduction". In *Malaysia's Original People: Past, Present and Future of the Orang Asli*, edited by Kirk Endicott, 1–38 (Singapore: NUS Press, 2016).

Hong, Lysa and Huang Jianli. *The Scripting of National History: Singapore and its Pasts* (Singapore: NUS Press, 2008).

J.J. "Malaya: The Straits Settlements and the Federated and Unfederated Malay States". *JMBRAS* 1, no. 2 (88) (1923): 388–89.

Kheng, C.B. *Malaysia: The Making of A Nation* (Singapore: ISEAS, 2002).

Kheng. "Writing Indigenous History in Malaysia: A Survey on Approaches and Problems". *Crossroads: An Interdisciplinary Journal of Southeast Asian Studies* 10, no. 2 (1996): 38–81.

Khoo, Kay Kim. "Local Historians and the Writing of Malaysian History in the Twentieth Century". In *Perceptions of the Past in Southeast Asia*, edited by Anthony Reid and David Marr, 299–312 (Singapore: Heinemann Educational Books (Asia), 1979).

Khoo, Benjamin, and Peter Borschberg. *Knowing Singapore: The Evolution of Published Information in Europe, c.1500–1819* (Kuala Lumpur: Malaysian Branch of the Royal Asiatic Society, 2023).

Kwa, Chong Guan. "From Temasek to Singapore: Locating a Global City-State in the Cycles of Melaka Straits History". In *Studying Singapore Before 1800*, edited by Kwa Chong Guan and Peter Borschberg, 179–205 (Singapore: NUS Press, 2018).

Kwa, Chong Guan, Peter Borschberg, Derek Heng, and Tan Tai Yong, eds. *Seven Hundred Years: A History of Singapore* (Singapore: Marshall Cavendish International (Asia), 2020).

Maier, Hendrik M.J. *In the Center of Authority: The Malay Hikayat Merong Mahawangsa* (New York: Southeast Asia Program, 1988).

Mansor, Suffian bin, Mardiana binti Nordin, and Ahmad Salehee bin Abdul Ishak bin Saidoo. *Sejarah Tingkatan* 2, edited by Abdul Ghani bin Abu and Md Shukuri bin Hamzah. Kurikulum Standard Sekolah Menengah (Kuala Lumpur: Dewan Bahasa dan Pustaka, 2022).

Milner, Anthony, and Wilbert W. W. Wong. "Winstedt, Colonialism and the Malaysian History Wars". *Indonesia and the Malay World* 52, no. 133 (2024): 1–20.

Mills, L.A. "British Malaya: 1824–1867". *JMBRAS* 3, no. 2 (1925): 1–339.

Mills. "British Malaya: 1824–1867". *JMBRAS* 33, no. 3 (1960): 1–424.

Raja Haji Ali. *Tuhfat Al-Nafis: Sejarah Melayu-Islam*, edited by Virginia Matheson Hooker (Kuala Lumpur: Dewan Bahasa dan Pustaka, 1991).

"Sijil Pelajaran Malaysia 2019. Sejarah. Kertas 3". Lembaga Peperiksaan Malaysia, November 2019.

Skinner, A.M. "Outline History of the British Connection with Malaya". *JSBRAS*, no. 10 (1882): 269–280.

Singapore: A Journey Through Time, 1299–1970s. (Singapore: Star Publishing Pte Ltd, 2021).

Soda, Naoki. *Conceptualizing the Malay World* (Kyoto: Kyoto University Press, 2020).

Soda. "The Malay World in Textbooks: The Transmission of Colonial Knowledge in British Malaya". *Southeast Asian Studies* 39, no. 2 (2001): 188–232.

Swettenham, Frank. *British Malaya* (London: Bodley Head, 1907).

Syed, Nasir bin Ismail, ed. *Hikayat Merong Mahawangsa* (Kuala Lumpur: Dewan Bahasa dan Pustaka, 1968).
Turnbull, Constance Mary. *A History of Modern Singapore: 1819–1975* (Kuala Lumpur: Oxford University Press, 1977).
Wheatley, Paul. *The Golden Khersonese* (Kuala Lumpur: University of Malaya Press, 1961).
Wilkinson, R.J., ed. "A History of the Peninsular Malays with chapters on Perak and Selangor". Third Edition (London: Oxford University Press, 1923), 15–151.
Winstedt, Richard O. "A History of Johore (1365–1895 A.D.)". *JMBRAS* 10, no. 3 (1932): 1–167.
Winstedt. "A History of Johore (1673–ca. 1800 A.D.)". *JMBRAS* 10, no. 1 (1932): 164–201.
Winstedt. "A History of Kedah". *JSBRAS* 81 (1920): 29–35.
Winstedt. "A History of Malaya". *JMBRAS* 13, no. 1 (1935): 1–270.
Winstedt. "A History of Selangor". *JMBRAS* 12, no. 3 (October 1934): 1–34.
Winstedt. *Kitab Tawarikh Melayu*. Third Edition (Singapore: Kelly & Walsh, 1921).
Winstedt. *Malaya and its History* (London: Hutchinson, 1948).
Winstedt, ed. *Malaya: The Straits Settlements and the Federated and Unfederated Malay States* (London: Constable, 1923).
Winstedt. "Negeri Sembilan: The History, Polity and Beliefs of the Nine States". *JMBRAS* 12, no. 3 (1934): 37–111.
Winstedt. "The Malay Annals of Sejarah Melayu". *JMBRAS* 16, no. 3 (1938): 1–226.
Winstedt. *The Malays: A Cultural History* (Singapore: Kelly & Walsh, 1947).
Winstedt, and Abdul Hamid bin Tengku Muhammad Salleh Daing. *Kitab Tawarikh Melayu*. First Edition (Singapore, 1918).
Winstedt, and R.J. Wilkinson. "A History of Perak". *JMBRAS* 12, no. 3 (1934): 1–34, 112–14.
Zainal, Abidin bin Ahmad. "'Modern Developments' an additional chapter to R.O. Winstedt 'A History of Malay Literature'". *JMBRAS* 17, no. 3 (1939): 142–63.

Author Biographies

Wang Gungwu

Professor Wang is an internationally renowned historian famed for his scholarship on the history of the Chinese diaspora in Southeast Asia, as well as the history and civilization of China and Southeast Asia. He was a History Professor at the University of Malaya (1963–68) and the Australian National University (1968–86), and the Vice-Chancellor at the University of Hong Kong (1986–95). Professor Wang is a Professor Emeritus at the Australian National University and University Professor at the National University of Singapore (NUS), the highest academic title conferred by NUS.

Professor Wang was the founding Chairman of NUS' Lee Kuan Yew School of Public Policy, Director (1997–2006) and Chairman (2006–19) of Singapore's East Asian Institute, and Chairman of the ISEAS–Yusof Ishak Institute. His international awards include the Commander of the British Empire (CBE) in 1988, the Tang Prize in Sinology in 2020, and the Singapore government's Distinguished Service Order in 2020. He earned his BA and MA in history from NUS when it was previously the University of Malaya and holds a PhD from the School of Oriental and African Studies, University of London.

Kwa Chong Guan

Professor Kwa Chong Guan is an Adjunct Associate Professor at the History Department, National University of Singapore, Senior Fellow at the S. Rajaratnam School of International Studies, Nanyang Technological University, and an Associate Fellow at the Archaeological Unit of the ISEAS–Yusof Ishak Institute. Kwa's expertise lies in exploring extended historical cycles and emerging deep histories of Southeast Asia. He started his career working on policy analysis in the Ministry of Foreign Affairs and then the Ministry of Defence, before being assigned to reorganize the Oral History Department in the National Archives and, concurrently, the old National Museum. In addition, he was previously Head of the old Department of Strategic Studies at the SAFTI Military Institute, where he taught military history and strategic studies. Today, he continues to examine the implicit narratives underpinning the framing of current regional security issues.

Syed Farid Alatas

Professor Syed Farid Alatas is a Professor of Sociology at the National University of Singapore, where he has been since 1992. Alatas previously taught at the University of Malaya in the Department of Southeast Asian Studies. A Malaysian national, he obtained his PhD in sociology from Johns Hopkins University in 1991. His areas of interest are historical sociology, the sociology of social science, the sociology of religion, and inter-religious dialogue. Among his works are *Alternative Discourse in Asian Social Science: Responses to Eurocentrism* (Sage, 2006), *Ibn Khaldun* (Oxford University Press, 2013), and *Applying Ibn Khaldun: The Recovery of a Lost Tradition in Sociology* (Routledge, 2014).

Peter Borschberg

Peter Borschberg, FRHistS, FRGS, completed his PhD at Cambridge and is currently in the Department of History at National

University of Singapore. He is the author of numerous books and articles about the history of Singapore and its surrounding region, and pioneered the use of non-English European archives to fill in the gaps for the fifteenth to eighteenth centuries—a period once thought to be lost to history. His books include *Mapping Singapore Before 1819* (NUS Press, 2018) and *Reconstructing Singapore, c.1500–1800* (NUS Press, forthcoming).

Tim Hannigan

Dr. Tim Hannigan was born in Penzance in Cornwall in the far west of the United Kingdom. He worked as a chef, an English teacher, and a tour guide before becoming a full-time writer and academic. He is the author of several narrative history books with a particular focus on Indonesia and is widely published as a travel journalist. His recent books include *The Travel Writing Tribe* and *The Granite Kingdom*. Dr. Hannigan has also engaged in radio and television documentaries, particularly those focused on Asian history. He received his PhD from the University of Leicester for a critical-creative investigation of ethical issues in contemporary travel literature, and his academic work generally focuses on nineteenth-century and contemporary travel literature. He teaches writing and literature at the Atlantic Technological University in Sligo, Ireland.

Christopher Hale

Christopher Hale is a documentary producer and the author five non-fiction books, including *A Brief History of Singapore and Malaysia* (2023). He was educated at Sussex University and has an LLM/Master's from the University of Edinburgh. Hale is currently a PhD student at De Montfort University, researching the legal dimensions of genocide.

Benjamin Khoo

Benjamin J.Q. Khoo, MA, is currently an independent scholar based in Singapore. He has published several articles on the history of Singapore before 1800. His research interests include the circulation of knowledge, as well as cross-cultural and diplomatic encounters in early modern Asia.

Mohamed Effendy

Dr Mohamed Effendy Bin Abdul Hamid is a Lecturer at the Department of Southeast Asian Studies, National University of Singapore. He holds a PhD in History, specializing in Southeast Asian Studies. He earned his doctorate from the University of Hawaii at Manoa, where his research focused on the history of the Cham community from the seventeenth to nineteenth centuries. Dr Effendy is a dedicated historian with a diverse range of research interests and expertise in Pre-colonial and Colonial Southeast Asian History. His research also extends to Martial Arts Studies, a field that combines historical research with the study of martial arts traditions and practices in Southeast Asia.

Wilbert Wong

Wilbert W.W. Wong is a Malaysian historian currently based at the Australian National University (ANU), where he teaches history, political science, international relations, and security. He also teaches history at the University of New South Wales, Canberra. His doctoral research, completed within the School of History in the Research School of Social Sciences at ANU, examined the colonial construction of Malaya and its enduring legacies. The thesis was shortlisted for the 2023 Australian Historical Association General History Prize and received high commendation. In 2016, he was awarded the Lee Kong Chian Research Fellowship at the National Library of Singapore. Wong maintains an active research profile focused on the history of colonialism in Asia, with particular interest in colonial discourse, intellectual history, cross-cultural encounters, and the legacies of colonialism in the Malay Peninsula.